Walter Melville Patton

Ahmed Ibn Hanbal and the Mihna

A biography of the Imam including an account of the Mohammedan Inquisition 218-234 A.H.

Walter Melville Patton

Ahmed Ibn Hanbal and the Mihna
A biography of the Imam including an account of the Mohammedan Inquisition 218-234 A.H.

ISBN/EAN: 9783743382770

Manufactured in Europe, USA, Canada, Australia, Japa

Cover: Foto ©Lupo / pixelio.de

Manufactured and distributed by brebook publishing software (www.brebook.com)

Walter Melville Patton

Ahmed Ibn Hanbal and the Mihna

AḤMED IBN ḤANBAL

AND

THE MIḤNA.

A BIOGRAPHY OF THE IMÂM INCLUDING AN ACCOUNT OF THE MOḤAMMEDAN INQUISITION CALLED THE MIḤNA, 218—234 A. H.

BY

WALTER M. PATTON, B. D., Ph. D.
Professor in the Wesleyan Theological College, Montreal, Canada.

LIBRAIRIE ET IMPRIMERIE
CI-DEVANT
E. J. BRILL
LEIDE — 1897.

PRINTED BY E. J. BRILL, AT LEYDEN.

TO MY WIFE.

INTRODUCTORY REMARKS.

The following pages contain the record of the Imâm Aḥmed ibn Ḥanbal and of a struggle [1]) with which he stood connected, whose issues were so great as to warrant a close study of all that is involved in the movement. The history of Dogma in Islâm as written by Western writers has given us an idea of the questions which were being disputed at this time, and the outward history of events has recorded in very meagre outline the most important public occurrences of our narrative; but there has been, so far, no use made of the rich opportunity presented in the biography of Aḥmed ibn Ḥanbal to see the theological controversies of Islâm in their connection with the outward history of the State. This kind of historical study is the more interesting, because from it we are enabled to understand the relation of the State to religion at that time, and the place occupied by religion and its teachers in the State.

1) The Miḥna. This term, meaning in general usage a 'testing' or 'trial', whether by the accidents of fortune or the actions of men, is often used, (together with the VIII Form of the verb محن) with reference to a religious test with a view to obtaining assent to some particular belief or system of beliefs. We find this special usage largely illustrated in the records of the Muʿtazilite inquisition, the account of which is to appear in the sequel. It is also found in the accounts of the Orthodox inquisition under the Khalif Ḳâhir 200 years later. Most commonly, the whole persecution extending from the year 218 A. H. to 234 A. H. is called the Miḥna.

We have referred above to the issues of the Miḥna, as the persecution inaugurated by al-Maʾmûn is called. The importance of them lies in the fact that they settled the orthodox character of Islâm for all following ages; and in the preservation of orthodoxy lies the preservation of Islâm itself, in our judgment. Had Rationalism succeeded in bringing about by persecution a general abandonment of orthodoxy, it is probable that the principle of free thought, without recognition of authority, would have had a disintegrating effect within Islâm itself, and would have made it much more susceptible to modifying and reforming influences from without; so that, in time, we should have seen standards of faith and life, which contravene our reason as the Ḳorân and Tradition do, given up for something more satisfying to reason and moral judgment. We need not enter into the question whether any good came from the preservation of orthodoxy, further than to say that if Islâm was to continue to be Islâm, to preserve orthodoxy was the best way to accomplish such a result.

We ought to give Rationalism credit for having asserted the principle, un-Islâmic though it be, that thought must be free in the search for truth. The abuse of free-thinking, however, in a love of speculation for speculation's sake, and in an inordinate desire of controversial victory is, in the history of this period, abundantly exemplified.

Aḥmed ibn Hanbal during his whole career subsequent to the death of the Imâm al-Shâfiʿî (204 A. H.) was the most remarkable figure in the camp of Mohammedan orthodoxy, and during the course of the Miḥna did more than any other individual to strengthen the resistance of his party to the repressive efforts of the Khalifs and their officers. He stood for the standing or falling of orthodoxy in its time of trial; and there is little exaggeration in the statement, made more than once concerning him, that 'all men were looking to him for an example, that as he decided on the test as to the Ḳorân being applied to him, so they might follow'.

We have some interesting circumstantial evidence of

Aḥmed's position and influence among the people from the way in which he was treated by the Khalifs. Al-Maʾmûn had made up his mind to cite him to appear with the first seven men to whom he put the test, but even the violent bigot Aḥmed ibn Abû Dowâd the Chief-Kâḍî advised his master not to summon him, doubtless recognizing that success with the seven men would be much more difficult should Aḥmed be with them, and feeling that the result of their trial would better determine whether or not it would be wise to attack one greater than they. Al-Maʾmûn's letter to his governor in Baghdâd after the latter had examined the doctors treats with gentleness Aḥmed ibn Ḥanbal, when one reads what he had to say about most of the other doctors there alluded to. In the case of al-Muʿtaṣim, we must bear in mind that he did not scourge Aḥmed until he had exhausted every means to save him, by threats, arguments and entreaties. He declared that had al-Maʾmûn not ordered him to deal with him and such as he, he would have had nothing to do with the infliction of the punishment. Furthermore, the scourging took place in the court-yard of the palace unknown to the mass of the people, who stood outside waiting for the announcement as to how the trial had ended. As soon as they suspected that their Imâm was being tortured, there was a tremendous excitement; and it seemed as if the Khalif's palace would become an object of assault, when al-Muʿtaṣim had Aḥmed's uncle ʾIsḥâḳ brought out, and had this man falsely intimate to them that he had not harmed his nephew in the least. To make himself still more secure against the danger of a popular uprising, al-Muʿtaṣim kept Aḥmed within the precincts of the palace until the evening, and then dressed him up in gala costume and sent him under cover of dusk to his dwelling. We may consider it as significant of Aḥmed's standing among the people that there were no further attempts to coerce him during the remaining fifteen years of the Miḥna, though we are assured that he was active in teaching and as popular as he ever had been, or even more so. Al-Wâthiḳ's treatment furnishes some evidence to shew how he regarded Aḥmed's influence. We are told that, despite the urging of Ibn Abû Dowâd, he would not cite Aḥmed for examination before him, but sent word to the Imâm to remove from his country; a good proof that Aḥmed had great power with the people. The biographer adds that he does not know whether the Khalif refrained from dealing with Aḥmed because of admiration for his steadfastness, or because of fear that evil consequences might come upon him should he lay violent hands upon so holy a man. For al-Mutawakkil we need say little here. His attention to Aḥmed and the messages which he sent him point clearly to his popularity and influence.

The religious sentiment in the Muslim populace had not much sympathy with the loose views and free living of the liberal teachers. Hence it was that they idolized as they did a man like Aḥmed ibn Ḥanbal. His intense devotion to the things most venerated and cherished by the people: God, the Prophet, the Ḳorân, the Tradition, the Sunna of the Prophet, and the Communion of the Faithful, endeared him to the mass of the common folk. He was, also, a remarkable example of an effort which always excited reverence in the breast of the Muslim, namely, the effort 'to bring himself near to God and thus secure a good reward from him'. Those who are familiar with the stock expressions of Mohammedan piety will understand what this means in the case of a sincere and earnest religionist. Judging by the record of a host of extravagant visions of blessedness in Paradise which men had of the Imâm Aḥmed after his departure from the world, one cannot doubt that all good Muslims believed him to have obtained even more than the good reward for which he had hoped.

That Aḥmed ibn Ḥanbal has come to be regarded as the founder of the Ḥanbalite Madhhab, or School, is not to be wondered at, though it is not because of any intention on his part, as far as I can see. He was a great saint and defender of orthodoxy, and it is due to this fact that his pupils and admirers, after his death, sought to give form to their master's teachings and compacted themselves into a sect or school of theology. I do not believe that Aḥmed himself had the idea that such would occur. That a school was formed spontaneously is a testimony to the powerful impression of the man's personality upon his own age and that following. The things which the Muslims reckon to Aḥmed's praise are his personal life, his intensely orthodox teaching, and his maintenance of his teaching in the face of persecution. He was learned in only one direction, that is, in the Ḳorân, Tradition, the Consensus of usage and opinion among the Faithful. These things he knew thoroughly; of worldly learning he does not appear to have had any great store. The kind of knowledge he had, supplementing great courage and firmness and much natural shrewdness, was his effective weapon in the controversial warfare which he had to wage. Aḥmed's great book the Musnad is the best monument to that knowledge in which he especially excelled. It exercised such an influence, in itself and in the works derived from it, for the maintenance of Tradition in its worthy place as a basis of theology, that its author's career ought to be known. We will then see the real life which was so steadying in its effect upon Mohammedan religious thought, and which was but followed up in its effect by the book which it produced.

Some native biographers and historians have noticed the man and the persecution in which he suffered for his faith with too flattering recognition of Aḥmed's worth and services. Others whose interest is more secular and who record, for the most part, only the outward events of civil history have often passed over the religious movement of Aḥmed's time with little or no notice. But there is a significance about the man and the movement which the greatest of the chroniclers, such as Ṭabarî, have not been slow to recognize. Abu'l-Maḥâsin, who professes to be writing the annals of Egypt, but whose interest in religious persons and events is evident on almost every page of his work, has done full justice to the general course of events in connection with the Miḥna and to the public career of Aḥmed ibn Ḥanbal.

In the narrative which follows, I have sought to give the connected story of my subject's life from its beginning to its close. The account expands, however, at that point where his life becomes a factor in the public history of the time, in order that we may have a fair impression of the whole course of religious events then transpiring, and may, also, see more clearly Aḥmed ibn Ḥanbal in the arena where he, more than elsewhere, won for himself that great fame which has placed him among the chief heroes and saints of his faith.

It should be remarked that European writers have too often written their accounts in a spirit of antipathy toward the orthodox theology of Mohammedanism, and have given more than a due share of commendation to the Muʿtazilites (Rationalists). They were, it is true, advocates of the freedom of thought, but were, none the less, in many cases, too self-indulgent and pleasure-loving to be credited with the highest moral aims or earnestness. It is doubtful whether, in most instances, their championship of free thinking was from any lofty conception of what constitutes true freedom. It would appear to be rather the motive of convenience that moved them to take the course they took. They preached the gospel of Freedom because they felt the Law and the Commandment to impose an inconvenience upon them, so that they could not do as they wished. All praise is due to the sincere men who loved freedom and sought it as the right of every man, but the sequel will shew not many of such men in that field of history which it covers.

The characters of the four Khalifs al-Maʾmûn, al-Muʿtaṣim, al-Wâthiḳ and al-Mutawakkil will receive some additional light from the narrative which follows; as a result, probably that of the first and last named will receive a different judgment from that which has been passed hitherto. Al-Maʾmûn, the scholar and patron of scholars, the first free-thinking Khalif who took a real interest in religion, will be more fully discovered as a man intolerant toward those who differed from him, even to the degree of becoming an intense persecutor. As to his liberal tendencies, it is not likely we shall find any reason to change our judgment. He had a quick and very capable mind, and hated to be fettered. He believed he had the right to think to the full extent of his opportunity, and to make opportunity for mental ranging where he had none. Had he stopped at this point, he would have presented to us a record of great service to his fellow-men accomplished by moral means; but when he rejected what he deemed a spiritual tyranny, only to turn spiritual and physical tyrant himself, the pure quality of his early aspirations is for us sadly spoiled.

Al-Mutawakkil is a Khalif whose character cannot possibly be what European historians have made it out to be — darker than the plague of darkness itself. He was orthodox, but his treatment of liberals will easily bear comparison with his predecessors' treatment of the orthodox theologians; while the attitude he assumed toward Aḥmed ibn Ḥanbal does not present to us a man without redeeming qualities. It is not to be understood that we condone his terrible treatment of individuals, and the gloating satisfaction with which he sometimes related his own barbarities. Nor would we soften terms over his treatment of Jews and Christians. But the man was a fanatical religionist, and many of his deeds must be viewed from the religious standpoint to a greater extent than they have been heretofore.

It will be seen that, in regard to some other points, I have indicated in a footnote here and there a difference of opinion from some of the modern authorities whose works have been consulted. But, none the less, I avail myself of the present opportunity to say that the books of scholars like Steiner, von Kremer, Houtsma and Goldziher have been of great service to me, and that I am fully appreciative of the service their contributions have rendered to our knowledge of that period of Mohammedan history with which my sketch professes also to deal.

In my work I have derived most of the material used

from three manuscripts in the Library of the University of Leiden; 1) Cod. 311 *a*, which, with its companion Cod. 311 *b*, represents the 5th and 4th vols, respectively, of a five volume Ms. of the حلية الاولياء or حلية الابرار of Abû Nu^caim Aḥmed ibn Abdallah al-'Ispahânî (d. 450). 2) Cod. 73 *a*, which was not in the University collection of Mss. at the time that Dozy prepared his Catalogue, and is, therefore, not described. Its companion volume, Cod. 73 *b* Gol., is however described. The two volumes form together one transcript of the work of Tâju'd-Dîn Abdu'l-Wahhâb ibnu'l-Subkî (d. 771), entitled طبقات الشافعية: 3) Cod. 1917, which is likewise not described in the University Catalogue, but will be found in the Catalogue of Landberg, "Catalogue de Manuscrits arabes provenant d'une Bibliothèque privée à el-Medîna et appartenant à la Maison E. J. Brill, Leide", p. 53, Cod. 188, Aḥmed el-Maqrîzî († 845) مناقب احمد بن حنبل *Autographe de l'auteur.*

The biography of Aḥmed ibn Ḥanbal in Abû Nu^caim is found pp. 138—161 and in al-Subkî pp. 132—143. I have made most extensive use of the former of these two, as being the most detailed and circumstantial account of my subject's life. It is the oldest account of the three, and shews that fact in the amount of gossip and personal detail which it records, and which the later accounts have omitted. The narrative in al-Subkî affords a great deal of matter touching Aḥmed's part in the Miḥna, but not so much for the biography before and after that time. Al-Maḳrîzî's contribution is almost sure to be a portion of his Mokaffa, and is a good piece of biographical writing, well-arranged, concise in expression, and covering fully the life and relations of Aḥmed. Considered as a literary production, it is a better account than that of Abû Nu^caim, because of its compactness and system; but, for one who is gathering materials to compose a sketch having itself a similar purpose to Maḳrîzî's, as might be expected, the more diffuse narrative of Abû Nu^caim, with its accumulation of traditional accounts bearing on many minor points in Aḥmed's career, has much more to offer.

As is pointed out in a footnote Ṭabarî's Annales have been followed for the letters of the Khalif al-Ma'mûn. The same source, also, has afforded some useful information touching matters of more public interest during the progress of the Miḥna.

My endeavor has been to use the materials gathered from these and other sources in such a way as to make many witnesses contribute each something complementary to the testimony of his fellows, and yet have the whole convey the impression of a continuous narration.

To my greatly esteemed Professor, Doctor M. J. De Goeje, Professor of Arabic in the University of Leiden, I am indebted for direction, advice, and encouragement without which it would have been impossible to have accomplished the result that is here presented. I am very thankful to him for this, as also for his great courtesy as Interpres Legati Warneriani in placing at my disposal the three manuscripts which have been used in the preparation of the work.

Leiden, Feby 4th, 1897.

WALTER M. PATTON.

AḤMED IBN ḤANBAL AND THE MIḤNA.

I.

Aḥmed's Birth and Family Connections.

Aḥmed ibn Ḥanbal was born in the month of Rabiᶜ the first, 164 A. H. [1]). The home of his parents was in Khorasân [2]). His father Moḥammed ibn Ḥanbal was one of the descendants of a captain in the Abbaside army in Khorasân which fought to overthrow the Omayyads [3]). The family left Khorasân to take up residence in Baghdâd, however, and Aḥmed was born a few days or months after their arrival in the latter city [4]). We are not informed what family his parents had beside himself, and in none of the sources of information to which I have had access is there, excepting of a brother of his father's, ʾIsḥâḳ ibn Ḥanbal [5]) and a son of this man, Ḥanbal ibn ʾIsḥâḳ ibn Ḥanbal [6]), any mention of a relative of his father's or his own generation. His lineage was of pure Arabic stock [7]) from the family of Shaibân of the great tribe of Bekr ibn Wâʾil. Aḥmed is rarely called 'ibn Moḥammed', the name

1) Ibn Chall. N°. 19, Dhahabî, Liber Class. 8, N°. 18, Abuʾl-Maḥâsin I, 735 ff.

2) Jâcût II, 777.

3) Abû Nuᶜaim, Leiden Ms. 311*a*, 150*b*, وكان ابوه من ابناء قواد خراسان

4) Ibn Chall. N°. 19, Dhahabî, Liber Class. 8, N°. 18, Al-Nawawî, Biog. Dicty. p. ١٤٩.

5) Abuʾl-Maḥ. I, 771.

6) Abuʾl-Maḥ. II, 76; cf. p. 26, l. 5 infra.

7) Al-Maḳrîzî, Leiden Ms, 1917, p. 1, واصله من العرب قال يحيى بن معين ما رايت خيرًا من احمد ما افتخر علينا قط بالعربية ولا ذكرها

of his paternal grandfather taking the place of that of his father, probably from the fact that the latter died at thirty years of age while his son was still in infancy. On the death of the father, the responsibility for Aḥmed's care and training devolved upon his mother, whose name and history we do not know [1]).

Years of Study and Teachers.

We are without any details of his early years and know merely that he continued to reside in Baghdâd until the year 179 A. H. In this year, when fifteen years of age, he began the study of the Tradition [2]). He first went to the lecture-room of Abdallah ibn al-Mubârak, who came to Baghdâd for the last time in 179 A. H. He was too late in going, however, as Ibn al-Mubârak had left the city to take part in an expedition to Tarsus [3]). Mâlik ibn ʾAnas, too, died in the very year in which Aḥmed began to study; and the latter used to say that he had been deprived of Mâlik ibn ʾAnas and Hammâd ibn Zaid, but that God had given him in their place Sofyân ibn ʿUyaina and ʾIsmâʿîl ibn ʿUlayya [4]). His first teacher was Hushaim ibn Bashîr al-

---

1) That Aḥmed's father did not die before his boy was born will appear from the following: Abû Nuʿaim, p. 138 *b*, وتُوُفِّي ابوه محمد بن حنبل وله ثلثون سنة فولِيَتْه أُمه قال ابى كان قد ثقب أُذنىّ الخ

2) Dhahabî, Lib. Class. 8, N°. 18.

3) Abû Nuʿaim, 138 *a*, وكان ابن المبارك قَدِمَ فى هذه السَّنة وهى اخر قَدمَة قَدِمَها وذهبتُ الى مجلسه فقالوا خرج الى طرسوس فتوفّى سنة احدى وثمانين

Abdallah ibn al-Mubârak d. 181 A. H., al-Nawawî Biog. Dicty ٣٦٥.

4) Al-Maḳrîzî, p. 2, وكان رضّه يتاسّفُ على عدم اجتماعه بالامام مالك لان مالك رضّه توفى السنة التى طلب الامامُ احمدُ فيها الحديث وهى سنة تسع وسبعين ومائة فكان يقول فاتَنى مالك فأَخلفَ الله

Sulamî, to whom he went in the year 179. With Hushaim he studied in this year and, then, to receive more particular instructions in difficult traditions, he continued to study with him three years longer and part of a fourth year up to the time of Hushaim's death, which occurred in the year 183 A. H. From Hushaim's dictation he wrote the كتاب الحج, containing about 1000 traditions, a part of the تفسير, the قضاء and some minor writings. He is said to have learned from this teacher in all more than three thousand traditions [1]. For the study of tradition he visited Kûfa and Baṣra, Mecca, Medîna, Yemen, Syria and Mesopotamia [2] and among the other teachers under whom he studied were Sofyân ibn ʿUyaina († 198), ʾIbrâhîm ibn Saʿd († 183), Yaḥya ibn Saʿîd al-Kaṭṭân († 198), Wakîʿ († 196), Ibn ʿUlayya († 193), Ibn Mahdî († 198), Abd al-Razzâḳ († 211), Jarîr ibn Abd al-Ḥamîd († 188), al-Walîd ibn Muslim († 194), ʿAlî ibn Hishâm ibn al-Barîd, Muʿtamar ibn Suleimân († 187), Ghundar († 193), Bishr ibn al-Mufaḍḍal († 186), Ziyâd al-Bakâʾî, Yaḥya ibn Abû Zâʾida († 182), Abû Yûsuf the Kâḍî († 182), Ibn Numair († 234), Yazîd ibn Hârûn († 206), al-Ḥasan ibn Mûsâ al-ʾAshyab († 209), ʾIsḥâḳ ibn Râhawaih († 238), ʿAlî ibn al-Madînî († 234), and Yaḥya ibn Maʿîn († 233) [3].

علىّ سفيانَ بن عيينة وفاتنى حماد بن زيد فأخلف الله علىّ اسمعيل بن علية

1) Abû Nuʿaim, 139 *a*, [قال ابو الفضل صالح] قال ابى وكتبت عن هشيم سنةَ تسع وسبعين الا انى لم اعتقد بعض سماعى ولزمناه سنة ثمانين واحدى وثنتين وثلاثة ومات فى سنة ثلاثة وثمانين كتبنا عنه كتاب الحجّ نحوا من الف حديث وبعض التفسير والقضاء وكُتُبًا صغارا قال قلت تكون ثلاثة آلاف حديث قال اكثر

2) On the subject of travelling about to acquire a knowledge of traditions cf. Goldziher, Moh. Studien II, p. 176.

3) Cf. al-Nawawî Biog. Dict. ١٤٢ f.; al-Subkî, p. 133; Dhahabî, Lib. Class. 8, N°. 18. Dhahabî adds Bahr ibn ʾAsad. Abuʾl-Maḥ. I, 638, makes Ḳubaisa

He studied with al-Shâfiʿî the Fiḳh and the ʾUsûl al-Fiḳh [1]). We do not know much of the history of Aḥmed until the year 218 A. H. is reached. In that year the Miḥna was begun by the Khalif al-Maʾmûn and Aḥmed comes at once into prominence. He must have been studying with Abû Yûsuf the Kâḍî before 182 A. H. when Abû Yûsuf died. His personal intercourse with al-Shâfiʿî began in 195 A. H., when the latter came to Baghdâd, and lasted till 197 A. H., when al-Shâfiʿî went to Mecca. After a break it was renewed in Mecca, and after that, probably, for a brief space of time in Baghdâd, when al-Shâfiʿî returned there for a month in 198 A. H. before finally taking his departure from ʿIrâḳ [2]). We know that Aḥmed was in Baghdâd in this year. Wakîʿ ibn al-Jarrâh he knew very intimately before his death in 197 A. H. Aḥmed had such familiarity with this man's traditions that he gave his son liberty to take any of Wakîʿ's books that he pleased, and told him that, if he would give him any tradition whatever from it, he would give him the ʾIsnâd for it, or, if he would give him the ʾIsnâd, he would give him the tradition. Wakîʿ had his tradition from Sofyân from Salama, but Aḥmed seems to have been able to add to his own teacher's knowledge in respect to the traditions of Salama [3]). With Sofyân ibn ʿUyaina he studied in Mecca

---

ibn ʿOḳba one of Aḥmed's teachers; I, 681, Khalaf ibn Hishâm al-Bazzâr; I, 715, ʾIsmâʿîl ibn ʾIbrâhîm ibn Bistam; I. 734, Ḳutaiba ibn Saʿîd ibn Jamîl. By Shahrastânî Wakîʿ and Yazîd ibn Hârûn are classed as Shyites, Haarbr. Trans. I. 218.

1) al-Maḳrîzî, p. 2, واجتمع بالامام الشافعى رضه واخذ عنه الفقه واصوله

2) De Goeje, Z. D. M. G. XLVII, p. 115; Ibn Chall. N°. 569.

3) al-Subkî, p. 132, وقال قتيبة بن سعيد كان وكيع اذا كانت العتمة ينصرف معه احمد بن حنبل فيقف على الباب فيذاكره فاخذ ليلة بعضادتى الباب ثم قال يابا عبد الله [احمد] اريد ان القى عليك حديث سفيان قال هات قل تحفظ عن سفيان عن سلمة بن كهيل

before 198 A. H., in which year Sofyân died. We have no means of fixing the exact date when he studied with Sofyân. It was, no doubt, on the occasion of a pilgrimage, for Aḥmed performed the Hajj five times in all [1]). It was also during the residence of al-Shâfiʿî in Mecca, in all likelihood, for we have it recorded that ʾIsḥâḳ ibn Râhawaih on two occasions disputed there with al-Shâfiʿî during Aḥmed's residence there, and it would seem also in his presence [2]).

The following incident is characteristic of the man. While in Mecca, Aḥmed's clothes and effects were stolen during his absence from his lodgings in the hours when he was engaged in study with his teacher (Sofyân). On his return, the woman of the house told him of the theft, but his only enquiry was as to whether the writing-tablets had been preserved. On learning that they had, he asked for nothing more. Still, owing to the torn state of his clothes, he was forced

---

كذا قل نعم ثنا يحيى فيقول سلمة كذا وكذا فيقول ثنا عبد الرحمن فيقول وعن سلمة كذا وكذا فيقول انت حدثنا حتى تفرغ من سلمة ثم يقول احمد فتحفظ [عن] سلمة كذا وكذا فيقول وكيع لا فياخذ فى حديث شيخ شيخ قال فلم يزل قائمًا حتى جاءت الجارية فقالت قد طلع الكوكب او قالت الزهرة وقال عبد الله قال لى ابى خذ اى كتاب شئت من كتب وكيع فان شئت ان تسألنى عن شىء (marg. الكلام) حتى اخبرك بالاسناد وان شئت بالاسناد حتى اخبرك عن الكلام

1) al-Nawawî Biog. Dict., p. ١٤٤, l. 16.

2) al-Subkî, pp. 157, 158, مناظرة بين الشافعى واسحاق رضهما روى عن اسحاق بن راهويه قال كنا بمكة والشافعى بها واحمد بن حنبل ايضا بها الخ

مناظرة اخرى بينهما . . . . . . فسكت الشافعى فلما سمع ذلك احمد بن حنبل الخ

to remain away for several days from the lecture-room, until the anxiety of his fellow-students led them to seek him out and put him in the way of earning a little money to procure a change of garments. Their proferred gifts or loans he would not on any account accept [1]).

Abd al-Razzâḳ Aḥmed first met in Mecca. On one of his

1) Abû Nuʿaim, 143 *a*, [قال ابو نعيم] حدثنى ابى ثنا احمد قال املى علىّ عبد الله بن احمد [بن حنبل] من حفظه قال نزلنا بمكة دارا وكان فيها شيخ يكنى بابى بكر بن سماعة وكان من اهل مكة قال نزل علينا ابو عبد الله فى هذه الدار وانا غلام قال فقالت امى الزم هذا الرجل فاخدمه فانه رجل صالح فكنتُ اخدمه وكان يخرج يطلب الحديث فسرق متاعه وقماشه فجاء فقالت له أُمى دخل عليك السُراق فسرقوا قماشك فقال ما فعلت الالواح قالت له أُمى فى الطاق قال وما سأل عن شىء غيرها (142 *a*) حدثنا سليمان بن احمد ثنا عبد الله بن احمد بن حنبل ثنا على بن الجهم بن بدر قال كان لنا جار فاخرج الينا كتابا فقال اتعرفون هذا الخط قلنا نعم هذا خط احمد بن حنبل فقلنا له كيف كتب ذلك قال كنا بمكة مُقيمين عند سفيان بن عيينة ففقدنا احمد بن حنبل اياما لم نره ثم جئنا اليه نسأل عنه فقال لنا اهلُ الدار التى هو فيها هو فى ذلك البيت فجئنا اليه والباب مردود عليه واذا عليه خلقان فقلنا يابا عبد الله ما خبرُك لم نرك منذ ايام قال سُرِقَتْ ثيابى فقلت له معى دنانير فان شئت خذ قرضا وان شئت صلة فابى ان يفعل فقلت تكتب لى باجرة قال نعم فاخرجت دينارًا وابى ان ياخذه وقال اشتر لى ثوبا واقطعه نصفين فأومأ انه يأتزر بنصف ويرتدى بالنصف الآخر وقال جئنى ببقيته ففعلتُ فجئتُ بورق فكتب لى فهذا خطه

pilgrimages Yaḥya ibn Maᶜîn accompanied Aḥmed [1]), and they made up their minds that, after the completion of the pilgrimage, they would go to Sanᶜâ in Yemen and study Tradition with Abd al-Razzâḳ. On arriving at Mecca they met with the teacher, who had, like themselves, come to perform the Hajj. Yaḥya ibn Maᶜîn introduced Aḥmed to him, and, after making known their wish to study with him, an appointment was made by Ibn Maᶜîn in accordance with which they should receive his instructions in Mecca instead of going to Sanᶜâ. Ibn Maᶜîn told Aḥmed of this and the latter asked him why he had made such an arrangement. His reply was that it would save a month's journey each way and all the expenses of the trip. Aḥmed, however, declared that he could not allow such considerations to overcome his pious resolutions, and, in the end, they did go to Sanᶜâ and received there the traditions. He suffered great hardships on the way thither, for, though offered money sufficient to enable him to travel in comparative comfort, he refused to take it and hired himself to one of the camel drivers of a caravan going to the place. At Sanᶜâ, likewise, he lived in penury and suffering, though help was tendered him such as would have secured him against anything of the kind. Abd al-Razzâḳ himself said that Aḥmed remained with him almost two years, and that when he came he offered him money, saying that the country was one where trading was difficult and to gain his livelihood would be impossible. Aḥmed was inflexible, however, saying that he had a sufficiency for his needs. The traditions which he had from this teacher were those of al-Zuhrî from Sâlim ibn Abdallah from his father and the traditions of al-Zuhrî from Saᶜîd ibn al-Musayyib from Abû Huraira. Aḥmed was fortunate in having studied with Abd al-Razzâḳ before the year 200 A. H., for his reputation as a sound traditionist was impaired after that date. It is in keeping with Aḥmed's character that he should, as we are informed, have put into practice every tradition which he

---

1) Abu'l-Feda, Annales, Reiske ed, II. 186.

learned from Abd al-Razzâḳ, even to one in which the Prophet is represented as giving to Abû Ṭaiba, a surgeon, a dinâr for cupping him. Following this example Aḥmed, too, asked to be cupped and gave the surgeon a dinâr [1]).

---

1) al-Maḳrîzî, p. 7, حجّ احمدُ حجات رافق فى بعضها يحيى بن معين واتفقا على انهما بعد انقضاء الحج يمضيان الى صنعاء اليمن ياخذان الحديث عن عبد الرزاق فوجداه فى الطواف فلما فرغ اجتمعا عليه وكان احمدُ لا يعرف شخصه وانما يعرفه باسمه فقال له يحيى بن معين هذا اخوك احمد بن حنبل فقال حيّاهُ الله انه ليبلغنى عنه كلّ ما أُسَرُّ به ثبّته الله تعالى على ذلك ثم واعد يحيى الشيخ على قراءة فلما انصرفا عنه قال احمدُ لابن معين لـمَ اخذتَ على الشيخ الموعدَ فقال له يحيى قد اراحك الله مسيرة شهر ورجوع شهر والنفقة فقال الامام احمد ما كان الله ليرانى وقد نويت نية أُفسدها بما تقول ثم سافرا الى صنعاء اليمن واخذ عنه بها وصحّ عن الامام احمد انه قال ما كتبت حديثا الا وقد عملت به حتى مرّ بى ان رسول الله صلعم احتجم واعطى ابا طَيْبَة الحَجّام دينارًا فاحتجمتُ واعطيت الحجام دينارا. Abû Nuʿaim, 141 *b*, لما خرج احمد بن حنبل الى عبد الرزاق انقطعت به النفقة فاكرى نفسَه من بعض الجمّالين الى ان وافى صَنعآء وقد كان اصحابُه عرضوا عليه المواساةَ فلم يَقبل من احد شيئا. . . . يقول (عبد بن حُمَيْد) سمعت عبد الرزاق يقول قدم علينا احمد بن حنبل هاهنا فاقام سنتين الا شيئا فقلت له يابا عبد الله خذ هذا لِشَىْءِ دفعه اليه فانتفعْ به فانّ ارضنا ليست بارض متْجر ولا مَكْسَب واراناعبد الرزّاق كفّه مدها فيها دنانير فقال احمد انا بخير ولم يقبل منى. Abû Nuʿaim, 144 *a*, لما قدم احمد ابن حنبل مكة من عند عبد الرزاق رأيت به شحوبا وقد تبيّن

With Isḥâḳ ibn Râhawaih, who is called in the Kitâb al-Fihrist (I. 230) a leading Ḥanbalite, he corresponded for a length of time, until Isḥâḳ took a letter of recommendation which Yaḥya ibn Yaḥya had written for him to Abdallah ibn Ṭâhir, and received from the latter because of it both money and high position [1]).

Aḥmed's Period of Teaching. When still a youth Aḥmed ibn Ḥanbal was held in reverence as an authority on the Tradition, and in the assemblies of the sheikhs was looked up to with great respect [2]). We do not know when his most

---

عليه اثر النصّب والتعب فقلت [اى احمد بن ابراهيم الدورقى] يابا عبد الله لقد شققت على نفسك فى خروجك الى عبد الرزاق فقال ما اهون الشقّة فيما استفدنا من عبد الرزاق كتبنا عنه حديث الزهرى عن سالم بن عبد الله عن ابيه وحديث الزهرى عن سعيد بن المسيّب عن ابى هريرة رضّه .... قال ابى [اى ابو عبد الله] ما كتبنا عن عبد الرزاق من حفظه شيئًا الا مجلس الاول وذلك انا دخلنا بالليل فوجدناه فى موضع جالسا فاملى علينا سبعين حديثا ثم التفت الى القوم فقال لو لا هذا ما حدثتكم يعنى ابى [اى ابو عبد الله] قال ابى [ابو عبد الله] وجالس عبد الرزاق معمرا [مات سنة ١٥٣] تسع سنين فكان يكتب عنه كلّ شىء يقول قال عبد الله وكل من سمع من عبد الرزاق بعد المائتين فسماعه ضعيف وسمع منه ابى قديما

1) al-Nawawî Biog. Dict. ١٤٤ f. cf. al-Subkî, p. 156, فدخل الحاجب [الى ابن طاهر] فقال له رجل بالباب زعم ان معه رقعة يحيى بن يحيى الى الامير فقال يحيى بن يحيى قال نعم قال ادخله فدخل اسحق وناوله الرقعة فاخذها عبد الله وقبلها واقعد اسحق بجنبه وقضى دينه ثلاثين الف درهم وصيره من ندمائه

2) Abû Nuʿaim, 144 *b*, قال ابو نصر سمعت عبد بن حميد يقول كان فى مسجد اظنه ببغداد واصحاب الحديث يتذاكرون واحمد يومئذ شاب الا انه المنظور اليه من بينهم الخ

active period of teaching and literary work occurred, but he was established as the greatest traditionist of his time when al-Ma'mûn introduced the Miḥna, and continued to teach until shortly after al-Wâthiḳ came to the Khalifate when he was forced to give up teaching. He may have resumed teaching for a year or so after al-Mutawakkil came to power, but in 237 A. H. when he went to the camp he took an oath never to tell a tradition in its integrity as long as he lived, a vow which he appears to have kept[1]).

His Works. In regard to his books we know on the whole very little. He left at his death twelve loads and a half of books all of which he had memorized[2]). The names which have come down to us are the following: كتاب العلل - كتاب - كتاب الزهد - كتاب الناسخ والمنسوخ - كتاب التفسير - الفرائض - كتاب الفضائل - كتاب المسائل - كتاب الاشربة - كتاب الايمان كتاب المناسك - كتاب الردّ على الجهمية - كتاب طاعة الرسول - كتاب المسند[3]).

The Musnad. Of one book, his great work, the Musnad, we have more definite particulars. It comprised the testimonies of more than 700 Companions of the Prophet, and was selected and compiled from 700,000 traditions (or according to another account from 750,000) and contained 30,000 (in some accounts 40,000) traditions. Aḥmed boasted that whatever was in it was a reliable basis for argument, and that what was not contained in it was not to be regarded as a sound basis. He looked upon this book as an imâm which was to settle all differences of opinion about any Sunna of the Prophet[4]). It has always had the greatest reputation in Mo-

---

1) Cf. Chapter II near the end; Chapter III near the beginning.

2) al-Nawawî, Biog. Dict. ١٤٣.

3) Kitâb al-Fihrist I, ٢٢٩.

4) al-Subkî, p. 133, l. 20, والف مُسنده وهو اصل من اصول هذه الامة. l. 27 قال لنا [الامام] ان هذا الكتاب قد جمعته وانتقيته من اكثر من سبعمائة وخمسين الفا فيما اختلف فيه المسلمون من حديث رسول

hammedan theological circles, and has been used as a basis of many smaller works and as a source of information by many authors. Its immense size and the very inconvenient method of its arrangement have, however, done a great deal to prevent its becoming much more used than it actually has been. In fact, it has been rarely mastered by any one individual, and perhaps as rarely transcribed by one person. Hence it is that, whereas there are a number of partial copies of the work, only one complete manuscript is known to-day [1]).

The Musnad as compiled by Aḥmed ibn Ḥanbal is no longer extant [2]), nor does it seem to have survived his own age; for Abû Abd al-Raḥmân Abdallah Aḥmed's son, who edited, with some additions of his own, the work of his

---

الله صلعم فارجعوا اليه فان كان فيه والا ليس بحجة.... فقال عملت هذا الكتاب امامًا اذا اختلف الناس فى سنّة عن رسول الله صلعم رجع اليه وقال ايضا خرّج ابى المسند من سبعمائة الف حديث قال ابو موسى المدينى ولم يخرج الا عمّنْ ثبت عنده صدقه وديانته دون من طَعَنَ فى امانته [Cod. has these points. Read طُعِنَ?] ثم ذكر باسناده الى عبد الله ابن الامام احمد رحمة الله عليهما قال سالت ابى عن عبد العز[يز] ابن ابان فقال لم اخرج عنه فى المسند شيئًا لمّا حدّث بحديث المواقيت تركته قال ابو موسى فاما عدد احاديث المسند فلم ازل اسمع من افواه الناس انها اربعون الفا الى ان قرات على ابى منصور بن زريق ببغداد قال انا ابو بكر الخطيب قال قال ابن المنادى لم يكن فى الدنيا اروى عن ابيه منه يعنى عبد الله ابن الامام احمد لانه سمع المسند وهو ثلاثون الفا والتفسير وهو مائة الف وعشرون الفا الخ

The sum 40000 for the traditions is that given in the Kitâb al-Fihrist I, ٢٢٩, l. 22.

1) Goldziher, Z. D. M. G., L, 466 f.

2) Goldziher, Z. D. M. G., L, 473.

father after his death [1]), speaks of what he heard from his father, what he read to his father from his own copy of the original page, and what he had gathered from books and papers belonging to his father, as being embodied in the edition which he had made [2]). In some cases he says that he 'thinks' he had a tradition from his father in such and such a form, in such and such a manner of communication, or under such and such a heading. These evidences seem to point to the absence of any book which could have been used to verify what he had in mind. The Musnad as now preserved to us is in the revised form given it by the editorial labours of Abdallah ibn Aḥmed. It is mentioned, further, that an edition of the Musnad with certain supplementary traditions by the editor was made by Abû ʿOmar Moḥammed ibn Abd al-Wahîd († 345). A commentary in eighty sections making together ten volumes was prepared by Abu ʾl-Ḥasan ibn Abd al-Hâdî al-Sindî († 1139); an epitome called al-Durr al-Muntacad min Musnad Aḥmed was compiled by Zain ad-Dîn ʿOmar ibn Aḥmed al-Shammâ al-Ḥalabî [3]) and, finally, an edition of the Musnad ordered alphabetically according to the names of the Companions of the Prophet from whom the traditions take their origin was made by the Jerusalem scholar Abû Bekr Moḥammed ibn Abdallah al-Makdisî: ترتيب مسند احمد بن حنبل على حروف المعاجم [4]). A printed edition of the work, based chiefly on a manuscript in the Library of the Sâdat Wafâʿîya at Cairo was issued in 1896 [5]).

The great work according to the boast of Aḥmed himself was intended to be encyclopaedic in its aim, as far as traditions related to the Sunna of the Prophet were concerned. It apparently attempts to comprehend everything which in

---

1) Goldziher, Z. D. M. G., L, 472, 504.
2) Goldziher, Z. D. M. G., L, 497.
3) Ḥaj. Ḥal. V, 534 f.
4) Goldziher, Z. D. M. G., L, 470.
5) Goldziher, Z. D. M. G., L, 468.

the author's judgment could possibly contribute to a complete notion of what the Sunna was. All the reliable materials coming down from the Companions were meant to be included within the book. Hence, only the very broadest tests were applied to the traditions which were accepted by the author. The main criterion was that the Isnâd must be sound; that is, no man whose reputation for truthfulness or religious character was deemed unsatisfactory could be allowed to validate a tradition [1]). The test of conflict with clear teaching of the Prophet elsewhere found was also applied, but not with the most thorough consistency [2]); and, finally, the duplicate traditions were excluded, though here, also, Aḥmed's practice was not uniform [3]). In a work of such an aim we expect to find and in this work do find all kinds of traditions: those relating to ritual, legal precedents, moral maxims, fables, legends, historical incidents and biographical anecdotes [4]). Furthermore, we cannot find the same order which is observed in the great collections of al-Bokhârî and Muslim. Their material was much less in quantity than Aḥmed ibn Ḥanbal's and much narrower in its scope. They had a purpose much more special in view, which permitted of a real system being observed. But Aḥmed's aim was simply to store up genuine traditions and nothing more [5]).

In such a collection, too, as that found in the Musnad any one acquainted with the genesis of Mohammedan tradition can understand that there would appear all sorts of inconsistencies and contradictions. Such, in fact, are found in the book. Sayings are attributed to the Prophet which never could have been uttered by him. He is represented as having prescience of events occurring long after his time, and as lending his countenance to views whose later origin

1) Goldziher, Z. D. M. G., L, 478 & note 1); v. note 4, p. 19.
2) Goldziher, Z. D. M. G., L, 480; v. note 4, p. 19.
3) Goldziher, Z. D. M. G., L, 481.
4) Goldziher, Z. D. M. G., L, 474.
5) v. note 4, p. 19.

is clearly known; opposite opinions and parties alike find their support in distinct traditions of the Musnad [1]). It might seem that there was room to question the honesty of the author who would thus leave all kinds of discrepancies in his work; but reflection will shew that a dishonest man would hardly admit or allow to remain in his compilation such things, and that the aim of Aḥmed, comprehensive and unscientific as it was, sufficiently accounts for whatever of miscellaneous or contradictory character there appears. It is quite likely, too, that the Musnad was a collection brought together during many years, and one to which labor was not continuously devoted by the compiler. In the use of the work, also, after its completion there probably was no continuity observed. He would read a portion now and a portion again, a portion to this one and a portion to that one (only three persons are said to have heard it complete from Aḥmed himself). These facts would make it difficult for him to have in mind and eye the whole work at one time, so as to perceive the mutual harmony or discrepancy of the parts of which it was composed. He, thus, might easily admit and with difficulty correct such inconsistencies as those of which we have spoken. With his aim, as we conceive it, however, inconsistencies made very little difference. He was but collecting sound traditions, and not supporting particular opinions or movements. It was not his idea to constitute himself a harmonist. Dishonesty in connection with any of the contents of the Musnad lies properly with other and earlier authorities than Aḥmed. We have no record of his having been charged with fabricating traditions during his lifetime [2]). His great fault was the uncritical aim and method. Even in the Isnâds, where he was supposed to be an excellent critic,

---

1) Goldziher, Z. D. M. G., L, 478, 489 f.

2) During the trial before al-Muᶜtaṣim it was not objected that any of his traditional arguments were unsound. When he was charged with plagiarizing a tradition (which he had not there cited), he was angry and took pains to put his adversaries to confusion. Cf. a passage in the long Arabic note in Chapter II.

ıc appears to have been rather liberal. There are found ists of authorities with anonymous individuals even as the irst sources of the traditions cited; a few names are given :redit, also, who do not stand as reputable authorities in he opinion of many theologians. In the cases of most of he latter Aḥmed, however, makes a special note to the :ffect that he sees no reason to refuse the traditions furnished ›y them. And, lastly, he favours at times the Kuṣṣâṣ, who, vhile not altogether discountenanced as authorities, were ıot held in great repute [1]).

Abdallah, Aḥmed's son, did his part as editor with great :onscientiousness, noting carefully his own additions to the naterials gathered by his father, and inserting corrections .nd glosses with explicit statement of his own authorship of hem. The traditions which he added to the Musnad appear o have been afterwards brought together by him in a se›arate book which bore the title زوائد مسند الامام احمد بن حنبل لولده عبد الله الزاهد. In some cases where Abdallah ıad heard a tradition found in the Musnad from another eacher as well as his father, he wrote a note to that effect vhen putting in the tradition concerned [2]).

During his lifetime Aḥmed read the Musnad to his sons ›âliḥ and Abdallah and to his uncle Isḥâḳ ibn Ḥanbal, and hey alone formed the favoured circle who heard the com›lete work from the lips of its author [3]).

As may be inferred from what has been already said,

---

1) Goldziher, Z. D. M. G., L, 471 f, 478 f; Cf. De Goeje, Gloss. Belâdhorî nd Gloss. Fragm. Hist. Ar. قصّ. The Ḳuṣṣâṣ having as storytellers no very erious aim were naturally enough in discredit with serious traditionists, but may well have been that such men actually furnished some sound tradi.ons. According to the critical method then in vogue, the soundness of such :aditions would depend upon their contents to some extent, but more upon he Isnâds.

2) Goldziher, Z. D. M. G., L, 501 ff. Abdallah is said to have made aditions, likewise, to his father's كتاب الزهد.

3) v. note 4, p. 19.

the great work of Aḥmed is not arranged with any reference whatever to the subjects of the traditions it includes. Such an arrangement is found rather in that kind of tradition-collections called Musannafs, a class of works which properly belongs to a later development of Arabic literature than these Musnads. The latter class, of which Aḥmed's book is representative, is ordered according to the earliest authorities or first sources of the traditions cited, and according to the localities where the author obtained his materials. In such an arrangement we would expect to find traditions bearing a particular colour and evincing a similar tendency brought together, according to the predilection or bias of the original authorities or of the localities made responsible for the traditions. This feature, which is almost inevitable in employing such a method, is a mere accident of the classification, and forms no part of the author's intention. Such a miscellaneous arrangement and the mass of the materials brought together made these Musnads of little general value as works of reference on account of their inconvenience, and led to such an undertaking as that of al-Maḳdisî to bring a more convenient order into the book of Aḥmed ibn Ḥanbal. It does not diminish the awkwardness of his work, either, that the traditions of the same primitive authority should be found, some in a section classified according to the names of the men, and others in one or more sections classified according to the places in which the materials were gathered [1]).

The order of the Musnad of Aḥmed ibn Ḥanbal, as found in the recently published Cairo edition, is as follows;

Vol. I, pp. 2—195, Traditions of ten Companions of the Prophet, including the first four Khalifs.

Vol. I, pp. 195—199, Four other Companions (principle of separate classification not given).

Vol. I, pp. 199—206, The Ahlu ʾl-Bait.

---

1) Goldziher, Z. D. M. G., L, 469 ff.

Vol. I, p. 206 to the end, Vol. II and Vol. III to p. 400, The well-known Companions.
Vol. III, pp. 400—503, Traditions of Meccans.
Vol. IV, pp. 2—88, Traditions of Medînans.
Vol. IV, pp. 88—239, Traditions of Syrians.
Vol. IV, pp. 239—419, Traditions of Kûfans.
Vol. IV, p. 419—Vol. V, p. 113, Traditions of Baṣrans.
Vol. V, p. 113—Vol. VI, p. 29, The Anṣâr.
Vol. VI, pp. 29—467, The Women. (In pp. 383—403 of this section are put in some traditions (من مسند القبائل) [1]).

It should be carefully borne in mind that each one of the sections enumerated, as well as the whole work, is called a Musnad, e. g. The Musnad of the Meccans, the Musnad of the Anṣâr etc. [2]). Such is a general description of the long famous Musnad of the Imâm Aḥmed.

Aḥmed's Pupils. We have the names of some of those who heard the Tradition from him, among whom were his teachers Abd al-Razzâḳ, Ibn Mahdî and Yazîd ibn Hârûn. Other pupils were Abu'l-Walîd, ʿAlî ibn al-Madînî, al-Bokhârî, Muslim, Abû Dâûd, al-Dhuhlî, Abû Zurʿa al-Râzî, Abû Zurʿa al-Dimashkî, Ibrâhîm al-Ḥarbî, Abû Bekr Aḥmed ibn Moḥammed ibn Hânî al-Ṭâ'î al-Athram, al-Baghawî, Obaidallah ibn Moḥammed Abu 'l-Ḳâsim (his last pupil آخرهم [3]), Ibn Abî Dunya, Moḥammed ibn Isḥâḳ al-Ṣaghânî, Abû Ḥâtim al-Râzî, Aḥmed ibn Abi 'l-Hawârî, Mûsâ ibn Hârûn, Ḥanbal ibn Isḥâḳ, Othmân ibn Saʿîd al-Dârimî, Hajjâj ibn al-Shâʿir, Abd al-Malik ibn Abd al-Hamîd al-Maimûn, Baḳî ibn Makhlad al-Andalusî, Yaʿḳûb ibn Shaiba, Duḥaim al-Shâmî and his own sons Abdallah and Ṣâliḥ [4]). His method of teaching was to read the tra-

---

1) Goldziher, Z. D. M. G., L, 470.
2) Goldziher, Z. D. M. G., L, 472. On the Musnad cf., also, Goldziher, Moh. Studien II, 228, 230, 266, 270.
3) Dhahabî, Liber Class. 8, N°. 18.
4) al-Nawawî, Biog. Dict. ١٤٣. The name مُخلّد in al-Nawawî's list should be مَخْلَد; v. de Jong's ed. of Dhahabî's Muschtabih 74, Ḳamûs, and Abu'l-

ditions from a book rather than recite them [1]). He is not known to have taught in any other way except in the case of about one hundred traditions [2]). He adopted this method notwithstanding the fact that he had everything committed to memory and was generally regarded as being almost the first ḥâfiẓ of his time. On one occasion when he was delivering the tradition to some of his pupils, after they had learned it by heart, and were preparing to write it, Aḥmed exclaimed, 'the book is the best ḥâfiẓ' and with that he started up and brought a book [3]). His wish probably was to verify his memoriter recitation.

Aḥmed does not appear to have taken money from his disciples, either for his services as a teacher or for the writing materials etc. which he furnished [4]).

Relations with al-Shâfiʿi. For al-Shâfiʿî he always entertained the most affectionate regard. His testimony to him was that none in his day carried an ink-bottle or touched a pen but there was resting upon him an obligation to al-Shâfiʿî [5]). For thirty years he declared he had never prayed a prayer without offering in it a petition for his friend, and on his son's asking him what kind of a man al-Shâfiʿî was that he should pray for him so regularly, he replied that al-Shâfiʿî was like the sun to the world and like good health to mankind [6]). Al-Shâfiʿî, too, seems to have had a great

---

Maḥâsin II. ٣٢٨. رحيم الشامى I have added from al-Subkî, p. 133, l. 18, cf. Dhahabî Liber Class. 8, N°. 69.

1) al-Nawawî, Biog. Dict. ١٤٣.

2) Abû Nuʿaim, 139 *a*, يقول (عبد الله بن احمد بن حنبل) ما رايتُ ابى فى حفظه حدّث من غير كتاب الا باقلّ من مائة حديث

3) al-Nawawî, Biog. Dict. ١٤٤, cf. Goldziher, Moh. Stud. II, 196, 197.

4) al-Nawawî, Biog. Dict. ١٤٥, cf. Goldziher, Moh. Stud. II, 181.

5) al-Nawawî, Biog. Dict. ٩٣.

6) al-Nawawî, Biog. Dict. ٧٩. al-Maḳrîzî, p. 2, وقال الامام احمد ما صليت صلاة منذ ثلاثين سنة الا وانا ادعو للشافعى كذا فى الحلية

respect and affection for Aḥmed. He is said to have declared, 'O Abû Abdallah, whenever a tradition from the Messenger of God is sound in your judgment, tell it to us that we may conform to it'. Aḥmed is reported as saying that al-Shâfiʿî told him that he (Aḥmed) was more learned in the sound traditions than himself, and that his (al-Shafiʿi's) desire was to know from him what he regarded as sound that he might adopt it. Aḥmed's son Abdallah declared that, wherever al-Shâfiʿî says in his book 'a trustworthy person told me that', or 'a trustworthy person related that to me', he refers to his father. Abdallah said, further, that the book which al-Shâfiʿî composed in Baghdâd was more correct than the book which he composed in Egypt, because, when he was in Baghdâd, he asked Aḥmed and the latter suggested corrections to him, but when he was in Egypt and was inclined to adopt a weak tradition there was no one to correct him [1]. Al-Shâfiʿî

للحافظ ابى نعيم وقال الامام الغزالى فى الاحياء اربعين سنة ولكثرة دعائه له قال له ابنه اىّ رجل كان الشافعى حتى تدعو له كل هذا الدعاء فقال يا بنى كان الشفعى كالشمس للدنيا وكالعافية للناس

1) Abû Nuʿaim, 140b, حدثنا سليمان بن احمد قال سمعت عبد الله بن احمد بن حنبل يقول سمعت ابى يقول قال محمد بن ادريس الشافعى يابا عبد الله اذا صَحَّ عندكم الحديث عن رسول الله صلعم فاخبرونا به حتى نرجع اليه   حدثنا سليمان [ابن احمد] قال سمعت عبد الله بن احمد يقول سمعت ابى يقول قال لى محمد بن ادريس الشافعى انت اعلم بالاخبار الصحاح منا فاذا كان خبر صحيح فأعلمنى حتى اذهب اليه كوفيا كان او بصريا او شاميا قال عبد الله جميع ما حدث به الشافعى فى كتابه فقال حدثنى الثقة او اخبرنى الثقة فهو ابى رحمه الله، قال عبد الله وكتابه الذى صنّفه ببغداد هو اعدل من الكتاب الذى صنفه بمصر وذاك انه حيث

went to Egypt in the year 198, stayed probably two or three months and then returned to Mecca, whence he took his final journey to Egypt in the end of 199 or the beginning of 200. In ʿIrâḳ he composed the Book of the Hajj. His first visit to Baghdâd was in the year 195; he left there for Mecca in 197 and returned for a month to Baghdâd in 198 [1]). Al-Shâfiʿî said, 'I left Baghdâd and did not leave behind in it any one greater as a fakîh, or one more pious, self-denying, or learned than Aḥmed' [2]).

Other Contemporaries. Al-Haitham ibn Jamîl, one of Aḥmed's teachers in Baghdâd, thought highly of his pupil's authority. On one occasion he was told that Aḥmed ibn Ḥanbal differed from him in regard to a certain tradition and his reply was, 'My wish is that it may shorten my life and may prolong Aḥmed ibn Ḥanbal's life' [3]). It is worthy of note that Aḥmed gave apparently unreserved credit to *Yazîd ibn Hârûn.* Yazîd ibn Hârûn as a traditionist. At one time Mûsâ ibn Ḥizâm al-Tirmidhî was on his way to Abû Suleimân al-Jûzajânî to ask him some question about the books of Moḥammed ibn al-Ḥasan when Aḥmed met him and enquired whither he was going. On learning his object, Aḥmed remarked

---

كان هاهنا يسال الشيخ فيُغيّر عليه ولم يكن بمصر مَنْ يُغيّر عليه اذا ذهب الى خبرٍ ضعيف قال وسمعت ابى يقول استفاد منّا الشافعى ما لم نستفد منه

1) De Goeje, Z. D. M. G. XLVII. 115; Ibn Chall. N°. 569.

2) al-Subkî, p. 132, l. 9, قال فيه الشافعى فيما رواه حرملة خرجت من بغداد وما خلفت بها افقه ولا اورع ولا ازهد ولا اعلم من احمد cf. Ibn Chall. N°. 19.

3) Abû Nuʿaim, 141 *a*, حدّث الهيثم بن جميل بحديث عن هشيم فوهم فيه فقيل له خالفوك فى هذا قال مَن خالفنى قالوا احمدُ بن حنبل قال وددتُ انّه نقص من عُمرى وزاد فى عمر احمد بن حنبل

that it was a very strange thing that Ibn Ḥizâm should be ready to accept the testimony of three persons leading up to Abû Ḥanîfa, and yet refuse that of three authorities forming a chain of tradition to the Prophet. Ibn Ḥizâm did not grasp Aḥmed's meaning and asked for an explanation. Aḥmed answering said, "You will not receive the Isnâd 'Yazîd ibn Hârûn in Wâsiṭ said, Ḥomaid told me from Anas, saying, the Messenger of God said'; and, yet, you receive the Isnâd 'Such an one said, Moḥammed ibn al-Ḥasan told us from Yaᶜkûb from Abû Ḥanîfa". Mûsa adds that he was so impressed by the force of what Aḥmed said that he engaged a boat at once and went to Wâsiṭ to receive the Tradition from Yazîd ibn Hârûn [1]). When Aḥmed himself went to study with Yazîd, on the other hand, Yazîd ibn Saᶜîd al-Ḳaṭṭân enquired for him, and, on learning where he had gone, exclaimed, 'What need has he of Yazîd?' This was interpreted to mean that Aḥmed was more fit to be the teacher than the scholar of Yazîd ibn Hârûn [2]).

---

1) Abû Nuᶜaim, 144 *b*, (يقول موسى بن حزام الترمذى بترمذ) كنت اختلف الى ابى سليمان الجُوزَجانى [Cod. الخُوزجانى] فى كتب محمد بن الحسن فاستقبلنى احمد بن حنبل عند الجسر فقال لى الى اين فقلت الى ابى سليمان فقال لى احمد العجب منكم تركتم الى النبى صلعم ثلاثة واقبلتم على ثلاثة الى ابى حنيفة فقلت كيف يابا عبد الله قال يزيد بن هارون بواسط يقول حدثنا حميد عن انس قال قال رسول الله صلعم وهذا يقول ثنا محمد بن الحسن عن يعقوب عن ابى حنيفة قال موسى بن حزام فوقع قوله فى قلبى فاكتريت زورقا من ساعتى فانحدرت الى واسط فسمعت من يزيد بن هارون

2) Abû Nuᶜaim, 140 *a*, قال (عبد الله) سمعت ابى يقول كنت مقيما على يحيى بن سعيد القطان ثم خرجتُ الى واسط فسأل يحيى بن سعيد عنى فقالوا خرج الى واسط فقال اىّ شىء يصنع

ᶜAlî ibn al-Madînî. ᶜAlî ibn al-Madînî not only shewed great respect for Aḥmed, but received it, likewise, from him. It is said that when ᶜAlî came to Baghdâd he took a leading place among the traditionists, and at such times as men like Aḥmed and Yaḥya ibn Maᶜîn and Khalaf and al-Muᶜaiṭî were in difference of opinion on any point the voice of ᶜAlî was regarded as decisive. Aḥmed out of respect never called ᶜAlî by his proper name, but always by his kunya Abu ʾl-Ḥasan [1]). While Aḥmed was regarded as the best faḳîh of his time, Ibn al-Madînî was said to have superior knowledge of the different views held as to traditions [2]), and to be the most learned of the doctors of his day, as Yaḥya ibn Maᶜîn was the one who wrote the most, and Abû Bekr ibn Abû Shaiba was the greatest ḥâfiẓ [3]).

Yaḥya ibn Maᶜîn. Of Yaḥya ibn Maᶜîn Aḥmed said, that the hearing of Tradition from Yaḥya was healing for troubled breasts. He said, also, that Yaḥya ibn Maᶜîn was a man whom God created for the express purpose of exposing the lies of liars; and any tradition which Yaḥya did not know was no tradition. When he died Yaḥya left behind him one hundred and fourteen cases and four casks of books. This is in harmony with what has just been said as to his having written more traditions than any of his contemporaries [4]).

بواسِط قالوا يُقيم على يزيد بن هارون قال واى شىء يمنع عند يزيد ابن هارون قال ابو عبد الرحمن يعنى ابى هو اعلم منه

1) al-Nawawî, Biog. Dict. ۴۴۳, cf. Goldziher Moh. Stud. I. 267.

2) al-Subkî, p. 185, l. 1, وقيل لابى داود احمد اعلم ام على قال على اعلم باختلاف الحديث من احمد

3) al-Nawawî, Biog. Dict. ۱۴۴.

4) „ „ ۹۳۸; the word جبات should probably be read حِبَابٌ, *jars*, (sg. حُبّ) vid. De Goeje, Gloss. Bibl. Geog.

Al-Husain ibn ʿAlî al-Karâbîsî. One of the contemporaries of Aḥmed ibn Ḥanbal was al-Ḥusain ibn ʿAlî ibn Yazîd Abû ʿAlî al-Karâbîsî († 245 A. H.) This man was well known both as a faḳîh and as a traditionist. At first, he was a disciple of the Ra'y school, but, later, inclined to the views of al-Shâfiʿî, became a student of his teachings and received authorization [1]) to teach what he had learned. The Khatîb al-Baghdâdî tells that he was much disesteemed (lit. was very rare) as a traditionist because he had acquired a bad name with Aḥmed ibn Ḥanbal. This was owing to his strong leaning toward dialectical theology (علم الكلام) [2]), in general, and, more particularly, to his application of dialectics in order to come to his conclusions touching the Ḳorân. He was a professed believer in the uncreated existence of the Ḳorân, but could not satisfy Aḥmed ibn Ḥanbal by his profession of this doctrine, and much less by his utterances on the symbolic expression of the Ḳorân in articulate human sounds (لفظ القرآن) [3]). He appears to have trifled somewhat in his treatment of subjects that were to minds such as that of Aḥmed in the highest degree sacred and serious. For example, his declared faith in the created nature of the Lafẓ al-Ḳorân was on one occasion told to Aḥmed, who, though the profession was in full accord with his own conviction, declared it heresy, because the process by which it had been reached was that of reasoning and not that of submission to traditional authority. Aḥmed's judgment on him was made known to al-Karâbîsî, who changed his declaration of faith and professed that the Lafẓ al-Ḳorân was uncreated as well as the Ḳorân itself. Naturally enough,

---

1) اجازة cf. Goldziher, Moh. Stud. II. 189.

2) For origin and use of the term كلام vid. Houtsma, De Strijd over het Dogma, 87 f.; cf. Shahrastânî, Haarbr. transl'n II. 388 f.

3) The Lafẓ al-Ḳorân is used here with reference to the enunciation of the Ḳorân in human speaking; in the following paragraph we have taken it to have a wider scope.

this pleased Aḥmed no better and he vigorously declared that this, too, was heresy. The whole quarrel, as one can readily see, was with the method of al-Karâbîsî, far more than with his theological conclusions [1]).

---

1) al-Subkî, p. 172, الحسين بن على بن يزيد ابو على الكرابيسى كان
اماما جليلا جامعا بين الفقه والحديث تفقه اولا على مذهب اهل
الرأى ثم تفقه للشافعى . . . .
. . . . (قال داود الاصبهانى) قال لى حسين الكرابيسى لما قدم
الشافعى الى بغداد قدمته فقلت له تاذن لى ان اقرا عليك الكتب فابا-
وقال خذ كتب الزعفرانى فقد اجزتها لك فاخذها اجازة قال الخطيب
حديث الكرابيسى يعز جدا وذلك ان احمد بن حنبل كان يتكلم
فيه بسبب مسئلة اللفظ وهو ايضا كان يتكلم فى احمد فتجنب
الناس الاخذ عنه لهذا السبب قلت كان ابو على الكرابيسى من
متكلمى اهل السنة استاذ فى علم الكلام كما هو استاذ فى الحديث
والفقه وله كتاب فى المقالات قال ابو الخطيب الامام فخر الدين فى
كتاب غاية المرام على كتابه فى المقالات معول المتكلمين فى معرفة
مذاهب الخوارج وسائر اهل الاهواء قلت المروى انه قيل للكرابيسى
ما تقول فى القران قال كلام الله غير مخلوق فقال له السائل فما تقول
فى لفظى بالقران فقال لفظك به مخلوق فمضى السائل الى احمد بن
حنبل فشرح له ما جرى فقال هذه بدعة والذى عندنا ان احمد
رضه اشار بقوله هذه بدعة الى الجواب عن مسئلة اللفظ اذ ليست
مما يعنى المرء وخوض المرء فى ما لا يعنيه من علم الكلام بدعة فكان
السكوت عن الكلام فيه اجمل واولى ولا يظن باحمد رحمه الله انه
يدّعى ان اللفظ الخارج من بين الشفتين قديم ومقالة الحسين هذه
قد نقل مثلها عن البخارى والحارث بن اسد المحاسبى ومحمد بن
نصر المروزى وغيرهم وسيكون لنا عودة فى ترجمة البخارى الى الكلام
فى ذلك ونقل ان احمد لما قال هذه بدعة رجع السائل الى الحسين

Al-Bokhârî. We have interesting evidence of the doctrinal sympathy between al-Bokhârî and Aḥmed ibn Ḥanbal. A jealous rival of al-Bokhâri in Nîsâbûr charged the latter with heresy on the point of the Lafẓ al-Ḳorân, and the imputation was taken up by many. But it is clear that al-Bokhârî's silence on the question, from reluctance to be drawn into any reasoning on a point for which there was so little evidence pro or con in Tradition, was the only ground for suspecting his orthodoxy. His belief, as well as that of Aḥmed ibn Ḥanbal, was that the Ḳorân itself was not created, but the Lafẓ al-Ḳorân, by which he understood the human acts of writing,

---

فقال له تلفظك بالقران غير مخلوق فعاد الى احمد فعرفه مقالة الحسين ثانيا فانكر احمد ايضا ذلك وقال هذه ايضا بدعة وهذا يدلك على ما نقوله من ان احمد انما اشار بقوله هذه بدعة الى الكلام فى اصل المسئلة والا فكيف ينكر اثبات الشىء ونفيه فافهم ما قلناه فهو الحق ان شاء الله تعالى وبما قال احمد نقول فنقول الصواب عدم الكلام فى المسئلة راسا ما لم يدع الى الكلام حاجة ماسّة ومما يدلك ايضا على ما نقوله وان السلف لا ينكرون ان لفظنا حادث وان سكوتهم انما هو عن الكلام فى ذلك لا عن اعتقاده ان الرواة رووا ان الحسين بلغه كلام احمد فيه فقال لاقولن مقالة حتى يقول احمد بخلافها فيكفر فقال لفظى بالقران مخلوق وهذه الحكاية قد ذكرها كثير من الحنابلة وذكرها شيخنا الذهبى فى ترجمة الامام احمد وفى ترجمة الكرابيسى فانظر الى قول الكرابيسى فيها ان مخالفها يكفر والامام احمد فيما يعتقده لم يخالفها وانما انكر ان يتكلم فى ذلك فاذا تاملت ما سطرناه ونظرنا قول شيخنا فى غير موضع من تاريخه ان مسئلة اللفظ مما يرجع الى قول جهم عرفت ان الرجل لا يدرى فى هذه المضايق ما يقول وقد اكثر هو واصحابه من ذكر جهم بن صفوان وليس قصدهم الا جعل الخ

reading, reciting and all other acts connected with the use or preservation of the revelation, was created [1]).

---

1) al-Subkî, p. 214, قال الحسن بن محمد بن جابر قال لنا الذهلى لما ورد البخارى نيسابور اذهبوا الى هذا الرجل الصالح فاسمعوا منه فذهب الناس اليه واقبلوا على السماع منه حتى ظهر الخلل فى مجلس الذهلى فحسده بعد ذلك وتكلم فيه قال ابو احمد بن عدى ذكر لى جماعة من المشايخ ان محمد بن اسمعيل لما ورد نيسابور واجتمعوا عليه حسده بعض المشايخ فقال لاصحاب الحديث ان محمد بن اسمعيل يقول اللفظ بالقران مخلوق فامتحنوه فلما حضر الناس قام اليه رجل فقال يابا عبد الله ما تقول فى اللفظ بالقران مخلوق هو ام غير مخلوق فاعرض عنه ولم يجبه فاعاد السؤال فاعرض عنه ثم اعاد فالتفت اليه البخارى وقال القران كلام الله غير مخلوق وافعال العباد مخلوقة والامتحان بدعة فشغّب الرجل وشغّب الناس وتفرقوا عنه وقعد البخارى فى منزله قال محمد بن يوسف الفربرى سمعت محمد بن اسمعيل يقول اما افعال العباد فمخلوقة حدثنا على بن عبد الله ثنا مروان بن معاوية ثنا ابو ملك عن ربعى عن حذيفة قال قال النبى صلعم ان الله يصنّع كل صانع وصنعته وسمعت عبيد الله بن سعيد يقول ما زلت اسمع اصحابنا يقولون ان افعال العباد مخلوقة قال البخارى حركاتهم واصواتهم واكسابُهم وكتابتهم مخلوقة فاما القران المتلو المثبت فى المصاحف المسطور المكتوب الموعى فى القلوب فهو كلام الله ليس بمخلوق قال الله تعالى بل هو ايات بينات فى صدور الذين اوتوا العلم وقال يقال فلان حسنُ القراءة ولا يقال حسن القران ولا روىّ القران وانما ينسب الى العباد القراءة لان القران كلام الرب والقراءة فعل العبد وليس لاحد ان يشرع فى امر الله بغير علم كما زعم بعضهم ان القران بالفاظنا والفاظنا به شىء واحد والتلاوة هى المتلو او القراءة

Mohammed ibn Aslam. Another of Aḥmed's companions, whose highest compliment was that he resembled the great Imâm, was Moḥammed ibn Aslam Abû Ḥusain al-Kindî al-Tûsî

هى المقروءة فقيل له ان التلاوة فِعل القارئُ وعمل التالى فرجع وقال ظننتهما مَصدرين فقيل له هل لا امسكت كما أَمسك كثير من اصحابك ولو بعثت الى من كتب عنك واستردت ما اثبت وضربت عليه فزعم ان كيف يمكن هذا وقال قلتَ ومضى فقلت له كيف جاز لك ان تقول فى الله شيئا لا يقوم به شرحا وبيانا اذا لم تميّز بين التلاوة والمتلو فسكت اذ لم يكن عنده جواب وقال ابو حامد الاعمش رايت البخارى فى جنازة سعيد بن مروان والذهلى يساله عن الاسماء والكنى والعلل ويمر فيه البخارى مثل السهم فما اتى على هذا شهر حتى قال الذهلى الا من يختلف الى مجلسه فلا يأتِنا فانهم كتبوا الينا من بغداد انه تكلم فى اللفظ ونهيناه فلم ينتهِ فلا تقربوه قلت كان البخارى على ما رُوِىَ وسنحكى ما فيه ممن قل لفظى بالقران مخلوق وقال محمد بن يحيى الذُهلى من زعم ان لفظى بالقران مخلوق فهو مبتدع لا يجالس ولا يكلَّم ومن زعم ان القران مخلوق فقد كفر وانما اراد محمد بن يحيى والعلم عند الله ما اراده احمد بن حنبل كما قدمناه فى ترجمة الكرابيسى من النهى عن الخوض فى هذا ولم يرد مخالفة البخارى وان خالفه وزعم ان لفظه الخارج من بين شفتيه المحدثتين قديم فقد باء بغضب واثم عظيم والظن به خلاف ذلك وانما اراد هو واحمد وغيرهما من الائمّة النهى عن الخوض فى مسائل الكلام وكلام البخارى عندنا محمول على ذكر ذلك عند الاحتياج اليه فالكلام فى الكلام عند الاحتياج واجب والسكوت عند [عند dittography] عدم الاحتياج سنّة فافهم ذلك ودع خرافات المورخين واضرب صفحا عن تمويهات الضالّين الذين يظنون انهم محدثون وانهم عند السنة واقفون

(† 242 A. H.). This man was an earnest opponent of the Jahmî and Murjî [1]) sects, of the former because they professed that

---

وهم عنها مبعدون وكيف يظن بالبخارى انه يذهب الى شىء من
اقوال المعتزلة وقد صحّ عنه فيما رواه الفريدى وغيره انه قال انى
لاستجهل من لا يكفّر الجهمية ولا يرتاب المصنف فى ان محمد بن يحيى
لحقته آفة الحسد التى لم يسلم منها الا اهل العصْم وقد سال بعضهم
البخارى عما بينه وبين محمد بن يحيى فقال البخارى كم يعترى
محمد بن يحيى الحسد فى العلم والعلم رزق الله يعطيه من يشاء
ولقد ظرف البخارى وابان عن عظيم حكاية حيث قال وقد قال له
ابو عمرو الخفاف ان الناس قد خاضوا فى قولك لفظى بالقران مخلوق
يابا عمرو احفظ ما اقول لك من زعم من اهل نيسابور وقومس [والرقى
dittography] والرى وهمذان وبغداد والكوفة والبصرة ومكة والمدينة انى
قلت لفظى بالقران مخلوق فهو كذاب فانى لم اقله الا انى قلت افعال
العباد مخلوقة قلت تامل كلامه ما اذكاه ومعناه والعلم عندَ الله انى
لم اقل لفظى بالقران مخلوق لان الكلام فى هذا خوض فى مسائل
الكلام وصفات الله لا ينبغى الخوض فيها الا لضرورة ولكنى قلت افعال
العباد مخلوقة وهو قاعدة مُغنية عن تخصيص هذه المسألة بالذكر
فان كل عاقل يعلم ان لفظنا من جملة افعالنا وافعالنا مخلوقة فالفاظنا
مخلوقة ولقد افصح بهذا المعنى فى رواية اخرى صحيحة عنه رواه حاتم
ابن احمد الكندى فقال سمعتُ مسلم بن الحجاج فذكر الحكاية وفيها
ان رجلا قام الى البخارى فساله عن اللفظ بالقران فقال افعالنا مخلوقة
والفاظنا من افعالنا وفى الحكاية انه وقع بين القوم اذذاك اختلاف على
البخارى فقال بعضهم قال [قال dittography] لفظى بالقران مخلوق وقال
اخرون لم يقل قلت فلم يكن الانكار الخ

1) For the doctrines of Jahm ibn Ṣafwân, the founder of the Jahmîa sect, v.

the Ḳorân was created, of the latter because they held that faith was mere profession without the inward trust and experience of the heart. The argument which he adopted toward the Jahmîa was that of the Ḳorân verses in which God speaks in his own person to Moḥammed announcing his Mission, and to Moses declaring himself to be his Lord and the Lord of the worlds. In the former case it is implied that if the *word* of the speaker be not that of God, Moḥammed's Mission is called in question. If it be the word of God, then it is eternally potential in him and inseparable from any true conception of him, and, therefore, it must be uncreated. In the case of Moses, if the speaker to him be a creature, then Moses himself and the worlds also, have a second lord, — for one Lord is admitted without question, — and the professors of such a doctrine are at once convicted of Shirk (شرك); but, supposing God to have really spoken, then we have again the proceeding forth of a word which we must not regard as created with its utterance, but rather as an inseparable adjunct of the Divine Knowledge, for how otherwise could the Divine Knowledge become efficient or communicative? The sin of the Jahmîa is their Shirk; this is the result of the reasoning, and without reasoning, from the standpoint of the orthodox apologist, they are guilty, as well, of forging a lie against God (افتراء) by declaring that God did not speak to Moses though the Ḳorân says he did.

Against the Karramîya Murjiʾa Ibn Aslam maintained the

Shahrastânî Haarbrücker's transl'n I, 89; Houtsma, De Strijd over het Dogma &c. pp. 102, 123 f. On the Murjiʾa v. Houtsma, De Strijd &c. pp. 34 ff., 40; Shahrastânî, Haarbrücker's transl'n I, 156 ff. The Murjite belief as presented in Houtsma, p. 36, differs from that set forth by Moḥammed ibn Aslam, but agrees with the second class of the Karramite sects (Houtsma, p. 39) and with the Ṣifatîya Karramîya (Shahrastâni, Haarbr. transl'n I, 119 ff., especially p. 127). Aḥmed ibn Ḥanbal, it will be remembered, composed two works bearing the titles, respectively, كتاب الردّ على الجهميّة and كتاب الايمان, vid. p. 19.

doctrine that faith is a gift of God to the heart, a gift of illumination and of spiritual adornment, by means of which it is disposed to believe in God, his angels, his books, his messengers, the resurrection, the day of judgment, the final account, in foreordination to good and evil, in paradise and in hell-fire. This faith is given only to those upon whom God is pleased to bestow it, and is not complete without both the testimony of the lips as, at once, its expression and its confirmation, and the acts of the bodily members as the evidence that the confession of the lips and the antecedent faith of the heart are genuine. The testimony of the lips has for its subjects the things believed on by the heart. These it declares to be true; and, more specifically, it gives the formal confession that there is no God but Allah and that Moḥammed is his Prophet and his Messenger. The acts of the members lie in the performance of such things as God prescribes and in the abstention from such things as he forbids. These points are supported by arguments from the Ḳorân and Tradition; but by this man, as by others of the strict orthodox party, there is stress laid, as well, on arguments outside of either of these sources. For example, it is said by Moḥammed ibn Aslam that, should the Murjite view be proved correct, then the Prophet and the first Khalifs, who had not spent their whole lives in the confession of Islâm, but who had had true faith, notwithstanding, might be held inferior to any mere babbler of the sacred formulas who had been occupied long enough with his task. Those (also called Murji'a [1]) who held that works were the measure and substance of faith are opposed, too, and the argument of disparagement to the early worthies is applied here, likewise.

Moḥammed ibn Aslam was a believer in the eternal existence of the Divine attributes, but we have no record

1) Called especially الكَرّامية v. De Goeje, Gloss. Bibl. Geog.

of his method of proving his position in this respect, nor have we any exposition of what it involved [1]).

1) Abû Nuʿaim, 162 a ff, قال الشيخ واما كلامه فى النقض على المخالفين من الجهمية والمُرجِئة فشائعٌ ذائعٌ وقد كان رحمه الله من المثبتة لصفات الله انها ازلية غير محدثة فى كتابه المترجم بالرد على الجهمية ذكرت منه فصلا وجيزا من فصوله . . . .
محمد بن اسلم رحمه الله يقول زعمت الجهْمية انّ القرآن خلق وقد اشْركوا فى ذلك وهم لا يعلمون لان الله قد بين ان له كلاما فقال انى اصطفيتك على الناس برسالاتى وبكلامى وقال فى اية اخرى وكلّم الله موسى تكليما فاخْبَر ان له كلاما وانّه كلم موسى عليه السلام فقال فى تكليمه ايّاه يا موسى انى انا ربك فمن زعم ان قوله يا موسى انى انا ربك خلق وانه ليس بكلامه فقد اشرك بالله لانه زعم ان خلقا قال لموسى انى انا ربك فقد جعل هذا الزاعم ربا لموسى دون الله وقول الله تعالى ايضا لموسى فى تكليمه فاستمع لما يوحى انى انا الله لا اله الا انا فاعبدنى فقد جعل هذا الزاعم الهًا لموسى غير الله وقال فى اية اخرى لموسى فى تكليمه اياه يا موسى انى انا الله رب العالمين فمن لم يشهد انّ هذا كلام الله وقولَهُ تكلم به واللّهَ قاله وزعم انه خَلق فقد عَظُم شِركُه وافتراؤه على الله لانه زعم انّ خلقا قال لموسى يا موسى انى انا الله رب العالمين فقد جعل هذا الزاعم للعالمين ربا غير الله فاىّ شرك اعظم من هذا فتبقى الجَهْمية فى هذه القصة بين كُفْرين اثنين إنْ زعموا ان الله لم يكلم موسى فقد ردّوا كتاب الله وكفروا وان زعموا ان هذا الكلام يا موسى انى انا الله رب العالمين من خلق فقد اشركوا بالله ففى هولآء الايات بيان انّ القرانَ كلام الله وفيها بيان شرك مَن زعم ان كلامَ الله خَلق او قول الله خلق

Mystics and Ascetics. Al-Ḥârith al-Muḥâsibî.

Aḥmed ibn Ḥanbal had a predilection in favor of mystics and ascetics, but toward one of these, al-Ḥârith ibn Asad al-Muḥâsibî, he conceived a strong antipathy because this man was said to use reasoning in theological matters. The reconciliation between

---

او ما اوحى الله الى انبيائه خلق واما نَقْضُه رحمه الله على المُرجئة
الكرّامية التى زعمت ان الايمان هو القول باللسان من دون عقد القلب
الذى هو التصديق فقد صنَّف فى الايمان وفى الاعمال الدالّة على
تَصديق القلب و اماراته كتابا جامعا كبيرا . . . .
. . . . فقال رسول الله صلعم
الايمانُ ان تُومن بالله وملائكته وكتبه ورسله واليوم الاخر وبالقدرِ
كله خيره وشرّه الحديث وهذا اوّل حديث ذكره واستفتح به كتابه
وبنى عليه كلامه قال محمد بن اسلم فبدْءُ الايمان من قبل الله
قُرْبانًا ورحمةً ومنًّا يمنّ به على من يشاء من عباده فيَقذفُ فى قلبه
الايمانَ و يُحَبّبه اليه فاذا نَوَّر قلبه وزيّن فيه الايمان وحببه اليه
آمن قلبُه بالله وملائكته وكتبه ورسله واليوم الاخر وبالقدر كله
خيرِه وشرّه [وهذا الحديث اول حديث ذكره واستفتح به كتابه وبنى
عليه كلامه قال محمدُ بن اسلم فبدأ الايمان من قبل الله قربانا ورحمة
ومنّا يمنّ به على من يشاء من عباده فيقذف فى قلبه نورا a repetition
يُنور به قلبه ويَشرح به صدره ويوثر فى قلبه الايمان [of preceding matter
ويحببه (ويصحبه Codex) اليه آمن قلبه بالله وملائكته وكتبه ورسله
واليوم الاخر وبالقدر كله خيره وشرّه وآمن بالبعث والحساب والجنة والنار
حتى كانه ينظر الى ذلك و ذلك من النُور الذى قذفه الله فى قلبه فاذا
آمن قلبه نطق لسانه مصدقا لما آمن به القلب واقرّ بذلك وشهد ان

them does not seem to have ever been openly effected; but there is a story to the effect that Aḥmed took the opportunity of secretly hearing al-Ḥârith, when the latter with

---

لا اله الا الله وانّ محمدًا رسول الله صلعم وانّ هذه الاشياء التى آمن بها القلب حقّ فاذا آمن القلب وشهد اللسان عَملت الجوارح فاطاعت امرَ الله وعَملت بعَمل الايمان وادّت حق الله عليها فى فرائضه وانتهت عن محارم الله ايمانا وتصديقا بما فى القلب ونطق به اللسان فاذا فعل ذلك كان مُومنا وقد بيّن الله تعالى ذلك فى كتابه انّ بدْء الايمان من قلبه فقال ولكنّ الله حبّب اليكم الايمان وزيّنه فى قلوبكم وقال افمن شرح الله صدره للاسلام فهو على نور من ربه وقال الذين اوتوا العلم والايمان وقال كتب فى قلوبهم الايمان وقال رسول الله صلعم للحارث بن مالك عَبدٌ نوّر الله الايمان فى قلبه وقال نور يقذف فى القلب فينشرح وينفتح ثم بيّن الرسول انه تبين على المومن ايمانه بالعمل حين قيل له هل له علامة يُعرف بها قال نعم الانابة الى دار الخلود والتجافى عن دار الغرور والاستعدادُ للموت قبل نزوله الا ترون انه قد بيّن أن ايمانه يعرف بالعمل لا بالقول وقد بين ان الايمان الذى فى القلب يَنفعه اذا عَمل بعمل الايمان فاذا عَمل بعَمل الايمان تبيّن علامةُ ايمانه انهُ مومن فهذا كلامه الذى عليه البناء والكتاب وانّه جعل الاعمال علامة الايمان قال الايمان هو تصديق القلب وانّ اللسان شاهدٌ يشهد ومُعبّرٌ يعبّر عما فى القلب لا انّ الشاهد المعبر نفس الايمان من دون تصديق القلب على ما زعمت الكرّامية وضمن هذا الكتاب من الاثار المسندة وقول الصحابة والتابعين احاديث كثيرة قال محمد بن اسلم قال المرجئ الايمان واحد ويتفاضل الناس بالاعمال يُقال للمرجئ قولك يتفاضل الناس بالاعمال

his companions had been invited to a feast, and that he was then convinced that his earlier impressions of the man, however just when formed, did al-Ḥârith some injustice at

---

خطَأً لانّه زعم انّ من كان اكثر عملا فهو افضل من الذى كان اقل عملا فعلى زعمه انّ من كان بعد رسول الله كان افضلَ من رسول الله صلعم لانهم عَملوا بعدَه اعمالا كثيرة منَ الحجّ والعمرة والغَزو وَالصلاة وَالصيام والصدقة والاعمال الجسمية ورسول الله صلعم افضل منهم ثم من كان بعد ابى بكر قد عملوا اعمالا كثيرة لم يبلغها ابو بكر وابو بكر افضل منهم ثم من كان بعد عمر قد عملوا الاعمال الكثيرة التى لم يعملها عمر ولم يبلغها وعمر افضل منهم ثم من بعد اصحاب رسول الله صلعم من التابعين قد عملوا اعمالا كثيرة اكثر مما عملته الصحابة والصحابة افضل منهم واى خطأ اعظم من خطأ هذا المرجئ الذى زعم ان الناس يتفاضلون بالاعمال انّما الفضل بيد الله يوتيه من يشاء يُفضل من يشاء من عباده على من يشآء عدلا منه ورحمة فكلّ مَن فضّله الله فهو اعظم ايمانا من الذى دونه لانّ الايمان قسم من الله قسمه بين عباده كيف شاء كما قسم الارزاق فاعطى منها كل عبد ما شاء الا ترى الى قول عبد الله بن مسعود اذا احبّ اللهُ عبدا اعطاه الايمان فالايمانُ عَطيةٌ من الله يُعطيه من يشآء ويفضل من يشآء على من يشآء وهو قولُه ولكن الله حبب اليكم الايمان وزينه فى قلوبكم وقال افمن شرح الله صدره للاسلام فهو على نور من ربه افلا تَرون ان هذا التزيين وهذا النور من عَطيّة الله ورزقه يعطى من يشاء كما يشاء الا ترون ان الناس يَمُرون يوم القيامة على الصراط على قَدر نورهم فواحِد نُورُه مثل الجبل واخر نوره مثل بيت فكم بين الجبل والبيت من الزيادة والنقصان فاذا كان نور من خارج

that time. The change in Aḥmed's opinion does not seem to have been complete or to have saved al-Muḥâsibî from loss of credit in Baghdâd, for, at his death in 243 A. H., only four people attended his funeral. It is possible that this may, however, be explained as the consequence of some pious wish which he had expressed [1]).

مثل الجبل واخر مثل البيت فكذلك نورهما من داخل القلب على قدر ذلك فالمرجئة والجهمية قياسهما قياس واحد فانّ الجهمية زعمت انّ الايمان المعرفة فحسب بلا اقرار ولا عمل والمرجئة زعمت انه قول بلا تصديق قلب ولا عمل وكلاهما من شيعة ابليس وعلى زعمهم ابليس مؤمن لانه عرف ربه ووحّده حين قال فبعزتك لاغوينّهم اجمعين وحين قال انى اخاف الله رب العالمين وحين قال رب بما اغويتنى فاىّ قوم ابيَن ضلالة واظهر جهلا واعظم بدعة من قوم يزعمون انّ ابليس مؤمن فضلّوا من جهة قياسهم يقيسون على الله دينه ولا يقاس دينه فما عبدت الاوثان والاصنام الا بالقياس فاحذروا يا امة محمد القياس على الله فى دينه واتبعوا ولا تبتدعوا فانّ دين الله استنان اقتداء واتباع لا قياس وابتداع

1) v. Shahrastânî Haarbrücker's transl'n I, 97, II, 389. A different view is given of Aḥmed's quarrel with this man in von Kremer, Herrsch. Ideen des Islâms, 68, note 1. For his biography v. Ibn Chall. N°. 151. Al-Subkî, p. 230, l. 9. فاعلم ان الامام احمد رضى الله عنه كان يشدد النكير على من يتكلم فى علم الكلام خوفا ان يجرّ ذلك الى ما لا ينبغى ولا شكّ ان السكوت عنه ما لم تدع اليه الحاجة اولى والكلام فيه عند فقد الحاجة بدعة وكان الحارث قد تكلم فى شىء من مسائل الكلام قال ابو القاسم النصراباذى بلغنى ان احمد بن حنبل هجره بهذا السبب قلت والظن بالحارث انه ربما تكلم حيث دعت الحاجة ولكل مقصد والله اعلم يرحمهما الله وذكر الحاكم ابو عبد الله ان ابا بكر احمد بن

With Bishr al-Hâfî († 226) and with al-Sarî al-Saḳ [illegible] Aḥmed stood on terms of intimate friendship. He counted it his high privilege, indeed, to have seen some of the most holy men of his time in possession of little else than their piety and poverty. Those whose names are recorded beside the

---

اسحاق اخبره قال سمعت اسماعيل بن اسحاق السّرّاج يقول قال لى احمد بن حنبل يبلغنى ان الحارث هذا يكثر الكون عندك فلو احضرته منزلك واجلستنى من حيث ان لا يرانى فاسمع كلامه فقصدت الحارث وسالته ان يحضرنا تلك الليلة وان يحضر اصحابه فقال فيهم كثرة فلا تزدهم على الكسب والتمر فاتيت ابا عبد الله فاعلمته فحضر الى غرفة وَاجْتهد فى وِرده وحضر الحارث واصحابه فاكلوا ثم صلّوا العتمة ولم يصلّوا بعدها وقعدوا بين يدى الحارث لا ينطقون الى قريب نصف الليل ثم ابتدا رجل منهم فسال عن مسالة فاخذ الحارث فى الكلام واصحابُهُ يستمعُون كأنّ على رؤوسهم الطير فمنهم مَن يبكى ومنهم من يحنّ ومنهم من يزعق وهو فى كلامه فصعد[ت] فى الغرفة لأتعرّف حال ابى عبد الله فوجدته قد بكى حتى غشى عليه فانصرفت اليهم ولم يزل تلك حالهم حتى اصبحوا وذهبوا فصعدت الى ابى عبد الله فقال ما اعلم انى رايت مثل هؤلاء القوم ولا سمعت فى علم الحقائق مثل كلام هذا الرجل ومع هذا فلا ارى لك صحبتهم ثم قام وخرج وفى رواية ان احمد قال لا انكر من هذا شيئا قلت تامل هذه الحكاية بعين البصيرة واعلم ان احمد بن حنبل انما لم يرو لهذا الرجل صحبتهم لقصوره عن مقامهم فانهم فى مقام ضيق لا يسلكه كل احد فيخاف على سالكه والا فاحمد قد بكى وشكر الحارث هذا الشكر ولكل رأى واجبها وحشرنا اللهُ معهم اجمعين فى زمرة سيد المرسلين صلعم

mentioned are Abdallah ibn Idrîs († 192) Abû Dâûd al-Ḥafarî and Ayûb al-Najjâr [1]).

Dâûd ibn ʿAlî. Dâûd ibn ʿAlî, the founder of the Zahirite school, († 270) was one of Aḥmed's pupils. There was made to Aḥmed a very unlikely report against him to the effect that he had been teaching in Khorasân that the Ḳorân was created (by fashioning that which already existed محدث), and that his Lafẓ al-Ḳorân was created (by being made from nothing مخلوق). This influenced Aḥmed so that he refused to receive him, and we have no knowledge that he afterwards changed his decision; but the Zahirites are known to have been even more strict than Aḥmed on the uncreated nature of the Ḳorân, and it may be assumed that Dâûd did not long continue to be suspected by him. It is to be remarked that the informant of Aḥmed was Moḥammed ibn Yaḥya al-Dhuhlî, the same man who in jealousy accused al-Bokhârî of heretical views on the Lafẓ al-Ḳorân. Further, it should be noted that the incident is said to have occurred during the lifetime of Isḥâḳ ibn Râhawaih († 238 A. H.) when Dâûd must have been a comparatively young man. If the account be true his views must have undergone

---

1) al-Maḳrîzî, p. 1, ولقى خلقا كثيرا من الصالحين الزهاد وقال الامام ابو بكر المروزى سمعت احمد بن حنبل يقول ما أعدل بالفقر شيئا رايت قوما صالحين لقد رايت عبد الله بن ادريس وعليه جبة من لبود وقد اتى عليه السنون والدهور ورايت ابا داود الحفرى وعليه جبة مخرقة قد خرج القطن منها يصلى بين المغرب والعشاء وهو يترجح من الجوع ورايت ايوب بن النجار بمكة قد خرج مما كان فيه ومعه رشاء [Cod. رشا] يستقى به بمكة وقد خرج من كل ما كان يملكه وكان من العابدين وكان فى دنيا فتركها فى يدى يحيى القطان فى أناس أخر ذكرهم

change during the remaining years of his life. He was born in 202 A. H. and died in 270 A. H. [1]).

Ibrâhîm ibn Ismâʿîl al-Muʿtalizî. In the year 218 A. H. there died in Egypt Ibrâhîm ibn Ismâʿîl Abû Isḥâḳ al-Baṣrî al-Asadî al-Muʿtalizî, known as Ibn ʿUlayya. He was a professor of the doctrine that the Ḳorân was created and had discussions about Fiḳh with al-Shâfiʿî in Egypt, and with Aḥmed ibn Ḥanbal in Baghdâd about the Ḳorân. Aḥmed regarded him as a dangerous heretic [2]). The Ibn ʿUlayya al-Akbar whose name figures in the history of the Miḥna under al-Maʾmûn, appears to have been a different person, who was of orthodox reputation hitherto. Taken together with the similarity of the names, the seeming readiness with which Ibn ʿUlayya al-Akbar complied with the test as to the Ḳorân's creation might suggest, however, that he was in some way related to the party here mentioned. But this is only hypothetical.

II.

MIḤNA. *Historical Development.* In the beginning of the second century of Islâm al-Jaʿd ibn Dirham, teacher of the Khalif Marwân II, held the doctrine that the Ḳorân was created, and, at that time, imaginative adversaries of the belief declared themselves to be able to trace the steps of Tradition by which the heresy was to be carried back from Jaʿd to Lebîd, a Jew, whom the Prophet had declared to have bewitched him and thereby produced in him a sickness [3]). However the doctrine came to him, Jaʿd was put to death by Khâlid ibn Abdallah, Governor of ʿIrâḳ, at the command of the Khalif Hishâm. After this we hear no more of the doctrine until the time of the Abbaside Hârûn al-Rashîd [4]). The account of the

1) Goldziher, Zahiriten, p. 134. The incident is also found in al-Subkî, p. 232.
2) Abu'l-Maḥâsin I, 647.
3) Weil, Moḥammed, 94, note 121.
4) Houtsma, De Strijd over het Dogma, 101 f.

historical development (of the doctrine of the creation of the Ḳorân) [1]) which led up to the inquisition under al-Maʾmûn and his successors is given by Abuʾl-Faraj ibn al-Jauzî, († 598 A. H.) as follows: Men did not cease to follow the good rule of the fathers of Islâm and their confession that the Ḳorân was the uncreated Word of God, until the Muʿtazilites (freethinkers) [2]) appeared, professing the creation of the Ḳorân. This they did secretly until the time of al-Rashîd. Then, they ventured to teach their view more openly, until al-Rashîd said one day, 'I have heard that Bishr al-Marîsî [3]) says that the Ḳorân is created; now, verily, if God give him into my hand, I will kill him in such a way as I have never yet killed anyone'. On learning this Bishr remained hidden for about twenty years during the days of al-Rashîd. (This would carry back his public profession of the doctrine in question to about 173 A. H.) When al-Rashîd died, the matter remained in the same position during the time of his son al-Amîn; but when al-Maʾmûn succeeded, some of the Muʿtazilites led him astray and made the doctrine of the creation of the Ḳorân to appear plausible to him [4]).

---

1) On this subject cf. Weil, Chalifen II, 262, note 1; von Kremer, Herrsch. Ideen des Islâms, 233 ff. and chronological note 20, p. 127, in the same work.

2) On the name Muʿtazila and the rise of the sect, vid. Steiner, Die Muʿtaziliten, 25 f.; Houtsma, De Strijd over het Dogma, 51. On the history of the sect, Steiner, 48 ff.; Dozy, Het Islamisme, 183, 184. On their doctrines, Maçoudî VI, 20 ff.; Steiner, 3 ff.; Houtsma, 55, 80, 89, 121 f.; Haarbrücker's transl'n of Shahrastânî I, 40. On their doctrine of the Ḳorân, Steiner, 75 ff.; Houtsma, 104 f.

3) Von Hammer, Lit. Geschichte III, 205; Abuʾl-Maḥ. I, 647 and note 9; Ibn Chall. N°. 114; Steiner, Die Muʿtaziliten, 78. He is called by Houtsma, De Strijd over het Dogma, 79 (cf. note 1), one of the leading Murjites of his time. By Shahrastânî, Haarbr. I, 94, he is called, as the result of false pointing of the letters, Bishr ibn Attâb, instead of Bishr ibn Ghiyâth al-Marîsî. For his views vid. Shahrastânî, Haarbr. I, 161, 162, cf. I, 243.

4) al-Maḳrîzî, p. 3, فصل فى محنة الامام رضى الله عنه وما وقع فيها على سبيل الاختصار قال الحافظ ابو الفرج بنُ الجَوْزى لم يزل الناس على قانون السلف وقولهم انّ القران كلام الله غير مخلوق حتى نبغت

A Prediction by al-Shâfiʿî. It is reported that the Imâm al-Shâfiʿî, before his death in 204, had a dream, in which he was forewarned by the Prophet of the trial, in years to come, of Aḥmed ibn Ḥanbal for the sake of the Ḳorân. He is alleged to have sent word to Aḥmed informing him of the communication he had received, and report says that Aḥmed, on reading the letter, exclaimed, 'I hope that God will verify that which al-Shâfiʿî says' [1]). We may, probably, infer from

---

المعتزلة فقالوا بخلق القران وكانوا ويتستّرون بذلك الى زمن الرشيد حتى ان الرشيد قال يوما بلغنى ان بِشْر المَريسى يقول القران مخلوق والله علىّ ان اظفرنى الله بـه لأقتلنه قِتلة ما قتلتها احدا فاقام بشر مُتواريا ايام الرشيد نحوًا من عشرين سنة فلما توفى الرشيد كان الامر كذلك فى زمنِ ولده الامين فلما وَلِىَ المامون خالَطه قوم من المعتزلة فحسّنوا له القول بخلق القران

1) al-Makrîzî, p. 3, فصل فى بشارة النبى صلعم له بالمحنة قبل وقوعها بسنين على لسان الامام محمد بن ادريس الشافعى رضى الله عنه كان الامام الشافعى رضى الله عنه لما دخل مصر راى النبىّ صلعم فى المنام واخبرَه ان الامام احمد سيُمتحن قال الربيع بن سليمان فكتَب الشافعى على يَدى كتابا الى ابى عبد الله احمد بن حنبل ثم قال لى ياابا سليمن انْحَدِر بكتابى هذا الى العراق ولا تقراه فاخذتُ الكتاب وخرجت من مصر حتى قدمتُ العراق فوافيتُ مسجدَ احمد ابن حنبل فصادفته يصلى الفجرَ فصلّيت معه وكنتُ لم اركع السُّنة فقمت أركَع عقيب الصلاة فجعل ينظر الىّ مَليّا حتى عرفنى فلما سلمت من صلاتى سلمت عليه واوصلت الكتاب اليه وقلت له هذا كتاب اخيك الشافعى من مصر فجعل يسالنى عن الشافعى طويلا قبل ان ينظر فى الكتاب ثم قال لى نظرتَ فيه قلت لا ففكّ ختمه

this incident that the doctrine of the creation of the Ḳorân had already begun to make some stir when al-Shâfiʿî was in Baghdâd, and that Aḥmed was at this early stage a vigorous opponent of the tenet.

Al-Maʾmûn. The interest of al-Maʾmûn in theology is emphasized by all the historians [1]). He had been thoroughly trained in the knowledge of Tradition, of the Ḳorân sciences, and of the Ḳorân itself from early childhood, and had had among his teachers Mâlik ibn Anas, Hushaim ibn Bashîr and his own father [2]). His ability as a pupil soon brought him

---

وقراه حتى اذا بلغ مَوضعا منه بكى وقال ارجو الله تعالى ان يحقق ما قاله الشافعى قلت يابا عبد الله اى شىء قد كتبَ اليك قال ذكرَ فى كتابه انه راى النبى صلعم فى نومه وهو يقول له يابنَ ادريس بَشِّر هذا الفتى ابا عبد الله احمد بن حنبل انه سيُمتحن فى دين الله ويُدْعى ان يقول القران مخلوق فلا يَفعل فانه سيُضرب بالسياط وان الله عز وجل ينشر له بذلك عَلمًا لا يُطوى الى يوم القيامة فقلت بشارة فاى شىء جائزتى عليها وكان عليه ثوبان فنزع احدهما فدفعَه الىّ وكان مما يلى جلده واعطانى جواب الكتاب فخرجت حتى قدمت على الشافعى فاخبرته بما جرى قال فاين الثوب قلت هُوذا فقال ليس نفجعُك به ويُروى ان الشافعى رضى الله عنه قال للربيع لا نبتاعه منك ولا نستهديه ولكن اغسِله وجئنا بمائه قال فغسلته وحملت ماءه اليه فجعله فى قِنّينة وكنت اراه فى كل يوم ياخذ منه فيمسح على وجهه تبركا باحمد بن حنبل

1) Cf. Abuʾl-Maḥâsin I, 644; Hammer-Purgstall, Lit. Gesch. III, 26; al-Suyûtî, Tarîkh al-Kholafâ, Calcutta, 1857, p. 310; Dozy, Het Islamisme, 1880, p. 152. The notices of al-Maʾmûn's character found in al-Subkî, p. 144, and al-Maḳrîzî, p. 3, are in accordance with the accounts found in the works just mentioned.

2) Houtsma, De Strijd over het Dogma, 13, says that al-Maʾmûn first

to a foremost place as a theologian, but a mind eager for much wider ranging than was afforded within the narrow bounds of the orthodoxy of Islâm, soon shewed its sympathy with the revived philosophy which had begun to be popular under the dominion of the Khalifs, and with the different branches of Arabic letters and sciences. Following his bent of mind [1]), he gathered to his court from different parts of his empire, philosophers and men of more liberal tendency of thought than had been found among the companions of his predecessors [2]). Al-Ma'mûn, however, is not looked upon as a man naturally impious nor was his interest in sacred subjects one merely controversial in its character. It is related of him that he used to complete 33 recitations of the Korân in the month of Ramaḍân [3]). He also gave special gifts of money to relieve the needs of the teachers of Tradition, and all accepted of his beneficence except Aḥmed ibn Ḥanbal [4]). The letters written by al-Ma'mûn in connection with the Miḥna, however, do not give us a favorable impression of his character. The orthodox historians say that his companions at Court were wholly responsible for al-Ma'mûn's

---

attended the lectures of the Mutakallims and later took an interest in orthodoxy. He does not cite his authority for the remark, and it does not harmonize with what I have been able to gather from the authorities I have consulted. They invert the order, and I have followed them in my narrative.

1) Steiner (Die Muʿtaziliten, p. 16) expresses the opinion that the tendency toward liberal theological views, which was so strongly advanced by the influence of the Greek Philosophy, had already set in before the Arabs became acquainted with Greek philosophical thought.

2) For the patronage of letters and philosophy by the Abbaside sovereigns with its direct effect in the rise of the men of the Kalâm, and its indirect or reactionary effect in increasing the zeal in study of the men of the Tradition, vid. Houtsma, De Strijd over het Dogma, 86 f.

3) Goldziher, Moḥ. Studien II, 58, 59; Von Kremer, Herrsch. Ideen d. Isl. 301, note 15; Steiner, Die Muʿtaziliten, 6, note 5; Al-Subkî, p. 144, قيل ختم فى رمضان ثلاثا وثلاثين ختمة.

4) Abû Nuʿaim, 143 b, دفع المامون مالا فقال اقسمه على اصحاب الحديث فان فيهم ضعفآء فما بقى احد الا اخذ الا احمد بن حنبل

he[illegible]xy in theology, and for the consequent persecution of the stricter theologians on which he entered. It would appear to be more in accordance with the facts, to say that al-Ma'mûn himself found the atmosphere of orthodoxy oppressive and sought relief by surrounding himself with men whose minds were of his own liberal cast [1]). That these men should then put forth this or that doctrine is not so much to be considered as that the Khalif himself found heterodoxy a more congenial environment than orthodoxy. That Aḥmed ibn Abî Dowâd, the Chief-Ḳâḍî, was responsible for the inquisition known as the Miḥna may be said [2]); but it should not be forgotten that before Ibn Abî Dowâd obtained his ascendency over the mind of al-Ma'mûn, the latter would himself have set on foot the Miḥna for the creation of the Ḳorân had he not been afraid to do so. The Khalif's public adoption of the doctrine of the Ḳorân's creation dates from Rabî^c I, 212 A. H. (827 A. D.) [3]).

The following incident shews clearly the state of al-Ma'mûn's mind previous to this date. Yazîd ibn Hârûn, who is mentioned in connection with the incident, died in 206 A. H., six years before al-Ma'mûn publicly professed the doctrine that the Ḳorân was created, and twelve years before the beginning of the Miḥna. Yaḥya ibn Aktham related; "Al-Ma'mûn said to us, 'If it were not for Yazîd ibn Hârûn I would assuredly make public declaration of the doctrine that the Ḳorân is created'. On this one of his courtiers said, 'Nay! but who is Yazîd ibn Hârûn that the Commander of the Faithful

---

1) Cf. Houtsma, De Strijd over het Dogma, 108.

2) Cf. Abu'l-Maḥ. I, 733; De Goeje, Fragm. Hist. Arab., 547; Al-Subkî, p. 136, وكان معظما عند المامون امير المومنين يقبل شفاعاته ويصغى الى كلامه واخباره فى هذا كثيرة فدسّ ابن ابى دواد له القول بخلق القران وحسّنه عنده وصيّره يعتقده حقّا مبينا الى ان اجمع رايه فى سنة ثمان عشرة ومائتين على الدعاء اليه

3) Ṭab. III, ١٠٩٩.

should fear him?' His reply was, 'I am afraid, [illegible] it publicly, that he will retort upon me, and m[illegible]ke h[illegible] at discord in their opinions, and thus there will come t[illegible]uble, to which I am averse'. One of those who were present then said to al-Ma'mûn, 'I will make trial of the matter with Yazîd ibn Hârûn'. So this man went down to Wâsiṭ and, coming upon Yazîd in the Mosque, said to him, 'O Abû Khâlid, the Commander of the Faithful greets thee and would inform thee that he wishes to make public declaration that the Ḳorân is created'. Yazîd answered, 'You lie against the Commander of the Faithful! If you speak the truth, wait here until the people come together to me'. So next day when the people came to him, the Khalif's messenger repeated what he had said the day before, and asked, 'What have you to say about the matter?' Yazîd retorted, 'You have lied against the Commander of the Faithful. The Commander of the Faithful will not force men to profess that which they have not hitherto known, and which none of them has ever professed'. After this passage the man returned to the Commander of the Faithful, told him of the result, and acknowledged that al-Ma'mûn had been more accurate in his forecast than he himself had been. Al-Ma'mûn replied, 'He has made jest of you" [1]).

---

1) al-Maḳrîzî, p. 3, [قال البيهقي († 458)] قال يحيى بن اكثم قال لنا المأمون لولا مكانُ يزيد بن هرون لَأُظهرنّ القول بخلق القران فقال له بعض جلسائه ومَن يزيد بن هرون حتى يَتَّقِيَه امير المومنين فقال انى اخاف ان اظهرته يَرُدّ علىّ فيختلف الناس وتكون فتنة وانا اكره الفتنة فقال الرجل للمامون انا أَخْبُرُ ذلك مِن يزيد بن هرون فخرج الى واسط فجاء الى يزيد فدخل عليه المسجد فقال ياابا خالد ان امير المومنين يقرئك السلام ويقول لك انى اريدُ ان اظهرَ القول فى ان القران مخلوق فقال له كذبت على امير المومنين فان

The public adoption of the doctrine that the Ḳorân was created was conjoined with the public declaration of the superiority of ᶜAlî over Abû Bekr and ᶜOmar. Al-Maʾmûn was a pro-ᶜAlyite Khalif [1]), even as al-Mutawakkil, who revoked the royal edict announcing the Ḳorân's creation, was an anti-ᶜAlyite Khalif. The Shyites were, in fact, Muᶜtazilites in theological opinion, and it is not surprising that the ruler who gave out their tenet touching the Ḳorân should, at the same time, prefer their great leader before the orthodox Abû Bekr and his successor, even as it is not surprising that the ruler who revoked their tenet should restore to the orthodox Khalifs their primacy. Political capital was made out of both events by partisans, but in both cases it seems to us that the intention of the Khalifs was primarily to effect a religious reform [2]).

For six years al-Maʾmûn was undecided as to whether or not he should make the tenet that the Ḳorân was created obligatory upon his subjects; finally, when he had deposed Yaḥya ibn

---

كنت صادقا فاصبر الى ان يجتمع علىّ الناسُ قال فلما كان الغدُ
واجتمع عليه الناس قلت يا ابا خالد انّ امير المومنين يقرئك
السلام ويقول لك انى أُريدُ ان أُظهر القول بخلق القران فما عندك
فى ذلك قال كذبت على امير المومنين اميرُ المومنين لا يَحمل الناس
على ما لا يعرفونه وما لم يَقل به احد قال الرجل فلما رجعت الى
امير المومنين قلت له يا امير المومنين انك كنت اعلمَ بالامر مِنا
كان من القصة كيت وكيت فقال امير المومنين انه تلعّب بك

cf. von Hammer, Lit. Gesch. III, p. 159, Yazîd ibn Hârûn.

1) Houtsma, De Strijd etc. 97. Al-Maʾmûn, who had hoped to effect something by political alliance with the ᶜAlyites, found in time that there was nothing to be gained and much to be lost by such an alliance and gave it up, though still friendly to the ᶜAlyite party and favorable to many of its views. Houtsma, 99.

2) Houtsma, De Strijd etc. 99 f. On this subject cf. Weil, Chalifen II, 258 ff.; von Kremer, Herrsch. Ideen, 333 ff.

Aktham, in the year 217 A. H., from the Chief-Ḳâḍî's office [1]) and appointed Aḥmed ibn Abî Dowâd as his successor, he was encouraged to take the step by his new favorite until, in the last year of his life 218 A. H., he ordered the application of the Miḥna, or test [2]).

Ibn Abî Dowâd. Aḥmed ibn Abî Dowâd, who held a position of great power under the three Khalifs, al-Maʾmûn, al-Muʿtaṣim and al-Wâthiḳ, and was the most vigorous advocate of the Miḥna during their reigns [3]), is pictured in the accounts given by the orthodox biographers of Aḥmed ibn Ḥanbal in much too unfavorable a light. He was a learned man, gifted in the Kalâm, — he studied the Kalâm with Hayyâj ibn al-ʿAlâ al-Sulamî, a pupil of Wâçil ibnʿAṭâ [4]), — and was the first who publicly employed it in speaking before the Khalifs, though he refrained from employing it in the presence of Ibn al-Zayyât the Vizier. The Khalif al-Muʿtaṣim was completely under the power of Ibn Abî Dowâd.

---

1) De Goeje, Fragm. Hist. Arab. 376.

2) p. 52, note 2.

3) Steiner, Die Muʿtaziliten, 78.

4) for Wâçil ibn ʿAṭâ cf. Dozy, Het Islamisme, 133 f.; Steiner, Die Muʿtaziliten, pp. 25, 50. Houtsma (De Strijd etc. 103) says that Wâçil ibn ʿAtâ does not appear to have taught the creation of the Ḳorân.

al-Subkî, p. 136, كان القاضى احمد بن ابى دواد ممن نشا فى العلم وتضلع بعلم الكلام وصحب فيه هياج بن العلاء السلمى صاحب واصل بن عطآء احد رووس المعتزلة وكان ابن ابى دواد رجلا فصيحا قال ابو العَيناء ما رايت رئيسًا قط افصح [Cod. no points; cf. Abu'l-Maḥâsin, I 475, 733] ولا انطق منه وكان كريمًا ممدحا وفيه يقول بعضهم لقد أَنْسَت مساوِىَ كل دهرٍ، محاسنُ احمد بن ابى دُؤادِ، وما طوّفت فى الافاق الّا، ومن جدواك راحلتى وزادِى، يقيم الظن عندك والامانى، وأرقلت [Cod. وان قلت Abu'l-Feda Ann. II, 678, corrects as in text] ركابى فى البلاد،

He entered the service of al-Ma'mûn in the year 204 A. H., on the recommendation of Yaḥya ibn Aktham, and at this Khalif's death was warmly recommended by him to his successor, al-Muʿtaṣim. In the very beginning of al-Mutawakkil's reign Aḥmed was paralyzed, and his son Moḥammed was made Chief-Ḳâḍî in his place, but was deposed in the same year, 232 A. H. Ibn Abî Dowâd was an eloquent man and a poet whose praises were loudly celebrated by poets and others. He was, also, a man of large generosity, and a lover of good living and entertainment [1]). In contrast to this estimate of the man is the representation of him as an impetuous, ignorant and narrow bigot, which we find in most of the orthodox accounts. In 236 or 237 A. H. Ibn Abî Dowâd came into disfavor at the Court, and was imprisoned and his property confiscated; later, he was sent to reside in Baghdâd, where he lived till his death. Both father and son died in disgrace in the year 240 A. H., the son twenty days before his father [2]).

First Letter of al-Ma'mûn to Baghdâd. The first step taken by al-Ma'mûn to secure conformity to the view which he had adopted was to send a letter to his lieutenant at Baghdâd, Isḥâḳ ibn Ibrâhîm, cousin of Ṭâhir ibn al-Ḥasan, ordering him to cite before him the ḳâḍîs and traditionists, and to demand of them an answer to the test as to the

---

1) On the luxurious life of the chief Muʿtazila cf. Houtsma, De Strijd etc. 81 f.; Steiner, Die Muʿtaziliten, 10 infra.

2) Weil, Chalifen II, 334; Goldziher, Moh. Stud. II, 58; Maçoudî VI, 214; Ibn Chall. N°. 31; Abu'l-Maḥ. I, 733; De Goeje, Fragm. Hist. Arab. 547; cf. Abû Nuʿaim, 152a, وجَعل يَعقوب وعتاب يصبران اليه فيقولان له يقول لك امير المومنين ما تقول فى ابن ابى دؤاد فى ماله فلا يجيب فى ذلك بشىء وجَعل يعقوب وعتاب يخبرانه بما يحدث فى امر ابن ابى دواد فى كل يوم ثم احدر ابن ابى دواد الى بغداد بعدما اشهد عليه ببيع ضياعه

creation of the Ḳorân. This letter ran as follows [1]: That which God has laid upon the imâms of the Muslims, their Khalifs, is to be zealous in the maintenance of the religion of God, which he has asked them to conserve; in the heritage of prophecy, which he has granted them to inherit; in the tradition of knowledge, which he has asked them to hold in charge; in the government of their subjects according to right and justice, and in being diligent to observe obedience to God in their conduct toward them. Now, the Commander of the Faithful asks God to assist him to persevere in the right way and to be energetic in it, to act justly, also, in those interests of his subjects over which God by his grace and bounty has appointed him to have rule. The Commander of the Faithful knows that the great multitude, the mass of the insignificant folk, and the vulgar public, who, in all regions and countries, are without insight and deep reflection, and have not a method of reasoning by means of such proof as God approves under the guidance which he gives, and no enlightenment by the light of knowledge and its evidences, are a people ignorant of God and too blind to see him, too much in error to know the reality of his religion, the confession of his unity and the belief in him; perverted, also, so as not to recognize his clear tokens, and the obligation of his service; unable to grasp the real

---

1) The text on which I have based all the translations of the Khalif al-Ma'mûn's letters in relation to the Miḥna is that found in the Leiden edition of Ṭabarî's Annales III (2nd vol.), ١١١٢—١١٣٣. It has the appearance of being a verbal copy of the letters, while the text in Abu'l-Maḥâsin I, ٦٣٧—٦٤١, De Goeje, Fragm. Hist. Arab. II, ٤٦٥, Abu'l-Feda Annales II, 154 f., and in al-Subkî, 136 ff. represents the letters in greatly abridged form. The later writers appear to have used Ṭabarî for their text, for all shew much the same variations from the extended form of the letters found in his work; that is, where they furnish the same portions of the letters (for some of the authorities mentioned have abridged more than others, and in some there is but one or, it may be, two letters found). The above mentioned authorities, beyond the help already gathered from the collation with Abu'l-Maḥâsin, do not afford any assistance to improve the text found in Ṭabarî.

measure of God, to know him as he really is, and to distinguish between him and his creation, because of the weakness of their views, the deficiency of their understandings, and their turning aside from reflection and recollection; for they put on an equality God and the Ḳorân which he has revealed. They are all agreed and stand unequivocally in accord with one another that it is eternal and primitive, and that God did not create it, produce it, or give it being; while God himself says in his well-ordered Book, which he appointed as a healing for what is within the breasts and as a mercy and right guidance for the believers, 'We have made it a Ḳorân in the Arabic tongue' [1]), and everything which God has made he has created. He says, also, 'Praise be to God who *created* the heavens and the earth and *made* the darkness and the light' [2]). He speaks also thus, 'We will tell thee tidings of that which went before' [3]); he says here that it is an account of things *after* whose happening he *produced* it, and with it he followed up their lead. Then he says, آلر, 'A book whose verses were well-ordered, and, then, were divided by order of a Wise and Knowing One' [4]). Now, for everything that is ordered and divided there is one who orders and divides; and God is the one who orders well his Book and the one who divides it, therefore, he is its creator and producer. They, also, are those who dispute with false arguments, and call men to adopt their view. Further, they claim to be followers of the Sunna, while in every chapter of God's Book is an account, which may be read therein, that gives the lie to their position, declares their invitation [to adopt their opinions] to be false, and thrusts back upon them their view and their religious pretentions. But they give out, in spite of that, that they are the people of the truth and the [real] religion and the communion of believers, all others being the people of falsehood, unbelief and schism; and they boast themselves of

1) Ḳorân, 43. 2.
2) Ḳorân, 6. 1.
3) Ḳorân, 20. 99.
4) Ḳorân, 11. 1.

that over their fellows, so deceiving the ignorant, until persons of the false way, who are devoted to the worship of another God than Allah, and who mortify themselves for another cause than that of the true religion, incline toward agreement with them and accordance with their evil opinions, by that means getting to themselves honour with them, and procuring to themselves a leadership and a reputation among them for honorable dealing. Thus they give up the truth for their falsehood, and find apart from God [1]) a supporter for their error. And, so, their testimony is received, because they [sc. the ignorant or people of the false way] declare them [sc. those who *pretend* to be the people of the truth] to be veracious witnesses; and the ordinances of the Ḳorân are executed by them [sc. those who pretend to be the people of the truth] notwithstanding the unsoundness of their religion, the corruption of their honour, and the depravation of their purposes and belief. That is the goal unto which they are urging others, and which they seek in their own practice and in [their] lying against their Lord, though the solemn covenant of the Book is upon them that they should not speak against God except that which is true, and though they have learned what the condition is of 'those whom God has made deaf and whose eyes he has blinded. Do they not reflect upon the Ḳorân? or are there locks upon their hearts?' [2]) The Commander of the Faithful considers, therefore, that those men are the worst and the chief in error, being deficient in the belief in God's unity, and having an incomplete share in the faith — vessels of ignorance, banners of falsehood, the tongue of Iblîs, who speaks through his friends and is terrible to his enemies who are of God's religion; the ones of all others to be mistrusted as to their truthfulness, whose testimony should be rejected, and in whose word and deed one can put no confidence. For one can only do good works after assured persuasion, and there [really] is assured persuasion

1) cf. Ḳorân, 9. 16.	2) Ḳorân, 47. 25—26.

only after fully obtaining a real possession of Islâm, and a sincere profession of the faith in God's unity. He, therefore, who is too blind to perceive his right course and his share in the belief in God and in his unity, is, in other respects, as to his conduct and the justness of his testimony, still more blind and erring. By the life of the Commander of the Faithful, the most likely of men to lie in speech and to fabricate a false testimony is the man who lies against God and his revelation, and who does not know God as he really is; and the most deserving of them all to be rejected when he testifies about what God ordains and about his religion is he who rejects God's testimony to his Book and slanders the truth of God by his lying. Now, gather together the ḳâḍîs under thy jurisdiction, read unto them this letter of the Commander of the Faithful to thee, and begin to test them to see what they will say, and to discover what they believe concerning the creation of the Ḳorân by God and its production by God. Tell them, also, that the Commander of the Faithful will not ask assistance in his government of one whose religion, whose sincerity of faith in God's unity, and whose [religious] persuasion are not to be trusted; nor will he put confidence in such a man in respect to what God has laid upon him and in the matter of those interests of his subjects which he has given into his charge. And when they have confessed that [sc. that the Ḳorân is created] and accorded with the Commander of the Faithful, and are in the way of right guidance and of salvation, then, bid them to cite the legal witnesses under their jurisdiction, to ask them in reference to the Ḳorân, and to leave off accepting as valid the testimony of him who will not confess that it is created and produced, and refuse thou to let them [the ḳâḍîs] countersign it. Write, also, to the Commander of the Faithful the reports that come to thee from the ḳâḍîs of thy province as to the result of their inquisition and their ordering that these things be done. Get acquainted with them and search out their evidences, so that the sentences of God may not be carried out, except on the testimony of such as have insight into real religion and are sincere in the belief in God's unity, and then, write unto the Commander of the Faithful of what comes of it all.

This letter was writen in the month of Rabîᶜ I, 218 A. H., before al-Maᵓmûn set out on his last expedition to the frontiers, and about four months before his death. It must be confessed that the spirit of the document is that of the bigot, rather than that of a broad and liberal mind. Nor can we suppose that a man of al-Maᵓmûn's character would let a document of this kind be composed in any spirit but his own. Its indications all point to arrogant intellectual self-sufficiency coupled with a contempt of opinions different from those held by himself. The contemptuous Khalif would appear to have been convinced by those about him that he could now safely terrorize the orthodox, securing assent to his own views from such as were weak enough to be frightened by his threats or tortures, and blotting out the obstinate ones from the face of the earth, when they were found incorrigible.

The Beginning of the Mihna elsewere. Egypt.

This letter was sent to all the provinces. The copy of that which was addressed to Kaidar, governor of Egypt, is practically the same as that whose translation has been given, but it did not reach Egypt until the month of Jumâdâ II. The Ḳâḍî in Egypt at this time was Hârûn ibn Abdallah al-Zuhrî. He gave in his assent on the test as to the Ḳorân being applied to him, as did also the constituted witnesses except some whose testimony was by their refusal rendered invalid. Kaidar had made a beginning with the examination of the faḳîhs and ᶜulamâ, but had evidently adopted no harsh measures, when the news of al-Maᵓmûn's death came to him in the month after the receipt of the order for the Miḥna. On the receipt of this news the inquisition was suspended[1].

There is mention of some trials for the sake of the Ḳorân at Damascus, but there, as well as in other provinces, little appears to have been done, for the notices are

---

1) Abu'l-Maḥ. I, 636, 637.

very slight; and, from the way in which Abu'l-Maḥâsin's record reads, one might infer that the order for the Miḥna to places outside of ᶜIrâḳ and Egypt came later than to these places. If this inference be just the time of the inquisit in these other parts must have been short, at least, in t Khalifate of al-Maᵓmûn. It is to be concluded, too, that th success of the persecution at Baghdâd led al-Maᵓmûn to orde a general introduction of the Miḥna throughout his empire.

Damascus. In the year 218 A. H., al-Maᵓmûn went in person to Damascus, probably on his last expedition to Asia Minor, and personally conducted the testing of the doctors there concerning the freedom of the will (عَدْل) and the divine unity, the second of which in his view involved a test as to the creation of the Ḳorân [1]). The governor of Damascus unde al-Maᵓmûn, as well as under his successors, al-Muᶜtaṣim anc

---

1) al-Jaᶜqûbî II, 571, The Muᶜtazila called themselves the Ahlu't-Tauhî wa'l-ᶜAdl, the men of the Divine Unity and Righteousness, chiefly fo the reason that they, on the one hand, rejected the orthodox view of th Divine attributes and of the Ḳorân as out of harmony with the unitaria faith of Islâm; and held, instead, that the so-called attributes were onl empty names, or were not real and distinct existences, but particular present ations of the Divine essence itself: that is, God as wise, God as powerfu etc. They, on the other hand, rejected the orthodox doctrine of the Divin foreordination of the actions and destinies of men as inconsistent with th absolute righteousness of God, and held that the human will was free, an man thus the determiner of his own destiny. Hence it is that in polemi literature Ahlu't-Tauhîd wa'l-ᶜAdl has a much more special meanin than that indicated in the beginning of this note, generally standing for thos who believe, 1) in the non-existence of the attributes of God or their identit with his essence, and in the creation of the Ḳorân (اهل التوحيد). 2) in th freedom of the will (اهل العدل); cf. Houtsma, De Strijd etc. 55, 92, 133 Steiner, Die Muᶜtaziliten, 30, 50 and note 3); Shahrastânî, Haarbrücker' transl'n I, 39, 42.

If Jaᶜqûbî be correct, Houtsma's statement (p. 108) "dat hij [al-Maᵓmûn niet den vrijen wil ook meteen [with the creation of the Ḳorân] als staats dogma vaststelde" must be modified. The probabilities are in favour of th Khalif's having done what Jaᶜqûbî says, though we, in general, do not fin Jaᶜqûbî a very satisfactory authority as far as the Miḥna is concerned. Hi usual accuracy in recording events is seemingly wanting at this point.

al-Wâthiḳ, was Isḥâḳ ibn Yaḥya. During the Khalifate of al-Muᶜtaṣim, that Khalif wrote him a letter ordering him to urge the Miḥna on the people under his authority. He, however, dealt leniently with them in regard to the order he had received. In 235 A. H., this man was appointed governor of Egypt by al-Mutawakkil [1]).

Kûfa. When the order came to Kûfa there was a great assembly of the sheikhs in the general mosque of the city, and, on the Khalif's (the name of the Khalif is not given) letter being read to them, the feeling was against yielding to the order it contained. Abû Nuᶜaim al-Faḍl ibn Dukain, a Kûfite, who died in 219 A. H., said that he had met over 870 teachers, from the aged al-Aᶜmash to those who were young in years, who did not believe the Ḳorân to be created, and that such teachers as were inclined to the heterodox view were charged by their fellows with being Zindîḳs (atheists) [2]). Abû Nuᶜaim ibn Dukain was present at the opening of the Miḥna in Kûfa. This fact shews us the approximate date of the event there, for this man, as we have said, died in the year 219 [3]).

Citation of the Seven Leaders. The result of the letter of al-Maʾmûn to Baghdâd was to produce, as we may justly conjecture, a feeling of resistance, the most zealous inciter of

1) Abu'l-Maḥ. I. 711 f.

2) On the origin of the name and its use among the orthodox v. Houtsma, De Strijd etc. 75.

3) al-Maḳrîzî, p. 13, واما الحافظ ابو نعيم الفضل بن دكين فروى الحافظ ابو الفرج بسنده الى محمد بن احمد بن عمرو بن عيسى قال سمعت ابى يقول ما رايت مجلسا انبل من مجلسٍ اجتمع فيه المشايخ بجامع الكوفة فى وقت الامتحان فقرئَ عليهم الكتاب الذى فيه المحنة فقال ابو نعيم ادركت ثمانى مائة شيخ ونيفا وسبعين شيخا منهم الاعمش فمَن دونه فما رايت احدا يقول بهذه المقالة يعنى بخلق القران ولا تكلم احد بها الا رُمى بالزندقة

which would be Aḥmed ibn Ḥanbal [1]). Still, al-Ma'mûn did not yet venture to apprehend the latter. His next step was one which was calculated to shew him just how far he was safe in going in his enforcement of conformity to his views.

Second Letter of al-Ma'mûn. He wrote a second letter to Isḥâḳ ibn Ibrâhîm, the governor of ᶜIrâḳ, ordering him to send seven of the leading traditionists of Baghdâd that he might test them himself. For his purpose, this was a sagacious move. Away from the moral support of their fellow-traditionists, and face to face with the state of the Court and the terrors which the Khalif brought to bear upon their minds, resistance was much more difficult than it would have been at Baghdâd. And the compliance of these leaders being secured, smaller men needed not to be feared. The name of Aḥmed ibn Ḥanbal was, at first, upon the list bearing the names of the seven referred to, but was erased at the instance of Ibn Abî Dowâd, — at least, so the latter claimed [2]).

Those now summoned [3]) to the Court were Moḥammed ibn Saᶜd the secretary of al-Wâḳidî, Abû Muslim the amanuensis of Yazîd ibn Hârûn, Yaḥya ibn Maᶜîn, Zuhair ibn Ḥarb Abû Khaithama, Ismâᶜîl ibn Dâûd, Ismâᶜîl ibn Abî Masᶜûd and Aḥmed ibn Ibrâhîm al-Dauraḳî. These seven men all yielded assent under the pressure which al-Ma'mûn used with them. Having obtained his desire, the Khalif sent the men back to Baghdâd, where Isḥâḳ ibn Ibrâhîm, acting under al-Ma'mûn's orders, had them repeat their confession before the faḳîhs and traditionists [4]).

Its Effect. The fall of these seven men from orthodoxy was a source of much grief to Aḥmed ibn Ḥanbal. His judgment

---

1) The Baghdâd people had in the year 215, and even earlier, protested against al-Ma'mûn's heterodoxy touching the Ḳorân, cf. Abu'l-Maḥ. I, 631.

2) Vid. p. 82.

3) Ṭabarî ١١١٩, text of letter not given.

4) Ṭabarî ١١١٩ f. A biographical notice of Moḥammed ibn Saᶜd is found Ibn Chall. N°. 656; of Yaḥya ibn Maᶜîn, al-Nawawî, Biog. Dict. p. 628; of Aḥmed ibn al-Dauraḳî, Dhahabî Ṭabaḳât 8, N°. 98; of Zuhair ibn Ḥarb, id. 8, N°. 23. I have not been able to find notices of the other three.

was that if they had stood their ground nothing more would have been heard of the Miḥna in Baghdâd. Al-Ma'mûn would have been afraid to deal harshly with them seeing they were the leading men of the city; but, when they gave way, he had little hesitation in dealing with others [1]). Their assent was by themselves excused on the ground of Taḳîa (exemp- from observance of religious duty when it involved risk ie), but the real cause of their doing as they did was nc of execution if they had not done so. Yaḥya ibn Maʿîn fr ith weeping used to confess that this was the case [2]). It aṣ unfortunate that the seven leaders proved themselves .o weak, for it is not unlikely that their firmness might have deterred al-Ma'mûn from prosecuting further his effort for uniformity of belief; and after his death, the succeeding Khalifs were not such as would likely have revived an inquisition like this when it had once been given up.

Third Letter. A third letter from the Khalif was now sent to Baghdâd to Isḥâḳ ibn Ibrâhîm the governor. Its text was as follows [3]): That which God has a right to expect from his vicegerents (khalifs) on his earth [and] those entrusted by him with rule over his servants, upon whom he

---

1) al-Maḳrîzî, p. 4, [قال احمد بن حنبل] فاجابوا ولو كانوا صبروا وقاموا لله لكان انقطع الامر وحَذِرَهم الرجل يعنى المامون ولكن لمّا اجابوا وهم عين البلد اجترأ على غيرهم وكان ابو عبد الله اذا ذكرهم يَغتمّ ويقول هم اول مَن ثلَم هذه الثلمة

2) al-Subkî, p. 137, وسبب طلبهم انهم توقفوا اولا ثم اجابوه تقية وكتب الى اسحق بن ابراهيم بان يُحضِر الفقهاء ومَشايخَ الحديث ويُخبِرَهم بما اجاب به هٰؤلآء السبعةُ ففعل ذٰلك فاجابه طائفة وامتنع آخرون فكان يحيى بن معين [al-Sujûtî, 314, adds وغيره] يقول اجبنا خوفا من السيف

3) Ṭabarî III, ١١١٧ ff.

has been pleased to lay the maintenance of his religion, the care of his creatures, the carrying out of his ordinance and his laws, and the imitation of his justice in his world, is that they should exert themselves earnestly for God, do him good service in respect to that which he asks them to guard and lays upon them, make him known by that excellency of learning which he has entrusted to them a[illegible]h the knowledge which he has placed within them, gui[illegible]ight him the one who has turned aside from him, bring [illegible]tious him who has turned his back on his command, mark [illegible]n- for their subjects the way of their salvation, tell them abo[illegible]e the limits of their faith and the way of their deliverance, and protection, and discover to them those things which are hidden from them, and the things which are doubtful to them [clear up] by means of that which will remove doubt from them and bring back enlightenment and clear know- ledge unto them all. And [part of that which he claims of them is] that they should begin that by making them go in the right way, and by causing them to see [things] clearly, because this involves all their actions, and comprehends their portion of felicity in this world and the next. They [the Khalifs] ought to reflect how God is one who holds himself ready to question them about that for which they have been made responsible, and to reward them for that which they have done in advance and that which they have laid up in store with him. The help of the Commander of the Faithful is alone in God, and his sufficiency is God, who is enough for him. Of that which the Commander of the Faithful by his reflection has made plain, and has come to know by his thinking, and the great danger of which is clear, as well as the seriousness of the corruption and harm which will come to religion thereby, are the sayings which the Muslims are passing round among themselves as to the Ḳorân, which God made to be an imâm and a lasting monument for them from God's Messenger and elect Servant, Moḥammed, and [another thing is] the confusedness of the opinion of many of them about it [sc. the Ḳorân] until it has seemed good in their opinions and right in their minds that it has not been cre. and, thus, they expose themselves to the risk of denyi. the creating by God of all things, by which [act] he is distinguished from his creation. He in his glory stands apart in the bringing into being of all things by his wisdom and the creation of them by his power, and in his priority in time over them by reason of his being Primitive Existence, whose beginning cannot be attained and whose duration cannot be reached. Everything apart from him is a creature from his creation, — a new thing which he has brought into existence. [This perverted opinion they hold] though the Ḳorân speaks clearly of God's creating all things, and proves it to the exclusion of all difference of opinion. They are, thus, like the Christians when they claim that ʿIsâ ibn Maryam was not created because he was the Word of God [1]). But God says, 'Verily we have made it a Ḳorân in the Arabic language' [2]); and the explanation of that is, 'Verily we have created it', just as the Ḳorân says, 'And he made from it his mate that he might dwell with her' [3]). Also, it says, 'We have made the night as a garment and the day as a means of gain' [4]). 'We have made every living thing from water' [5]). God thus puts on equal footing the Ḳorân and these creatures which he mentions with the indication of 'making'. And he tells that he alone is the One who made it, saying, 'Verily it is a glorious Ḳorân (something to be read) on a well-guarded table' [6]). Now, he says that on the supposition that the Ḳorân is limited by the table, and only that which is created can be limited (by surrounding bounds) [7]). He says, likewise, to his Prophet, 'Do not move in it thy tongue to make haste in it' [8]). Also, 'That which came to them was a newly created religion (ذكر) from their Lord' [9]).

---

1) cf. Sura 112; cf. Steiner, Die Muʿtaziliten, p. 90 and note.
2) Ḳorân, 43. 2.
3) Ḳorân, 7. 189.
4) Ḳorân, 78. 10.
5) Ḳorân, 21. 31.
6) cf. Ḳorân, 85. 21—22.
7) cf. Shahrastânî, Haarbrücker's transl'n I, 72, l. 20 ff.
8) Ḳorân, 75. 16.
9) Ḳorân, 21. 2.

has ,' 'And who is a worse liar than the man who inventeth the lie against God or charges his verses with being false' [1]. He tells, too, about men whom he blames because of their lying, in that they say, 'God has not sent down [by revelation] to men anything' [2]. Then, by the tongue of his Messenger he declares them liars, and says to his Messenger, 'Say, who sent down the book which Moses brought?' [3]. So God calls the Ḳorân something to be read, something to be kept in memory, a faith, a light, a right guidance, a blessed thing, a thing in the Arabic language, and a narration. For he says, 'We relate unto thee a most beautiful narration in that which we reveal unto thee, — this Ḳorân' [4]. Furthermore, he says, 'Say, surely, if men and jinns were gathered together to bring forth such as this Ḳorân, they could not bring forth one like it' [5]. Also, 'Say, bring ten suras fabricated like it' [6]. Also, 'Falsehood shall not come up to it either from before or after it' [7]. Thus, he puts [at least, by possibility] something before and after it, and so indicates that it is finite and created. But these ignorant people, by their teaching concerning the Ḳorân, have made large the breach in their religion and the defect in their trustworthiness; they have also levelled the way for the enemy of Islâm, and confess fickleness and heresy against their own hearts, [going on] even till they make known and describe God's creation and his action by that description which appertains to God alone, and they compare him with it, whilst only his creation may be the subject of comparison. The Commander of the Faithful does not consider that he who professes this view has any share in the real religion, or any part in the real faith and in well-grounded persuasion. Nor does he consider that he should set any one of them down as a trustworthy person in regard to his being admitted as

---

1) Ḳorân, 6. 21.
2) Ḳorân, 6. 91.
3) ibid.
4) Ḳorân, 12. 3.
5) Ḳorân, 17. 90.
6) Ḳorân, 11. 16.
7) Ḳorân, 41. 42.

امين — عَدْل or شاهد or as one to be relied upon in speech or report, or in the exercise of authority over his subjects. Now, if any of them seem to act with equity, and to be known by his straightforwardness, still, the branches are to be carried back to their roots, and the burden of praise or blame is to be according to these. Thus, whosoever is ignorant in the matter of his religion, concerning that which God has commanded him in reference to his unity, he, as regards other things, is still more ignorant, and is too blind and erring to see the right way in other matters. Now, read the letter of the Commander of the Faithful unto thee to Jaʿfar ibn ʿIsâ and Abd al-Raḥmân ibn Isḥâḳ the ḳâḍî, and cite them both to answer for their knowledge respecting the Ḳorân, telling them that the Commander of the Faithful in the affairs of the Muslims will not ask the assistance of any but those in whose sincerity of faith and whose belief in God's unity he has confidence; and that he has no belief in God's unity who does not confess that the Ḳorân is created. And, if they profess the view of the Commander of the Faithful in this particular, then, order them to test those who are in their courts for the giving of evidence touching rights of claimants, and [order them] to cite them to answer for their profession in respect to the Ḳorân. He who does not profess it to be created, let them declare his testimony invalid and refrain from giving sentence on what he says, even if his integrity be established by the equity and straightforwardness of his conduct. Do this with all the ḳâḍîs in thy province, and examine them with such an examination as God can cause to increase the rightmindedness of the rightminded, and prevent those who are in doubt from neglecting their religion. Then, write unto the Commander of the Faithful of what thou hast done in this matter.

Citation of the Doctors in Baghdâd. Following out the instructions of this letter, Isḥâḳ ibn Ibrâhîm summoned to his presence a number of the faḳîhs, doctors and traditionists [1]). Among

1) Ṭabarî III, ١١٢١ ff. is followed throughout the passage.

those summoned were Aḥmed ibn Ḥanbal, Bishr ibn al-Walîd al-Kindî, Abû Ḥassân al-Ziyâdî, ᶜAlî ibn Abî Muḳâtil, al-Faḍl ibn Ghânim, Obaidallah ibn ᶜOmar al-Ḳawârîrî, ᶜAlî ibn al-Jaᶜd, al-Ḥasan ibn Ḥammâd al-Sajjâda [1]), al-Dhayyâl ibn al-Haitham, Ḳutaiba ibn Saᶜîd, who seems to have been only temporarily in Baghdâd, Saᶜdawaih, Saᶜîd ibn Suleimân Abû ᶜOthmân al-Wâsiṭî [2]), Isḥâḳ ibn Abî Isrâʾîl, Ibn al-Harsh, Ibn ᶜUlayya al-Akbar, Moḥammed ibn Nûḥ al-Maḍrûb al-ᶜIjlî [3]), Yaḥya ibn Abd al-Raḥmân al-ᶜOmarî, Abû Naṣr al-Tammâr, Abû Maᶜmar al-Ḳatîᶜî, Moḥammed ibn Ḥâtim ibn Maimûn, a sheikh of the descendants of ᶜOmar ibn al-Khaṭṭâb who was ḳâḍî of al-Raḳḳa, Ibn al-Farrukhân, al-Naḍr ibn Shumail, Abd al-Raḥmân ibn Isḥâḳ, Ibn Bakkâ al-Akbar, Aḥmed ibn Yazîd ibn al-ᶜAwwâm Abu 'l-Awwâm al-Bazzâz, Ibn Shujâ and Moḥammed ibn al-Ḥasan ibn ᶜAlî ibn ᶜÂsim. Others are mentioned in the account of the investigation which follows.

When these men were brought before Isḥâḳ ibn Ibrâhîm, he read to them twice al-Maʾmûn's letter until they grasped its meaning and, then, asked them for their assent to the doctrine which the Khalif propounded. At first, they tried subterfuges and would neither affirm nor deny that the Ḳorân was created. The first to whom Isḥâḳ ibn Ibrâhîm put the test was Bishr ibn al-Walîd. 'What dost thou say respecting the Ḳorân?' he asked; and Bishr replied, 'I have more than once made my view known to the Commander of the Faithful'. Isḥâḳ said, 'But this letter is a new thing from the Commander of the Faithful. What is your view?' Bishr answered, 'I say the Ḳorân is the Word of God'. Isḥâḳ. 'I did not ask thee for that. Is it created?' Bishr. 'God is the creator of everything'. Isḥâḳ. 'Is not the Ḳorân a thing?' Bishr. 'It is a thing'. Isḥâḳ. 'And, there-

Bishr ibn al-Walîd.

1) Abu'l-Maḥ. I. 638 and al-Maḳrîzî, p. 4, supply the name of Sajjâda الحسن بن حماد المعروف بسجّادة.

2) Abu'l-Maḥ. I, 665, supplies the name of Saᶜdawaih.

3) Abu'l-Maḥ. I, 648; al-Subkî, p. 138, adds المضروب.

fore, created?' Bishr. 'It is not a creator'. Isḥâḳ. 'I did not ask for this. Is it created?' Bishr then confessed that he had yielded as far as he could yield, and could give no further answer; he contended, moreover, that the Khalif had given him a dispensation from speaking his mind on the subject. The governor now took up a sheet of paper that lay before him and read and explained it to Bishr. Then, he said, 'Testify that there is no God but Allah, one and alone, before whom nothing was and after whom nothing shall be and like to whom is nothing of his creation, in any sense whatsoever or in any wise whatsoever' [1]). Bishr said, 'I testify that and scourge those who do not testify it'. Isḥâḳ then turned to the secretary and said, 'Write down what he has said'.

ᶜAlî ibn Abî Muḳâtil. Turning next to ᶜAlî ibn Abî Muḳâtil he asked for his confession. He replied, 'I have told my opinion about this to the Commander of the Faithful more than once, and have nothing different to say'. The written test was then read to ᶜAlî and he gave the confession it required. Then the governor said, 'Is the Ḳorân created?' ᶜAlî answered, 'The Ḳorân is God's Word'. Isḥâḳ, as in the case of Bishr, told him he had not asked for that, and ᶜAlî answered, 'It is the Word of God; if, however, the Commander of the Faithful command us to do a thing we will yield him obedience'. Again, the scribe was bidden to record what had been said.

The next was al-Dhayyâl whose replies were in the same strain as those of ᶜAlî.

Abû Ḥassân. In the reply of Abû Ḥassân there is something naïvely submissive. 'The Ḳorân is the Word of God', he said, 'and God is the creator of everything; all things apart from

1) Houtsma (De Strijd etc. 108 infra) seems to imply that this written 'credo', which was to be subscribed by those to whom it was put, contained a confession that the Ḳorân was created. As Ṭabarî presents the case the document demanded only a profession of faith in God's unity. Its purpose was evidently to support the separate oral test as to the Ḳorân. None seem to have had any scruples about giving assent to the written test, while all would have avoided the other, had it been possible.

him are created. But the Commander of the Faithful is our imâm, and through him we have heard the whole sum of learning. He has heard what we have not heard, and knows what we do not know. God also has laid upon him the rule over us. He maintains our Hajj and our prayers; we bring to him our Zakât; we fight with him in the Jihâd, and we recognize fully his imâmate. Therefore, if he command us we will perform his behest, if he forbid us we will refrain, and if he call upon us we will respond'. Isḥâḳ said, 'This is the view of the Commander of the Faithful'. Abû Ḥassân rejoined, 'True! but sometimes the view of the Commander of the Faithful is one concerning which he gives no command to people, and which he does not call upon them to adopt; if, however, you tell me that the Commander of the Faithful has commanded thee that I should say this, I will say what thou dost command me to say, for thou art a man to be trusted and one on whom reliance is to be placed in respect to anything you may tell me from him. If, then, you order me to do anything, I will do it'. The governor's reply was, 'He has not commanded me to tell thee anything'. Abû Ḥassân said, 'I mean only to obey; command me and I will perform it'. Isḥâḳ said, 'He has not commanded me to command thee, but only to test thee'. The examination of Abû Ḥassân ends here.

Aḥmed ibn Ḥanbal. In the case of Aḥmed ibn Ḥanbal, Ibn Bakkâ al-Asghar suggested to Isḥâḳ ibn Ibrâhîm that he should ask him about the expression of the Ḳorân, 'He is the Hearing and Seeing One', which Aḥmed had used in his confession. Aḥmed, in harmony with the principles of men of his class, answered only, 'He is even as he has described himself'. Being further pressed to explain the words, he said, 'I do not know; he is even as he has described himself'. He was firm in adhering to the confession that the Ḳorân was the Word of God, and would add nothing to it by way of compromise or admission. Those who were examined subsequently all followed Aḥmed's example, except Ḳutaiba, Obaidallah ibn Moḥammed ibn al-Ḥasan, Ibn

ʿUlayya al-Akbar, Ibn al-Bakkâ, Abd al-Munʿim ibn Idrîs ibn Bint Wahb ibn Munabbih, al-Muẓaffir ibn Murajjâ, another man not a faḳîh who happened to be present, Ibn al-Aḥmar and the ʿOmarî Kâḍî of al-Raḳḳa. The answers of these are not furnished us but the implication seems to be that they compromised themselves. On this occasion when Aḥmed perceived the assent of his companions as the test was applied he was intensely angry [1]). Ibn al-Bakkâ al-Akbar also compromised himself, but not fully, and with better grace than some of his fellows, for he stood on the ground of the Ḳorân text in making the admissions which he made. These admissions were that the Ḳorân was, on the one hand, something 'made' (مَجْعُول) and, on the other hand, something 'newly produced' (مُحْدَث). For the former position the text adduced was one cited by the Khalif in arguing that the Ḳorân was created (مَخْلُوق), namely, Ḳor. 43 : 2, 'Verily we have made it a Ḳorân (reading) in the Arabic language'. For the latter position the text was, likewise, one cited by the Khalif in his argument, Ḳor. 21 : 2, 'What came to them from their Lord was a newly produced religion (ذِكْر)'. Isḥâḳ asked Ibn al-Bakkâ if the term مَجْعُول were not the same in meaning as مَخْلُوق,

Ibn al-Bakkâ.

1) Abû Nuʿaim, 146 *b* حدثنا سليمان بن احمد ثنا عبد الله ابن احمد بن حنبل حدثنى ابو معمر القطيعى قال لما احضرنا فى دار السلطان * ايام المحنة وكان ابو عبد الله احمد ابن حنبل قد أُحضِر فلما رأى الناس يجيبون وكان ابو عبد الله رجلا لينا فلما رأى الناس يجيبون انتفخت اوداجه واحمرت عيناه وذهب ذلك اللين الذى كان فيه فقلتُ انه قد غضب لله قال ابو معمر فلما رايتُ ما به قلتُ يابا عبد الله أبْشِرْ

and he answered that it was. 'Then the Ḳorân is created (مَخْلُوق)?' said the governor. 'Nay, that I will not say. I say it is something made (مَجْعُول)', was the answer.

After all the other cases had been disposed of Ibn al-Bakkâ al-Asghar remarked that 'the two ḳâḍîs', whom we assume to be Abd al-Raḥmân ibn Isḥâḳ and Jaᶜfar ibn ᶜIsâ, should be examined; but the governor said they held to the same profession as the Commander of the Faithful. Ibn al-Bakkâ suggested that if they were ordered to tell their opinion it could be reported to the Khalif for them. The governor, however, seems to have been determined to avoid the examination of the two ḳâḍîs, probably, to save one who may have been his own son from exposure and humiliation. He simply said to the provoking questioner, 'If thou wilt serve as witness [1]) before them thou shalt know their opinion'.

Fourth Letter. Isḥâḳ ibn Ibrâhîm then wrote to al-Maʾmûn a detailed account of the answers received, and after a delay of nine days again summoned the doctors to hear the Khalif's reply. The following is a version of the letter [2]); — The Commander of the Faithful has received your answer to his letter touching that which the ostentatious among the followers of the Ḳibla and those who seek among the people of religion a leadership for which they are not the right persons, believe about the doctrine of the Ḳorân, in which letter of his the Commander of the Faithful commanded thee to test them, and discover their positions and put them in their right places. Thou dost mention thy summoning of Jaᶜfar ibn ᶜIsâ and Abd al-Raḥmân ibn Isḥâḳ on the arrival of the Commander of the Faithful's letter, together with those whom thou didst summon of those classed as faḳîhs and known as doctors of Tradition and who set themselves up to give legal

---

1) ان شهدت عندهما بشهادة.

2) Ṭabarî III, ١١٢٥ ff.

decisions in Baghdâd, and [thou dost speak of] thy reading unto them all the letter of the Commander of the Faithful. [Thou hast mentioned], too, thy asking of them as to their faith touching the Ḳorân and [thy] pointing out to them their real interest; also, their agreeing to put away anthropomorphic conceptions and their difference of view in the matter of the Ḳorân; further, thy ordering of those who did not confess it to be created to refrain from Tradition and from giving decisions in private or in public. [Thou hast mentioned], too, thy giving orders unto al-Sindî and Abbâs the client of the Commander of the Faithful, to the same effect as thou didst give orders concerning them unto the two ḳâḍîs, even the same which the Commander of the Faithful prescribed to thee, namely, the testing of the statutory witnesses who are in their courts. Again, [thou hast mentioned] the sending abroad of letters unto the ḳâḍîs in the several parts of thy province that they should come to thee, so that thou mightest proceed to test them according to that which the Commander of the Faithful has defined, whilst thou hast put down at the end of the letter the names of those who were present and their views. Now, the Commander of the Faithful understands what thou hast reported, and the Commander of the Faithful praises God much, even as he is the One to whom such belongs; and he asks him to bless his Servant and his Messenger, Moḥammed, and he prays God to help him to obey him, [sc. God] and to give him [sc. the Khalif], by his grace, effectual aid in his good purpose. The Commander of the Faithful has also thought over what thou hast written relating to the names of those whom thou hast asked about the Ḳorân, and what each of them answered thee touching it, and what thou hast explained as his view. As for what the deluded Bishr ibn al-Walîd says about putting away anthropomorphic conceptions, and that from which he keeps himself back in the matter of the Ḳorân's being created, while he lays claim to leave off speaking on that subject as having had an engagement [to that effect] with the Commander of the Faithful,

Bishr has lied about that, and has acted as an unbeliever, speaking that which is to be refused credit and false; for there has not passed a compact or exchange of opinion in respect to this or any other matter between the Commander of the Faithful and himself, more than that the Commander of the Faithful told him of his belief in the doctrine of the Ikhlâṣ [i. e. the belief in the unity of God] and in that of the creation of the Ḳorân. Call him before thee; tell him what the Commander of the Faithful has told thee in the matter; cite him to answer about the Ḳorân and ask him to recant; for the Commander of the Faithful thinks that thou shouldst ask to recant one who professes his view, seeing that such a view is unmixed infidelity and sheer idolatry in the mind of the Commander of the Faithful. Should he repent, then, publish it and let him alone; but, should he be obstinate in his idolatry and refuse in his infidelity and heterodoxy to confess that the Ḳorân is created, then behead him and send his head to the Commander of the Faithful. In the same way, also, deal with Ibrâhîm ibn al-Mahdî. Test him as thou hast tested Bishr, for he professes his view and reports about him have reached the Commander of the Faithful; and, if he say that the Ḳorân is created, then publish it and make it known; but, if not, behead him and send his head to the Commander of the Faithful [1]). As for ʿAlî ibn Abî Muḳâtil, say to him, "Art thou not the man who said to the Commander of the Faithful, 'Thou art the one to declare what is lawful and unlawful'? and who told him what thou didst tell him?" the recollection of which cannot yet have left him [sc. ʿAlî]. And as for al-Dhayyâl ibn al-Haitham, tell him that what should occupy his mind is the corn which he formerly stole in al-Anbâr, when he administered the government in the city of the Commander of the Faithful, Abuʾl-Abbâs [2]); and that, if he were a follower in the footsteps of his forefathers, and went in their ways only, and

1) On death penalty for heresy cf. Goldziher, Moh. Stud. II, 216.

2) cf. Ṭabarî III, ٨٠, l. 18, seq.; De Goeje, Bibl. Geog. VII, ٣٣٧, 5 seq.

pushed on in their path, surely he would not go off into idolatry after having believed. As for Aḥmed ibn Yazîd, known as Abu'l-ʿAwwâm, and his saying that he cannot well answer about the Ḳorân, tell him that he is a child in his understanding, though not in his years, — an ignoramus; and that, if he do not see his way clear to answer he shall see his way clear to answer when he is disciplined, but should he not do it then, the sword will follow. As for Aḥmed ibn Ḥanbal and that which thou hast written about him, tell him that the Commander of the Faithful understands the import of that view and the manner of his conduct in it; and, from what he knows, he infers his ignorance and the weakness of his intellect. As for al-Faḍl ibn Ghânim, tell him that what he did in Egypt, and the riches which he acquired in less than a year are not hidden from the Commander of the Faithful, nor what passed in legal strife between him and al-Muṭṭalib ibn Abdallah about that; for a man who did as he did, and who has a greedy desire for dinârs and dirhems as he has, can be believed to barter his faith out of desire for money, and because he prefers his present advantage to everything else. [Remind him] that he, besides, is the one who said to ʿAlî ibn Hishâm what he did say, and opposed him in that in which he did oppose him. And what was it that caused his change of opinion and brought him over to another? And as for al-Ziyâdî, tell him that he is calling himself a client of the first false pretender in Islâm in whose case the ordinance of the Messenger of God was infringed. It is in harmony with his character that he should go in the way he goes. (But Abû Ḥassân denied that he was a client of Ziyâd or of anyone else, adding that he had the name of Ziyâd [ibn abîhi] for some other reason) [1]). As for Abû Naṣr al-Tammâr, the Commander of the Faithful compares the insignificance of his understanding with the insignificance of his business [date-merchant]. And as for al-Faḍl ibn al-

1) This parenthesis represents a gloss in Ṭabarî III, ١١٢٨, ll. 6—8, (line 7 read وَذَكَرَ for وذُكر).

Farrukhân, tell him that by the doctrine which he professes respecting the Ḳorân he is trying to keep the deposits which Abd al-Raḥmân ibn Isḥâḳ and others entrusted to him, lying in wait for such as will ask him to undertake trusts, and hoping to increase that which has come into his hand; for which there is no recovery from him, because of the long duration of the compact and the length of time of its existence. But say to Abd al-Raḥmân ibn Isḥâḳ, 'May God not reward thee with good for thy giving of power to the like of this man and thy putting of confidence in him, seeing that he is devoted to idolatry and disjoined from belief in God's unity!' And as for Moḥammed ibn Ḥâtim, and Ibn Nûḥ, and him who is known as Abû Maᶜmar, tell them that they are too much taken up with the devouring of usury to grasp properly the doctrine of the divine unity, and that, if the Commander of the Faithful had sought legal justification to attack them for the sake of God, and make a crusade against them on the sole ground of their practice of usury and that which the Ḳorân has revealed concerning such as they, he surely might have found it lawful; how will it be, then, now that they have joined idolatry to their practice of usury, and have become like the Christians? And as for Aḥmed ibn Shujâᶜ, tell him that not long ago thou wast with him, and thou didst extort from him that which he confiscated of the riches belonging to ᶜAlî ibn Hishâm; and [tell him] that his religion is found in dinârs and dirhems. And as for Saᶜdawaih al-Wâsiṭî, say to him, 'May God make abominable the man whose ostentatious preparing of himself for a 'colloquium doctum' on Tradition, while hoping to gain honour by that and desiring to be a leader in it, carries him so far that he wishes for the coming of the Miḥna, and thinks to ingratiate himself with me by it; let him be tried; [if he yield] he may still teach Tradition. And as for him who is known as Sajjâda and his denying that he heard from those traditionists and faḳîhs with whom he studied the doctrine that the Ḳorân is created, tell him that in his preparing of date-stones and his rubbing in order to improve his sajjâda [1]), and likewise in his care for the deposits which ʿAlî ibn Yaḥya and others left in trust with him lies that which occupies his attention so that he forgets the doctrine of the divine unity and that which makes him unmindful [of it]. Then ask him about what Yûsuf ibn Abî Yûsuf and Moḥammed ibn al-Ḥasan used to say, if he have seen them and studied with them. As for al-Ḳawârîrî, in what has been made known of his doings, in his receiving of gifts and bribes, lies that which sets in a clear light his real opinions, the evil of his conduct and the weakness of his understanding and his religion. It has also reached the Commander of the Faithful that he has taken upon himself the [settlement of] questions for Jaʿfar ibn ʿIsâ al-Ḥasanî; so, order Jaʿfar ibn ʿIsâ to give him up, and to abandon reliance upon him and acquiescence in what he says. And as for Yaḥya ibn Abd al-Raḥmân al-ʿOmarî, if he were of the descendants of ʿOmar ibn al-Khaṭṭâb, it is well known what would answer. And as for Moḥammed ibn al-Ḥasan ibn ibn ʿÂsim, if he were an imitator of his ancestors, he would not profess that profession which has been related of him [2]). He is yet a child and needs to be taught. Now, the Commander of the Faithful is sending to thee also, him who is known as Abû Mushir [3]), after that the Commander of the Faithful has cited him to answer in his testing about the Ḳorân; but he mumbled about it and stammered over it, until the Commander of the Faithful ordered the sword to be brought for him, when he confessed in the manner of one worthy to be blamed. Now, cite him to answer about his confession; and, if he stand fast in it, then, make it known and publish it. But those who will not give up their idolatry, and profess that the Ḳorân is created, of those whom thou hast named in thy letter to the Commander of the

1) Callous patch of skin on the forehead produced, when genuine, by oft-repeated religious prostrations; when an imposture, by rubbing the skin.

2) Ṭabarî, III, ١١٣٠. read حُكِيتْ.

3) d. 218 A. H. Dhahabî Tabaḳât 7, N°. 62.

Faithful and whom the Commander of the Faithful has mentioned or refrained from mentioning to thee in this letter of his, except Bishr ibn al-Walîd and Ibrâhîm ibn al-Mahdî, send them all in bonds to the camp of the Commander of the Faithful in charge of a watch and guards for their journey, until they bring them to the camp of the Commander of the Faithful and deliver them up to those to whom the delivery has been ordered [1]) to be made, so that the Commander of the Faithful may cite them to answer; and, then, if they do not give up their view and recant, he will bring them all to the sword. The Commander of the Faithful sends this letter by extra post [courier's letterbag] instead of waiting till all the letters have been gathered for the post, seeking to advance in the favor of God by the decree he has issued and hoping to attain his purpose, and to gain the ample reward of God thereby. So, give effect to the order of the Commander of the Faithful that comes to thee, and hasten to answer by extra p· iat [v. above] about that which thou hast done, not waiting' he the other letter-bags, so that thou mayest tell the Comma now of the Faithful of what they will do.

Recantation of the Doctors. On this letter being read all of those mentioned in it recanted, with the exception of Aḥmed ibn Ḥanbal, Sajjâda, al-Ḳawârîrî and Moḥammed ibn Nûḥ al-Maḍrûb. These four were then cast into prison in chains and next day were again brought before the governor and given a chance to recant. Of this chance Sajjâda availed himself and was set free [2]). The following day, also, they were brought from the prison and given another opportunity to yield, which Obaidallah ibn ʿOmar al-Ḳawârîrî embraced and received his liberty. *Aḥmed and Moḥammed ibn Nûḥ Refuse to Recant.* Thus Aḥmed and Moḥammed ibn Nûḥ alone of those cited to appear remained firm in their faith; the others Aḥmed always excused on the ground of the Taḳîa

---

1) Variant يوهرون adopted in the translation.

2) Abu'l-Maḥ. I, 738, says Sajjâda 'stood firm in the Sunna'.

as supported by Ḳorân, 16. 108, 'Except him who is forced, though he have no pleasure in it, while his heart rests in the faith [1]).

and are Cited to Tarsus.

Isḥâḳ the governor now wrote a letter giving the results of his examination of the doctors [2]). Shortly after this, al-Ma'mûn ordered Isḥâḳ ibn Ibrahîm to send Aḥmed ibn Ḥanbal and Moḥammed ibn Nûḥ in chains to him to Tarsus. On their journey when they were in the neighbourhood of al-Anbâr Abû Jaᶜfar al-Anbârî crossed the Euphrates to see Aḥmed in the khân where he was lodged, and reminded him of his responsibility as the leader to whom all men looked for an example. If he answered favorably, they, too, would assent to the doctrine; but should he refuse to assent, a great many, if not all, would be held back from recantation. He told him, besides, to remember that death would come to him in the natural course of things, and exhorted him, in view of what he had said, to maintain the integrity of his faith [3]).

---

1) Houtsma, De Strijd etc. 69 and note; al-Maḳrîzî, p. 4, وكان ابو عبد الله رحمه الله يُقيم عُذرهما ويقول اليس قد حُبسا وقُيّدا قال الله تعالى الا مَن اكرِه وقلبُه مطمئن بالايمان [Kor. 16. 108] ثم قال ابو عبد الله رحمه الله القيد كُرْه والحبس كُرْه والضرب كُرْه فأما اذا لم يُنَل بمكروه فلا عُذر له

2) Ṭabarî, III, ١١٣١.

3) al-Maḳrîzî, p. 4, ثم ورَد كتاب المامون الى اسحاق بن ابرهيم بحمل ابى عبد الله ومحمد بن نوح اليه ببلاد الروم فحُملا . . . . . وذكر ابن الجوزى بسنده الى ابى جعفر الانبارى [الابيارى al-Subkî, p. 136,] انه قال لما حُمِل احمد الى المامون اُخبرتُ فعبرت الفرات فاذا هو جالس فسلمت عليه فقال يابا جعفر تعَنّيت فقلت ليس فى هذا عَناء وقلت له انت اليوم راس والناس يقتدون بك فوالله لئِن اجبت

In pursuance of the Khalif's order the two unyielding theologians were borne on camels from Baghdâd, Aḥmed's companion in the maḥmal being a man called Aḥmed ibn Ghassân. As they were on the way Aḥmed told his companion that he had a firm conviction that the messenger of al-Ma'mûn, Rajâ al-Ḥiḍârî, would meet them that night; and, in fact, Rajâ al-Ḥiḍârî did meet them and the prisoners were transferred to his care, but he was not allowed to proceed far with his charge before the news of the Khalif's death relieved him of the obligation to bring the men to Tarsus. When he had conducted them as far as Adhana, and was just setting out with them at night, a man met them in the gate of the town with news that al-Ma'mûn had just died at the river Bodhandhûn [Ποδενδουν] in Asia Minor, after leaving as a last charge to his successor to prosecute vigorously the Miḥna [1]).

الى خلق القران ليُجيبن باجابتك خلق من خلق الله وان انت لم تجب ليمتنعن خلق من النّاس كثير ومع هذا فان الرجل يعنى المامون ان لم يقتلك تموت ولا بُد من الموت فثِق بالله ولا تجبهم الى شىء قال فجعل ابو عبد الله يبكى ويقول ما شاء الله ما شاء الله

1) Abû Nuʿaim, 147 *a*, 147 *b*, (al-Subkî, p. 139, cf. al-Makrîzî, p. 4 infra, a fuller account), قال احمد بن غسّان حُملتُ انا واحمدُ بن حنبل فى محمل على جَمل يُرادُ بنا المامون فلما صِرنا قُربَ عَانَة قال لى احمد قلبى يُحِسّ ان رجآء الحِضارى ياتى فى هذه الليلة فانْ اتى وانا نآئم فايقظنى وانْ اتى وانت نائم ايقظتك . . . . فلم يكن باسرع ان خَرَج علينا رجآء الحِضَارى فقال اين هولاء الاشقِياء فقال احمد يا عَدُوّ الله انت تقول القرانُ مخلوق ونكونُ نحن الاشقياء قال [احمد بن غسّان] فانزَلنا من المحامل وصيّرنا فى خيمة . . . . قال والله ما مضى الثلث الاول من الليل الا ونحن

Al-Ma'mûn Rejects the Plea of Taḳîa Offered by the Doctors.

In the meantime, al-Ma'mûn had received word that those who had recanted had done so claiming the Taḳîa as a justification, in accordance with the dispensation granted in the Ḳorân to such as are forced to confess a *false* faith, while their hearts continue to hold fast to the true [1]. This, of course, meant that what the Khalif believed and had propounded to them was false, a conclusion with which he was by no means satisfied, and, therefore, wrote again to Isḥâḳ

بصَيحة وضَجّة واذا رجاء الحصَارى قد اقبل علينا فقال صدقت يابا عبد الله القران كلام الله غير مخلوق قد مات والله اميرُ المومنين، [Aḥmed had previously prayed for a Divine interposition to demonstrate that he was in the right way].

فلما صِرْنا الى اذَنَة ورحلنا منها وذلك فى جوف الليل فُتِح لنا [147 *b*] بابُها فلقينا رجل ونحن خارجون من الباب وهو داخل فقال البُشرى قد مات الرجل قال ابى وكنتُ ادعو الله ان لا اراه قال ابو الفضل صالح فصار ابى ومحمد بن نوح الى طرسوس وجاء نَعى المامون من البذندُون فرُدّا فى اقيادهما الى الرَّقة واخرجا من الرقّة فى سفينة مع قوم مُحبّسين فلما صارا بعانات توُفّى محمّد بن نوح رحمه الله وتقدّم ابى فصَلّى عليه ثم صار ابى الى بغداد وهو مقيّد فمكث بالياسريّة اياما ثم صُيّر الى الحبس فى دار اكتُريت عند دار عُمارة ثم نقل بعد ذلك الى حَبْس العامة فى درب المَوصلية فمكث فى الحبس منذ اخذ وحُمل الى ان ضُرب وخلى عنه ثمانية وعشرين شهرا قال ابى فكنت اصلى بهم وانا مُقيد وكنت ارى بُوران يَحمل له فى زورق ماء باردا فيُذهب به اليه الى السجن،

1) Ṭabarî III, ۱۱۳۱ f.; De Goeje, Fragm. Hist. Arab. II, 465 f.; Abu 'l-Feda Annales II, 155.

ibn Ibrâhîm to tell Bishr ibn al-Walîd and the others who had pleaded that their case was similar to that of ᶜAmmâr ibn Yâsir contemplated in the Ḳorân's dispensation to recusants, that there was no similarity between the cases. He had openly professed a false religion, while at heart a Muslim; they had openly professed the truth while in their hearts believing what was false. To settle matters they must all be sent to Tarsus, there to await such time as the Khalif should leave Asia Minor. The following men were therefore sent after Aḥmed and his company: Bishr ibn al-Walîd, al-Faḍl ibn Ghânim, ᶜAlî ibn Abî Muḳâtil, al-Dhayyâl ibn al-Haitham, Yaḥya ibn Abd al-Raḥmân al-ᶜOmarî, ᶜAlî ibn al-Jaᶜd, Abuᵓl-ᶜAwwâm, Sajjâda, al-Ḳawârîrî, Ibn al-Ḥasan ibn ᶜAlî ibn ᶜÂṣim, Isḥâḳ ibn Abî Isrâᵓîl, al-Naḍr ibn Shumail, Abû Naṣr al-Tammâr, Saᶜdawaih al-Wâsiṭî, Moḥammed ibn Ḥâtim ibn Maimûn, Abû Maᶜmar, Ibn al-Harsh, Ibn al-Farrukhân, Aḥmed ibn Shujâ and Abû Hârûn ibn al-Bakkâ. They received the news of the Khalif's death when they arrived at al-Raḳḳa, and, on the order of ᶜAnbasa ibn Isḥâḳ, the Wâlî of the place, were detained there until they were sent back to Baghdâd in charge of the same messenger as had brought them thence. On arriving at Baghdâd, the governor Isḥâḳ ordered them to keep to their dwellings [1]), but afterwards relaxed his severity toward them and allowed them to go abroad. Some of those who had been sent, however, had the temerity to leave al-Raḳḳa and come to Baghdâd without having obtained permission. As might have been expected, they suffered for their boldness when they reached the latter place, for Isḥâḳ punished them. Those who thus procured trouble to themselves were Bishr ibn al-Walîd, al-Dhayyâl, Abuᵓl-ᶜAwwâm and ᶜAlî ibn Abî Muḳâtil.

and Orders Them to be Sent to Him.

Death of al-Ma'mûn and its Consequences.

---

1) On 'keeping to their dwellings' cf. Goldziher, Moh. Stud. II, 94.

Ahmed and Ibn Nûh Ordered back to Baghdâd. To return to Aḥmed and his companion Moḥammed ibn Nûḥ. These two were now sent back to al-Raḳḳa where they, also, remained in prison until the oath of allegiance was taken to the Khalif al-Muᶜtaṣim. After this event, they were taken in a boat from al-Raḳḳa to ᶜÂnât, at which place Moḥammed ibn Nûḥ died, and Aḥmed, after performing the offices of the dead over his friend, was brought back in bonds to Baghdâd [1]). At first, he was imprisoned, as it appears, in the street al-Yâsirîya for some days. From there he was transferred to the Dâr al-Sharshîr near to the Dâr ᶜUmâra and lodged in a stable belonging to Moḥammed ibn Ibrâhîm (brother of Isḥâḳ) which had been rented as a place of detention. It was very small and his stay there was short. He took sick in Ramaḍân, and was then transferred to the common prison in the Darb al-Mausilîya [2]).

Death of Ibn Nûh.

Among those who stood faithful in the inquisition during

---

1) See preceding note, p. 82, 1. Houtsma (De Strijd etc. 106) says that Moḥammed ibn Nûḥ, as well as Aḥmed ibn Ḥanbal, was scourged by al-Muᶜtaṣim, but he, in fact, never appeared before that Khalif.

2) al-Subkî, p. 139, قال صالح صار ابى الى بغداد مقيدا فمكث بالياسرية اياما ثم حبس بدار الشرشير عند دار عمارة ثم نقل بعد ذلك الى حبس العامة فى درب الموصلية [marg: Copy المفضلى] . . . . . . واما حنبل بن اسحق فقال حبس ابو عبد الله فى دار عمارة ببغداد فى اصطبل لمحمد بن ابراهيم اخى اسحق بن ابراهيم وكان فى حبس ضيق ومرض فى رمضانَ فحبس فى ذلك الحبس قليلا ثم حول الى سجن العامة فمكث فى السجن نحوًا من ثلاثين شهرا فكنا ناتيه وقرا علىّ كتاب الارجاء وغيره فى الحبس فرايته يصلى باهل الحبس وعليه القيد وكان يخرج رجله من حلقة القيد وقت الصلاة والنوم

Others who did not Recant. ʿAffân ibn Muslim.

the Khalifate of al-Maʾmûn, but whose name has not yet appeared, was ʿAffân ibn Muslim Abû ʿOthmân, whom the Khalif and Isḥâḳ ibn Ibrâhîm his lieutenant in ʿIrâḳ, in penalty for his refusal to obey the order to recant, deprived of the stipend which each of them granted to him. When asked what he had to say in reply to the demand made on him, he answered by reciting Sura 112, and enquiring whether that were created. His people were very angry with him for leaving them without means of support, for he had about 40 persons dependent on him. But the very day his stipend was cut off, a stranger brought to him a purse of 1000 dirhems (his stipend from al-Maʾmûn had been 500 per month), and promised him that he should receive the same amount each month from the same source. He died in Baghdâd in 220 A. H. During his life he was one of the leading men in Baghdâd and a friend of Aḥmed's who had much influence with him [1]). Another to whom the Miḥna was applied in

1) al-Maḳrîzî, p. 13, واما عفان بن مسلم فقال حنبل بن اسحاق كنت
حاضرا عند عفان بعد ان امتُحن فساله يحيى بن معين بحضور
ابى عبد الله احمد بن حنبل ونحن معه فقال يابا عثمن أخبرنا بما
قال لك اسحق بن ابراهيم فى المحنة وما رددت عليه فقال عفانُ لابن
معين يابا زكريا لم اسوّد وجهك ولا وجوه اصحابك يعنى انه لم يجب
الى القول بخلق القران فقال له فكيف كان فقال دعانى اسحق
ابن ابراهيم فلما دخلت عليه قرا الكتاب الذى كتبه المامون من
ارض الجزيرة الى الرَّقة [Cod. الرِّقة] فاذا فيه امتحن عفان وادّعه الى ان
يقول القرانُ كذا وكذا فان قال ذلك فأقِره على امره وان لم يجبك
فاقطع عنه الذى يجرى عليه وكان المامون يُجرى عليه فى كل شهر
خمس مائة درهم قال عفان فلما قرأ علىّ الكتاب قال لى ما تقول فقرات
عليه قُلْ هُوَ ٱللَّهُ أَحَدٌ [Kor. 112] الى اخرها وقلت امخلوق هذا

Abû Nu^c^aim al-Faḍl ibn Dukain. this Khalifate, and who did not yield was the Kûfite, Abû Nu^c^aim al-Faḍl ibn Dukain. When al-Ma'mûn's letter came to Kûfa he was told of its purport and exclaimed, 'It means only beating with whips'; and, then, taking hold of a button of his coat, he said, 'to me my head is of less consequence than that'. Of his trial we have no particulars, but he, at all events, does not appear to have died a violent death. He died in 219 A. H. [1]).

^c^Alî ibn al-Madînî. ^c^Alî ibn al-Madînî is classed with those who surrendered their faith at the time of the Miḥna, apparently about the beginning of its course. He bitterly regretted his weakness, however, and was firmly reestablished in the orthodox faith before his death in 234 A. H. [2]).

فقال لى اسحق ان امير المومنين امر ان لم تجبه بقطع عنك ما يجرى عليك وانْ قطع عنك امير المومنين قطعنا عنك نحن ايضا فقلت له قال الله تعالى وَفِى ٱلسَّمَآءِ رِزْقُكُمْ وَمَا تُوعَدُونَ [Kor. 51. 22] فسكت عنى اسحق وانصرفت فسُرّ ابو عبد الله ويحيى ومَن كان حاضرا فلما رجع الى داره عَذله اهل بيته وكان اربعين نفسا فبعد قليل دَقّ عليه البابَ انسان فدخل ومعه كيس فيه الف درهم فقال يابا عثمن ثبتك الله كما ثبّتّ الدين وهذا لك فى كل شهر

1) al-Makrîzî, p. 13, وقال الامام ابو بكر بن ابى شيبة لما جاءت المحنة الى الكوفة قال لى احمد بن يونس الق ابا نعيم فقل له فلقيته فقلت له فقال انما هو ضرب الاسياط [so Cod.] ثم اخذ زِرّ ثوبه وقال راسى اهونُ علىّ من هذا Abû Nu^c^aim al-Faḍl ibn Dukain was a Shyite according to Shahrastânî, Haarbrücker's transl'n I, 218.

2) al-Subkî, p. 185, وكان على المدينى ممن اجاب الى القول بخلق القران فى المحنة فنُقم ذلك عليه وزيد عليه فى القول والصحيح عندنا انه انما [Cod. انها] اجاب خشية السيف الخ . . . .

Aḥmed in Prison. In the common prison Aḥmed ibn Ḥanbal was confined for a considerable time, the whole period, from the time of his arrest until he was set free after being scourged by al-Muᶜtaṣim, being twenty-eight months. While in the prison he used to lead the prayers with the inmates, and engaged in the study of books which were provided for him by his friends. His good friend Bûrân did him the kindness to send him daily cold water, by means of a boat.

During the first part of his imprisonment, his uncle Isḥâḳ ibn Ḥanbal spoke to the officials and attachés of the governor seeking to secure a release of his nephew from prison; but, failing to obtain any satisfaction, he appealed to Isḥâḳ ibn Ibrâhîm in person. With a view to securing from Aḥmed a modification of his position, Isḥâḳ then sent his chamberlain to the prison with Aḥmed's uncle, ordering him to report whatever might pass between them. When they came to the prison, Isḥâḳ ibn Ḥanbal urged his nephew to yield an assent to the doctrine which was being pressed upon him. He reminded him that his companions, with much less reason, had recanted and that he had justified them in doing so on the ground of the Taḳîa. Why then should he not recant? After much fruitless disputation, they made up their minds to leave him in prison; and he went on to say that imprisonment was a matter of very little concern to him — a prison or his own house it was all the same. To be slain with the sword, too, was not a matter which caused him great anxiety; the one thing that he feared was to be scourged. If that should befall him, he could not answer for his holding out against it. One of the prisoners then reminded him that in the case of scourging he need have no fear, for after two strokes of the whip, he would never know where

---

وقال محمد بن عثمان بن ابى شيبة سمعت على المدينى يقول، قبل موته بشهرين القران كلام الله غير مخلوق ومن قال مخلوق فهو كافر

any that might follow would strike him. With this assurance the remaining anxiety of Aḥmed was completely dispelled [1]).

Another Citation before Isḥâḳ ibn Ibrâhîm. On the 17th of Ramaḍân, 219 A. H., that is, fourteen months from the time that he was stopped when on his way to al-Maʾmûn, he was brought from the common prison to the house of Isḥâḳ ibn Ibrâhîm, being bound with a single chain on his feet. While he was confined in the house of Isḥâḳ ibn Ibrâhîm, the latter sent

---

1) al-Maḳrîzî, p. 5, قال اسحاق ابن حنبل عمّ الامام احمد كنت اتكلم
مع اصحاب السلطان والقوّاد فى خلاص ابى عبد الله فلم يَتم لى امر
فاستاذنت على اسحاق بن ابراهيم فدخلت اليه وكلمته فقال
لحاجبه اذهب معه الى ابن اخيه ولا يكلمِ ابنَ اخيه بشىء الا
اخبرتنى به قال اسحاق فدخلت على ابى عبد الله ومعِى حاجبُه
فقلت يا ابا عبد الله قد اجاب اصحابك وقد اعذرت فيما بينك
وبين الله وبقِيت انت فى الحبس والضيق فقال ابو عبد الله يا عم
اذا اجاب العالم تَقِية والجاهل بجهل متى يتبين الحق قال فامسكت
عنه قال فذَكَر ابو عبد الله ما رُوِى فى التَّقية من الاحاديث فقال
كيف تصنعون بحديث خباب انّ من كان قبلكم يُنشر احدهم
بالمِنشار ثم لا يصُده ذلك عن دينه قال فيَئِسْنا منه ثم قال لستُ
أُبالى بالحبس ما هو ومنزلى الا واحد ولا قتلاً بالسيف انما اخاف فتنة
بالسوط واخاف ان لا اصبِر فسمعه بعض اهل الحبس وهو يقول ذلك
فقال لا عليك يابا عبد الله ما هُو الا سوطان ثم لا تدرى اين يقع
الباقى فلما سمع ذلك سُرّى عنه، قال ثم حُوّل ابو عبد الله الى دار
اسحاق بن ابراهيم فى شهر رمضان Abû Nuʿaim, 147b, adds [لليلة
سبع عشرة خلت منه] سنة تسع عشرة ومائتين

to him every day two men to reason with him; their names were, respectively, Aḥmed ibn Rabâḥ and Abû Shuaib al-Hajjâm. These two men used to argue with him, and, finding him immovable, as they turned to go away each day they called for an extra chain to be placed upon his feet, until, finally, there were four chains upon them. One of the discussions which Aḥmed had was about the Knowledge of God. He asked one of the two inquisitors for his opinion on the subject, and the man said that the Knowledge of God was created. On hearing this Aḥmed called him an infidel, and, though reminded that he was casting insult upon the messenger of the Khalif, he refused to withdraw the charge. Aḥmed's reasoning was that the names of God as symbols of his attributes were in the Ḳorân; that the Ḳorân was part of the Knowledge of God, which is one of his attributes; that, therefore, he who pretended that the Ḳorân was created had denied God, and, also, that he who pretended that the names of God were created had denied God. Here the argument seems to be: The names of God are not created; but the names of God form some part of the Ḳorân; therefore, it follows that some part of the Ḳorân, at least, is not created.

Aḥmed Ordered to al-Muᶜtaṣim. On the fourth night after he had been removed to the house of Isḥâḳ ibn Ibrâhîm, the messenger of the Khalif al-Muᶜtaṣim, Bughâ al-Kabîr, arrived after the last prayer, bringing the command of the Khalif to Isḥâḳ to send Aḥmed to him. When Aḥmed was brought in to Isḥâḳ before going to al-Muᶜtaṣim, the governor addressed him, reminding him that it was his life which was at stake, and that the Khalif had sworn that he would not kill him with the sword, but would scourge him stroke after stroke, and would throw him into a place where no light would ever reach him. Then, the governor proceeded to argue with him regarding the Ḳorân, quoting the text, 'Verily, we have made it a Ḳorân (reading) in the Arabic tongue', and he asked him, if there could be anything made unless it were created. Aḥmed answered with another text. 'He made them like grass to be eaten', and asked the governor, if he would conclude from such a text anything about their being created. In this case the argument turns upon the fact that the word جَعَلَ does not, necessarily, include the meaning of خَلَقَ.

Preparations were then made for bringing Aḥmed to al-Mu^ctaṣim. The interest of Bughâ, the messenger of the Khalif, in his prisoner and his cause was no very intelligent interest. He inquired of Isḥâḳ ibn Ibrâhîm's messenger what Aḥmed was wanted for, and, on learning, he declared that he knew nothing about such things; that the limits of his faith as a Muslim did not extend beyond the declaration that 'there is no God but Allah, that Moḥammed is the Apostle of God, and that the Commander of the Faithful is of the relationship of the Prophet of God'. At the gate of the royal park they disembarked after a short trip on the Tigris. Aḥmed was taken out of the boat and put upon a beast, from which he was in danger of falling off, owing to his helplessness because of the weight of his chains. He was brought under these circumstances into the palace precincts [1]) and made to alight at a house in a room of which he was confined, without any lamp to enable him to see at night [2]). During the night

---

1) al-Mu^ctaṣim's palace was in the eastern part of Baghdâd (vid. Ja^cqûbî, Bibl. Geogr. VII, ٢٥٥, 17). The general prison, if in the Darb al-Mufaḍḍal (but v. p. 85, note 2), was in the same quarter and Isḥâḳ the governor's residence may not have been at any great distance from this general prison. In any case it is clear that the trial and scourging took place in Baghdâd, where Aḥmed was well-known and had many admirers. Hence the popular demonstration against the Khalif when Aḥmed was flogged.

2) Abû Nu^caim, 147*b* f. حدثنا محمد بن جعفر وعلى بن احمد والحسين بن محمد قالوا ثنا محمد بن اسماعيل ثنا ابو الفضل صالح ابن احمد بن حنبل قال قال ابى رحمه الله لما كان فى شهر رمضان لليلة سبع عشرة خلت منه حُوِلت من السجن الى دار اسحاق

he is said to have had a vision of ᶜAlî ibn ᶜÂsim, and in-

ابن ابرهيم وانا مقيد بقيد واحد يُوَجّه النبى فى كل يوم رجلان سماهما ابى قال ابو الفضل وهما احمد بن رَباح وابو شُعَيب الحجام [al-Makrîzî الحجاج ,Cod. الحجاج] يكلمانى ويناظرانى فاذا ارادا الانصراف نُعى بقيد فقُيدت به فمكثت على هذه الحالة ثلاثة ايام وصار فى رجلى اربعةُ اقياد فقال لى [فقالى .Cod] احدهما فى بعض الايام فى كلام دارَ وسَالتُه عن علم الله فقال علم الله مخلوق فقلت له يا كافر كفرتَ فقال لى الرسول الذى كان يَحضُر معهم من قِبل ابى اسحاق هذا رسول امير المومنين قال فقلت له ان هذا قد كفر وكان صاحبُه الذى يجى معه خارجا فلما دخل قلت له ان هذا زعم ان علم الله مخلوق فنظر اليه كالمُنْكِر عليه ما قال ثم انْصَرفا قال ابى واسمآء الله فى القران والقران من علم الله فمن زعم ان القران مخلوق فهو كافر ومن زعم ان اسمآء الله مخلوقة فقد كفر قال ابى رحمه الله فلما كانت الليلة [اليلة .Cod] الرابعة* بعد العشآء الاخرة وجه المعتصم ببُغا الى اسحاق بن ابرهيم بامْره بحملى فأُدخلت على اسحاق فقال لى يا احمد انّها والله نفسُك انه قد حلف ان لا يقتُلك بالسيف وان يَضْربك ضَربا بعد ضرب وان يُلْقِيَك فى موضع لا ترى فيه الشّمس اليس قد قال الله تعالى انَّا جَعَلْنَاه قُرْانًا عَرَبِيًّا [Kor. 43. 2] افَيَكُونُ مجعولٌ الا وهُوَ مخلوق قال ابى فقلت له قد قال الله فَجَعَلَهُمْ كَعَصْفٍ مَأْكُولٍ [Kor. 105. 5] افخلقهم فقال اذهبوا به قال ابى رحمه الله فانزلت الى شاطئ دجلة وأُحدرتُ الى الموضع المعروف بباب البستان ومعى بُغَا الكبير ورسول من قبل اسحاق قال فقال بُغا لمحمد المحاربى بالفارسية ما تُريدون من هذا الرجل قال

terpreted it as being of good omen, assuring him of exaltation (علو) and protection from God (عصمة)[1].

Trial before al-Mu

Trial before al-Muᶜtaṣim. First Day. The next morning he was led to the palace in his chains and brought before the Khalif[2]). On this occasion, there were present with the Khalif Aḥmed ibn Abî Dowâd and his companions. It is said that

---

يُريدون منه ان يقول القرآنُ مخلوق فقال ما اعرِف شيئا من هذا الا قول لا اله الا الله وانّ محمدا رسول الله وقرابَةَ امير المومنين من رسول الله قال ابى فلما صِرنَا الى الشَط أُخرجت من الزورق فجُعلتُ على دابّة والاقياد علىّ وما معى احد يُمسكُنى فجعلت اكادُ اخرّ على وجهى حتى انتهى بى الى الدار فأُدخلت ثم عُرج بى الى حجرة فصُيِّرتُ فى بيت منها وغلق على الباب واقعِد عليه رجل وذلك فى جوف الليل وليس فى البيت سراج فاحتَجت الى الوُضوء فمَدَدْتُ يدى اطلب شيئا فاذا انا باناءٍ فيه ماء وطَسْتٍ [Cod. وطَسْتٌ] فتهيّأتُ للصّلاة وقُمتُ اصلى

1) al-Maḳrîzî, p. 4, قال حنبل بن اسحاق بن حنبل ابن عم الامام احمد سمعت ابا عبد الله يقول لما دعيت الى المحنة رايت فى المنام على بن عاصم فاوّلتها علوا وعصمة من الله عز وجل والحمد لله على ذلك

2) Abû Nuᶜaim, 148 *a* ff. With a few exceptions which are indicated, the narrative is now drawn from this source until we reach p. 111; cf. Abu'l-Feda Annales II, 168. There is a short and mutilated account of the proceedings before al-Muᶜtaṣim in al-Jaᶜqûbî II. 576, 577. فلما اصبحت جاءنى الرسول فاخذ بيدى فادْخلنى الدار واذا هو جالس وابنُ ابى دواد حاضر وقد جمع اصحابه والدّارُ غاصّة باهلها فلما دَنَوتُ منه سلمت فقال لى ادْنُهْ ادْنُهْ فلم يزل يُدنينى حتى قَرُبتُ منه ثم قال لى اجلِس فجلَستُ وقد اثقلتنى الاقياد فلما مكثت هُنَيهَة قلت تاذن فى الكلام فقال

when al-Muᶜtaṣim first saw Aḥmed, he said to those about

تكلم قلت الى ما دعا اليه رسول الله صلى الله عليه وسلم فقال الى شهادة ان لا اله الا الله قال فقُلت انا اشْهد ان لا اله الا الله ثم قلت له انّ جدّك ابنَ عباس يَحكِى انّ وَفْدَ عبد القَيْس لما قَدِموا على رسول الله صلى الله عليه وسلم امرهم بالايمان بالله فقال اتدرون ما الايمانُ بالله قالوا الله ورسوله اعلم قال شهادةُ ان لا اله الا الله وانّ محمدا رسول الله واقامُ الصلاة وايتآء الزكاة وصَوْمُ رمضان وان تعطوا الخُمس من المغنم قال ابو الفضل حدّثناه ابى ثنا يحيى بن سعيد عن شعبة قال حدثنى ابو جمرة قال سمعت ابن عباس قال انّ وَفْدَ عَبدِ القيس لما قَدموا على رسول الله صلى الله عليه وسلم امرهم بالايمان بالله فذكر الحديث قال ابو الفضل قال ابى فقال لى عند ذلك لولا انى وجدتك فى يد من كان قبلى ما تَعرّضت لك ثم التفت الى عبد الرحمن بن اسحاق فقال له يا عبد الرحمن الم آمُرك ان ترفع المحنة قال ابى فقلت فى نفسى الله اكبر انّ فى هذا لفرجًا للمسلمين قال ثم قال ناظروه وكَلّموه ثم قال يا عبدَ الرحمن كَلمه فقال لى عبد الرحمن ما تقول فى القران قال قلتُ له ما تقول فى علم الله فسكت قال ابى فجعل يُكلّمنى هذا وهذا فاردُّ على هذا واكلم هذا ثم اقول يا امير المومنين اعْطونى شيئا من كتاب الله او سنة رسول الله صلى الله عليه وسلم اقول به ما [Cod. omits] أراه قال فيقول ابن ابى دواد انت لا تقول الا ما فى كتاب الله او سنة رسول الله صلى الله عليه وسلم قال فقلتُ له تاوّلتَ تاويلا فانتَ اعلم وما تَناولتَ ما يُحبَس عليه ويُقيَّدُ عليه قال فقال ابن ابى دواد هو والله يا امير المومنين ضَالّ مُضل مبتدع * وهولاء قُضاتك والفقهآء فسَلْهم فيقول لهم ما تقولون

him reproachfully, ‘Did you not pretend that this was a

فيقولون يا امير المومنين هو ضال مضل مبتدع قال ولا يزالون يكلمونى
قال وجعل صوتى يعلو على اصواتهم وقال لى انسان منهم قال الله
مَا يَأْتِيهِمْ مِنْ ذِكْرٍ مِنْ رَبِّهِمْ مُحْدَثٍ [Ḳorân 21. 2] افيكون محدث الا
مخلوق قال فقلت له قال الله تعالى صٓ وَالْقُرْآنِ ذِي الذِّكْرِ [Ḳorân 38. 1]
فالذكر هو القرآن وتلك ليس فيها الف ولا لام قال فجعل ابن سمّاعة
لا يفهم ما اقول قال فجعل يقول لهم ما يقول قال فقالوا له انّه يقول كذا
وكذا قال فقال لى انسان منهم حديث خبّاب يا هناه تقرب الى الله
بما استطعت فانك لن تتقرب اليه بشىء هو احبُّ اليه من كلامه
قال ابى فقلتُ له نعم هكذا هو قال فجعل ابنُ ابى دواد ينظر اليه
ويلحظ متغيظا عليه قال ابى وقال بعضهم اليس قال الله خالق كل
شىء قال قلت قد قال تُدَمِّرُ كُلَّ شَىْءٍ [Ḳorân 46. 24] فدمّرت الا ما
اراد الله قال فقال بعضهم فما تقول وذكر حديث عمران بن حصين
انّ الله تعالى كتب الذكر فقال انّ الله خلق الذكر فقلت هذا
خطأ حدثناه غير واحد ان الله كتبَ الذكر قال ابى فكان اذا
انقطع الرجل منهم اعترض ابنُ ابى دواد فتكلم فلما قاربَ الزوال قال
لهم قُوموا ثم احتبس عبدَ الرحمن بن اسحاق فخلا بى وبعبد
الرحمن فجعل يقول لى اما تعرف صالحا الرشيدى كان مُودبى وكان
فى هذا الموضع جالسا واشار الى ناحية من الدار قال فتكلم وذكر
القران فخالفنى فامرتُ به فسُحبَ ووُطى ثم جعل يقول ما اعرِفك
الم تكن تاتينا فقال له عبد الرحمن يا امير المومنين اعرِفه منذ
ثلاثين سنة يرى طاعتك والحج والجهاد معك وهو ملازم لمنزله قال
فجعل يقول والله انه لفقيه وانه لعالم وما يسرّنى ان يكون مثله معى

يرد على اهلِ الملل ولـئـن اجابنى الى شىء له فيه ادْنى فَرج لاطْلقَن عـنـه بـيدى ولاطان عَقبه ولاركَبنّ اليه بجندى قل ثم يلتفت الىّ فيقول وَيْحَك يا احمد ما تقول قال فاقول يا اميرِ المومنين أَعطُونى شيئا من كتاب الله او سنة رسول الله صلى الله عليه وسلم فلما طال بنا المجلس ضجر فقام فرُددتُ الى الموضع الذى كنتُ فيه ثم وجه الىّ برجلين سماهما وهـمـا صاحبُ الشافعى وغَسّانُ من اصحاب ابـن ابى دواد يُناظرانى فيقيمان معى حتى اذا حضر الافطار وُجـه الينا بمآئدة عليها طعام فجعلا ياكلان وجعلتُ اتعلّل حتى تُرفع المآئدة و اقاما الى غد فى خلال ذلك يجىء ابن ابى دُواد فيقول لى يا احمد يقول لك امير المومنين ما تقول فاقول له اعطونى شيئا من كتاب الله او سُنة رسول الله صلى الله عليه وسلم حتى اقـولَ بـه فقال لى ابـن ابى دواد والله لـقـد كَتب اسمَك فى السَبعة فمحوتُه ولقد سآءنى اخذهم اياك وانّه والله ليس السَيف أنه ضَربٌ بعد ضَرب ثم يقولِ لى ما تقول فارُدُّ عليه نحوا مما ردَدْتُ عليهِ ثم يانينى رسولُه فيقول اين احمدُ بن عمّار اجِبْ للرجل [Cod. الرجل] الذى انزلتُ** فى حُجرته فيذهب ثم يَعُود فيقول لى يقول لك امير المومنين ما تـقول فأرُدُّ عليـه نحوا مما رَدَدْت على ابن ابى دواد فلا تزال رسله تاتى احمد بن عمار وهو يختلف فيما بينى وبينه ويقول يقول لـك امير المومنين اجبنى حتى اجى فاطلق عنك بـيدى قال فلما كان فى اليوم الـثـانى ادخِلت عليه فـقـال ناظروه وكلـموه قال فجعلوا يتكلمون هذا من هاهنا* وهذا من هاهنا فارد على هذا وهذا فاذا جاءوا بشىء من الكلام مما ليس فى كتاب الله ولا سنة رسول الله صلى الله عليه وسلم ولا فيه خبر ولا اثـر قلت ما ادرى ما هذا قال

**) Cod. انزلتَ, but if we read للرجل the correction is obviously necessary; i. e. 'pointing to the man in whose dwelling I had been lodged'.

فيقولون يا امير المومنين اذا توجّهتْ له الحجة علينا وثب واذا كلمناه بشىء يقول لا أدرى ما هذا قال فيقول ناظروه ثم يقول يا احمد انى عليك شفيق فقال رجل منهم اراك تذكر الحديث وتنتحله [Cod. تنجله] قال فقلت له فما تقول فى قول الله تعالى يُوصِيكُمُ ٱللَّهُ فِى أَوْلَادِكُمْ لِلذَّكَرِ مِثْلُ حَظِّ ٱلْأُنْثَيَيْنِ [Kor. 4. 12] فقال خص الله بها المومنين قال فقلتُ له ما تقول ان كان قاتلا او عبدا او يهوديا او نصرانيًّا فسكت قال انى فانما احتججت عليهم بهذا لانهم كانوا يحتجون علىّ بظاهر القران ولقوله اراك تنتحل الحديث وكان اذا انقطع الرجل اعترض ابن ابى دواد فيقول والله يا امير المومنين لئن اجابك لهو احب الىّ من مائة الف دينار ومائة الف دينار فيُعَدّدُ ما شآء الله اليه من ذلك ثم امرهم بعد ذلك بالقيام وخلا بى وبعبد الرحمن فيدور بيننا [Cod. فينا] كلام كثير وفى خلال ذلك يقول تدعوا احمد بن ابى دواد فاقول ذلك اليك فيُوَجه فيجى فيتكلم فلما طال بنا المجلس قام ورُددتُ الى الموضع الذى كنت فيه وجآءنى الرجلان اللذان كانا عندى بالأمس فجعلا يتكلمان فدار بيننا كلام كثير فلما كان وقت الافطار جىء بطعام على نحوٍ مما اتى به فى اول الليلة فافطروا وتعلّلْتُ وجعلتْ رسُلُه تاتى احمد بن عمار فيمضى اليه فيأتينى [Cod. يأتينى] برسالة على نحوٍ مما كان فى اوّل ليلة فجاء ابن ابى دواد فقال له انه قد حلف ان يضربك ضربا بعد ضرب وان يحبسك فى موضع لا ترى فيها الشمس فقلت له فما اصنع حتى اذا كدتُ ان اصبح قلت لخليقٌ ان يحدُثَ فى هذا اليوم من امرى شىء وقد كنتُ اخرجت تِكّتى من سراويلى فشددتُ به الاقياد احملها بها اذا توجهت اليه فقلت لبعض من كان معى

الموكّل بى أُريد لى خَيطا فجآءنى بخَيط فشَدَدْتُ بها الاقياد واعدت التكة فى سراويلى ولبستها كراهِيَة ان يَحدث شىء من امرى فأتعرى فلما كان فى اليوم الثالث أُدخلتُ عليه والقومُ حضور فجعلتُ أُدخَل من دار الى دار وقوم معهم السيوف وَقومٌ معهم السياط وغير ذلك من الزِى والسلاح وقد حُشيَت الدار بالجُند ولم يكن فى اليومين الماضيين كَبير احد من هولآء حتى اذا صِرت اليه قال ناظروه وكلموه فعادوا بمثل مناظرتهم فدار بيننا وبينهم كلامٌ كثير حتى اذا كان فى الوقت الذى كان يخلو بى فيه نحّانى ثم اجتمعوا وشاورَهم ثم نَحّاهم ودعانى فخلا بى وبعبد الرحمن فقال لى ويحك يَا احمد انا والله عليك شفيق وانى لأُشفِقُ عليك مثلَ شفَقَتِى على هرون ابْنى فاجبْنى فقلت يا امير المومنين اعطونى شيئا من كتاب الله او سُنّةِ رسول الله صلى الله عليه وسلم فلما ضَجر وطال المجلس قال عليك لَعنة الله لقد كنت طمِعتُ فيك خُذوه خَلِّعوه ثيابه اسحَبُوه قال فاخذت فَسُحبتُ ثم خلعت ثم قال العُقابين [قال لى العقاربين .Cod] والسِّيَاط فجىء بعُقابين [read ?بالعُقابين] والسياط فقال انى وقد كان صار الىّ شعرتان من شَعرِ النبى صلى الله عليه وسلم فصَررتهما فى كم قميصى فنظر اسحاق بن ابرهيمَ الى الصُرّة فى كم قميصى فوجّه الىّ ما هذا مصرور فى كم قميصك [Margin, variant كمك] فقلت شعر من شعر النبى صلى الله عليه وسلم وسَعَى بعض القوم الى القميص ليُخرقه فى وقت ما اقمت بين العُقابين فقال لهم لا تخرقوه انزِعوه عنه قال انى ظننت انه* درى عن القميص الخرق لسبب الشعر الذى كان فيه , صيرت بين العُقابين وَشدّت يدى وجِىء بكرسى فَوُضع له وابن ب; دواد قائم على راسه والناس اجمعون قيام مِمّن حضر فقال لى

انسان مِمَّن شدَّنـى خُـذ نابَي الخَشَبَتيْن بيدكَ وشُدَّ عليهما فلَم افهم ما قال قال فتخلعَتْ يـدى لما شُـددتُ ولم امسك الخشبتين قال ابـو الفضل ولم يـزَل ابـى رحمه الله يتَوجَّـع منهما من الرُسغ الى ان توفى ثم قال للجلّاديـن تـقـدموا فنظرِ الى السياط فـقـال ائتوا بغيرها ثم قال تقدمـوا فقال لاحدهم ادنه اَوْجع قطَع الله يدك فتقدم فضرَب سـوطين ثم تنحّى ثم قال ادنـه شـد قطع الله يدَك فتقدم فضَربنى سوطين ثم تنحى فلم يزَلْ يدعو واحدًا بعد واحد فيضربنى سَوطَين ثم يتنحى ثم قام حتى جاءنى وهم مُحدقون به فقال ويحك يا احمد تَقتُل نَفسَـك وَيْحكَ اجِبْنى اطـلـق عنك بـيـدى قال فجعل بعضهم يقول لى وَيحك اِمامُـك على راسك قآئم قال وجعل عُجَيفٌ يَنخُسُنى بقآئم سَيْفه ويقول تُريـد ان تغلب هؤلآء كلهم قال وجعَل اسحاق بن ابـرهيم يَـقول وَيْلـك الخليفة على راسـك قآئـم ثم يقول بعضهم يـا اميرَ المومنين دَمُه فى عُنقى قال ثم رجع فجلس على الكرسى ثم قال للجلّاد اَدْنُـه شـد قطعَ الله يدَك ثم لم يزَلْ يدعو جلّادا [Cod. جلّاد] بعد جلاد فيضربنى سـوطين ويتَنَحّى وهو يقولُ له شُدَّ قطع الله يدك ثم قام الـىَّ الثانية فجعل يقولُ يـا احمد اجِبْنى فجعل عبد الرحمن بن اسحاق يقول لى مَن صنَع بنفسه من اصحابك فى هذا الامر ما صنَعت هـذا يحيى بـن معين وهـذا ابـو خيثمة وابنُ ابى اسرائيل وجعل يُعددُ علىَّ من اجـاب وجَعل هو يقول ويحك اجِبنى قال فجعلت اقول نَحوا مما كنت اقوله لهم قال فرجع فجلس ثم جعل يقول للجلّاد شُدَّ قطع الله يـدك قال ابى فـذهـب عقلى وما عَقَلتُ الا وانـا فى حُجْر مطلق عـن الاقياد فقال انسان ممَّن حَـضَـر انا كبَّبناك على وجهك وطَـرَحْنَا على ظهرك بـاريَـة ودُسـنـاك قال ابى فقلت ما شَعرتُ بذا

قال فجاءونى بسويق فقالوا لى اشرب وتقيّأ فقلت لا افطر ثم جيء بى الى دار اسحاق بن ابرهيم قال ابى فنُودى بصلاة الظهر فصلّينا الظهر فقال ابن سَماعةَ صليت والدمُ يَسيلُ من ضَربك فقلت قد صلّى عُمر رضى الله عنه وجُرحه يَثعَبُ دما فسكت ثم خلى عنه فصار الى المنزل [Cod. omits قال?] ووُجه الىّ برجل من السجن ممن يُبصر الضرب والجراحات ويُعالج منها فنَظر اليه فقال أنا والله لقد رايتُ من ضُرب الف سوط ما رايت ضربا اشد من هذا لقَدْ جُرّ عليه من خلفه ومن قدامه ثم أدخل ميلا فى بعض تلك الجراحات وقال لم يُنقَب فجعل يأتيه ويُعالجه وقد كان اصحاتّ [cf. Tâj al-ʿArûs] وجهه غير ضربة ثم يمكث يعالجه ما شآء الله ثم قال له ان هاهنا شيئا أُريدُ انْ اقطعه فجآء بحديدة فجعل يُعلق اللحم بها ويقطعُه بسكين معه وهو صابر بذلك يحمد الله فى ذلك فبرأ منه ولم يزل يتوجع من مواضع منه وكان اثر الضرب بيّنا فى ظهره الى ان توفى رحمه الله، قال ابو الفضل سمعت ابى يقول والله لقد اعطيت المجهودَ من نَفْسى ولوددتُ انى انجو من هذا الامر كفافا لا على ولا لى قال ابو الفضل واخبرنى احد الرجلين اللذين كانا معه وقد كان هذا الرجل يعنى صاحب الشافعى صاحب حديث قد سمع ونظر ثم جآءنى بعد فقال يابن اخى رحمةُ الله على ابى عبد الله ما رايت احدا بِعَيْنى يشبهُه لقد جعلت اقول له فى الوقت ما يوجه الينا بالطعام يابا عبد الله انتَ صائم وانت فى موضع تقيّة* ولقد عَطِشَ فقال لصاحب الشراب نَاولنى نناوله قَدحًا فيه مآء وثلج فاخذه فنظر اليه هنيهة ثم ردّه عليه قال جعلت اعجب اليه من صَبْره على الجوع والعطش وما هو فيه من هول قال ابو الفَضْل وكنت التَمس واحتال ان اوصل اليه طعاما او

young man, but this man is not young' [his age was 54] [1]). The Khalif, on his entering, commanded him to draw near and bade him sit down. Then Aḥmed asked permission to speak, and, having received it, put the question, 'To what did the Messenger of God give invitation?' The Khalif said, "To the testimony 'that there is no God but Allah'." Aḥmed replied, 'I testify that there is no God but Allah'; and, after he had professed his adherence to the five cardinal points of Islâm, the Khalif told him that if he had not been apprehended by his predecessor in the Khalifate he would not have taken any action against him. Then, turning to Abd al-Raḥmân ibn Isḥâḳ, al-Muʿtasim asked him if he had not given him command to abolish the Miḥna. On hearing this, Aḥmed was overjoyed, supposing that it was really the Khalif's intention to deliver his subjects from the objectionable test. Following this, there was disputation, in which the Khalif ordered Abd al-Raḥmân ibn Isḥâḳ to take a part. This man then put the question to Aḥmed, 'What dost thou say about the Ḳorân?' Aḥmed returned him no direct answer, but, in turn, asked him 'what he had to say about the Knowledge of God'. To this Abd al-Raḥmân made no reply. During the Miḥna this question was, with Aḥmed, a favorite device in argument and one by means of which he generally put his opponents in embarrassment. The force of the argument lies in the fact that the Ḳorân is declared to be knowledge from God, and Aḥmed and such as he regarded this as equivalent to its being inseparable from the Knowledge of

---

رغيفا او رغيفين فى هذه الايام فلم اقدر على ذلك واخبرَنى رجل حضره قال تَفقَّدتُه فى هذه الايام وهم يناظرونه ويُكلمونه فما لحَن فى كلمة وما ظننت ان احدًا يكونُ مثل شجاعته وشدة قلبِه قدس الله روحه

1) al-Maḳrîzi, p. 5، فلما نظر اليّ المعتصم سمعته يقول لهم كالمنكِر عليهم اليس قد زعمتم انه حدث السن هذا شيخ مكتهل

God. 'If this Knowledge', say they, 'be uncreated then the Ḳorân must be uncreated'. Another point which Abd al-Raḥmân urged was that 'God existed when a Ḳorân did not exist'; to this Aḥmed replied with the same argument, 'Did God exist and not his Knowledge?' [1]).

During the passage between Abd al-Raḥmân ibn Isḥâḳ and Aḥmed, the latter asked Abd al-Raḥmân what his master al-Shâfiʿî had taught him about the ritual washing of the feet, and Ibn Abî Dowâd, in great astonishment, exclaimed, 'Behold a man who is face to face with death indulging in questions over Fiḳh!' [2]).

One of those in the room recited a tradition of ʿImrân ibn Ḥuṣain that God created الذكر and الذكر is the Ḳorân; to this Aḥmed answered that he had the tradition from more than one authority in the form, 'God wrote الذكر'. The bearing of this tradition as corrected by Aḥmed is to the effect that the substance and words of the Ḳorân were not created but that the earthly record was. Another tradition which was adduced was that of Ibn Masʿûd, 'God did not create in paradise, hell, heaven and earth anything greater than the Throne verse' (Ḳorân 2. 256). Aḥmed's rejoinder was that the creation applied only to paradise, heaven, hell and earth, but

---

1) al-Maḳrîzî, p. 6, فقال لى عبد الرحمن كان الله ولا قران فقلت له اكان الله ولا علم فأمسك ولو زعم ان الله كان ولا علم كفر

2) Abû Nuʿaim, 144*b*, الحسن يقول أدخل احمد بن حنبل على الخليفة وعنده ابن ابى دواد وابو عبد الرحمن الشافعى فاجلس بين يدى الخليفة وكانو هوّلوا عليه وقد كانوا ضربوا عنق رجلين فنظر احمد الى ابى عبد الرحمن الشافعى فقال اى شىء تحفظ عن الشافعى فى المسح فقال ابن ابى دواد انظروا رجلا هوذا يقدم لضرب العنق يناظر فى الفقه،

did not apply to the Ḳorân — a construction which is admissible [1]).

Someone introduced the verse, 'What came to them of ذِكْر from their Lord was a thing newly produced', and asked, 'Can anything be newly produced unless it be created?' Aḥmed said the Ḳorân, Sura 38, declares, 'By the Ḳorân, the possessor of الذكر'; so الذكر is the Ḳorân but there is in that other (ذِكْر) no article. Here the argument is to shew that الذِّكْر and the Ḳorân are identical in meaning, but ذِكْر without the article is not identical with the Ḳorân. Consequently, no argument can be based upon the declaration that ذكر was newly produced.

The words were cited, 'He is the creator of everything'. Against this Aḥmed quoted, 'Thou dost destroy everything'; and he added, 'Dost thou destroy except what God wills?' The argument is that the term 'everything' must be understood in harmony with declarations as to the unoriginate character of the Ḳorân found elsewhere within the Book itself.

It is said that, in the course of the discussion, Ibn Abî Dowâd lost his patience because Aḥmed insisted on keeping to the Ḳorân and the Tradition. Aḥmed's defence was to the effect that his course was justifiable, for Ibn Abî Dowâd was putting a construction upon the Ḳorân with which sincere minds could not agree, and, failing to agree, the men were being cast into prison and loaded with chains. With this Ibn Abî Dowâd called upon the Khalif to ask his ḳâḍîs and faḳîhs if Aḥmed were not a man misled, misleading

1) al-Maḳrîzî, p. 6, واحتجوا علىّ بحديث ابن مسعود وما خلق الله من جنة ولا نار ولا سماء ولا ارض اعظمَ من اية الكرسى [Ḳor. 2. 256] قال ابو عبد الله فقلت انما وقع الخلق على الجنة والنار والسماء والارض ولم يقع على القران

and heretical. On his enquiring of them they declared he was such. On this occasion Aḥmed repeatedly protested to the Khalif that his opponents were not adhering to the authorities which alone could settle such disputes [1]). Indeed, Aḥmed seems to have been the most vehement of all the disputants. Ibn Abî Dowâd shewed his zealot spirit, likewise, by frequently interjecting his opinion. On the first occasion of his interference, Aḥmed did not answer him, and, when al-Muᶜtaṣim rebuked him for it, he replied that he was not aware that Ibn Abî Dowâd was a man of learning [2]).

When it came to the time of closing the Khalif bade all present arise; and after the session was ended, the Khalif and Abd al-Raḥmân ibn Isḥâḳ had a private conference with Aḥmed, in which al-Muᶜtaṣim mentioned to him the punishment he had visited upon his own private tutor Ṣâliḥ al-Rashîdî for opposing him in regard to the Ḳorân. He complained, too, that Aḥmed had not given him any chance to learn his views or their vindication. Abd al-Raḥmân, however, explained that he had known Aḥmed for thirty years as a pious Muslim who observed the Hajj and the Jihâd and was a loyal subject of the Khalif. In view of what Abd al-Raḥmân said, and of what he himself had heard of Aḥmed's answers, al-Muᶜtaṣim then exclaimed, 'Surely, this man is a faḳîh! surely, he is a man of learning [ᶜâlim]! and I would that I had men such as he with me to take part in managing my affairs, and to effectually answer the advocates of other religions'. He, further, professed himself ready to suspend at once all action against Aḥmed, and to support him with all his power, if he would but give him the very slightest

1) cf. Dozy, Het Islamisme, 152.

2) al-Maḳrîzî, p. 6, قال ابو عبد الله كان القوم اذا انقطعوا عن الحجة عرّض ابن ابى دُواد فتكلم وكلمنى مرة فلم التفت اليه فقال لى المعتصم الا تكلمه فقلت لست اعرفه من اهل العلم فاكلمه قال ابو عبد الله وكان ابن ابى دواد من اجهل بالعلم والكلام

mission as a ground for doing so. To this Aḥmed made answer in harmony with what he had said before, asking for some justifying passage from the Ḳorân or from the Tradition of the Prophet.

This closed the first day's proceedings, and Aḥmed was sent back to his place of confinement, where two men, one a follower of al-Shâfiʿî and a certain Ghassân, of the following of Ibn Abî Dowâd, visited him and engaged in conversation and disputation with him until the next morning. In the meanwhile, the evening meal was brought in and the two visitors partook; but Aḥmed, though strongly pressed and though suffering from hunger, would not touch anything. Before the audience of the next day Ibn Abî Dowâd himself brought a message from the Khalif enquiring as to whether Aḥmed had changed his mind or not. Ibn Abî Dowâd, also, expressed his personal sorrow at his arrest, especially in view of the Khalif's resolution not to execute him with the sword, in case he should refuse to recant, but to scourge him stroke after stroke until he should be brought to a change of mind or should die under the lash. He assured Aḥmed that the Khalif al-Maʾmûn had written his name among the first seven who were summoned, but that he had been instrumental in securing its erasure [1]. To all these persuasions Aḥmed replied with the same plea for some satisfactory ground from either the Ḳorân or the Tradition on which to base a change of faith. The man in whose house he was detained, Aḥmed ibn ʿAmmâr, was, also, sent to him repeatedly with messages from the Khalif, but all in vain.

Second Day. On the second day, the proceedings were much the same as those of the previous audience. Whenever they used the Ḳorân or a tradition of recognized authority Aḥmed shewed himself ready to meet them, and appears to have been fully able to hold his own. When, however, they adopted any other method of argument, he refused absolutely to recognize the validity of their proofs, and maintained a

---

1) cf. p. 64.

stubborn silence. He carried this practice out so thoroughl that his opponents complained to the Khalif that, when ever the argument was in his favor he had his answer ready, but, on the contrary, whenever it went in their favor he simply challenged the testimonies which they adduced. It seems to have troubled him that they should have insisted, as they sometimes did, on the letter of the Ḳorân; and, to shew them that they ought not to be too slavish in their adherence to the Ḳorân, he asked one of the disputants what he had to say about the text, 'God commanded you concerning your children, the male's portion shall be the portion of two females'. The man replied that the text related specially to the believers. Aḥmed then asked him, what would be the rule if the man were a murderer, a slave, a Jew, or a Christian. To this his opponent made no answer. This argument Aḥmed apologized for using on the ground of their annoying manner of argument with him; and it would appear from this case that he was prepared to follow the text of the Ḳorân as closely as practical necessity would allow, but admitted the need, in special cases, of modification or expansion by means of additional light from some other source. This additional light he apparently would have borrowed only from well-established Tradition.

On this day, as on the previous one, Aḥmed Ibn Abî Dowâd, whenever opportunity offered, took an active part in the discussion. In one of Aḥmed ibn Ḥanbal's three examinations in this trial, probably in the first or second, when he had declared his faith in the Ḳorân as uncreated, it was retorted upon him that he was setting up a similar being to God (dualistic view)[1]). His reply was, 'He is one God, eternal; none is like him and none is equal. He is even as he has described himself'[2]). At the close of this session a private conference between the Khalif, Abd

1) Steiner, 77, cf. 90 f.

2) al-Maḳrîzî, p. 4, وكان ابو عبد الله اذا دُعى الى القول بخلق

al-Raḥmân and Aḥmed again occurred, to which Aḥmed ibn Abî Dowâd was afterwards called in. At its close, Aḥmed was returned to the place of detention, and the history of the first night was repeated. Messengers came and went, and the two men who had been with him before came back and stayed with him through the night. Before the next day came, Aḥmed had a premonition that an issue would surely be reached at the coming session, and prepared himself for it.

Third Day. When the messenger came the next day Aḥmed was brought to the palace of the Khalif, and his fear began to be confirmed as he saw the great display of pomp and of armed men, apparently prepared for some special occasion. First, there was an audience, in which the learned men disputed with him, and then followed another private conference in which the Khalif, as before, besought Aḥmed to yield, in however slight a degree, so that he might grant him his freedom. The Khalif assured him of his having as much compassion for him as he would have for his own son Hârûn in such a case. Aḥmed's reply was the invariable one, asking for some ground for a change of faith adduced from the only sources which he recognized as authoritative. Finally the Khalif lost all patience when he saw that his hopes of a ground for leniency toward his prisoner were to be disappointed, and he ordered him to be taken

Aḥmed Scourged. away and flogged. The flogging then ensued. Before it occurred, a little knot was noticed in the sleeve of Aḥmed's ḳamîṣ, and he was asked what might be the explanation of it. He said that it held two hairs of the Prophet [1]). On learning this Isḥâḳ ibn Ibrâhîm saved

---

القران وضُرب بالسياط يقول القران كلام الله غير مخلوق فاذا قيل له القول بذلك يؤدى الى التشبيه يقول احَد صمد لا شبيه له ولا عدل وهو كما وصف به نفسه

1) On hairs of the Prophet as charms cf. Goldziher, Moh. Stud. II, 358.

the ḳamîṣ from being destroyed. Before and during the course of the flogging, the Khalif sought to secure from Aḥmed a recantation, and seems to have been moved by compassion for him, though equally moved by a determination to drive him to repent of his obstinate refusal. Ibn Abî Dowâd and the leaders who were with him did their best, however, to move the Khalif to put Aḥmed to death. When bound, Aḥmed complained to the Khalif that the punishment he was inflicting upon him was unlawful according to the declaration of the Prophet, who had said that the blood and possessions of any man who confessed that there was no God but Allah, and that he was God's Messenger, were inviolable. Aḥmed Ibn Abî Dowâd, thinking his master inclined to weaken out of admiration for Aḥmed's spirit and courage and from the conviction wrought by his arguments, reminded al-Muʿtaṣim that, if he yielded, he would certainly be said to oppose the doctrines of the former Khalif al-Maʾmûn, and men would regard Aḥmed as having obtained a victory over two sovereigns, a result which would stimulate him to assume a leadership fraught with evil consequences to the dominion of the Khalifs [1]. As he was bound to the whipping-posts the lictors, one hundred and fifty in

---

1) al-Maḳrîzî, p. 7, قل ابو عبد الله وجُعلت بين العُقابين فقلت يا امير المومنين ان رسول الله صلعم قل لا يحل دم امرء مسلم يشهد ان لا اله الا الله وانى رسول الله الا باحدى ثلاث الحديث وقل رسول الله صلعم امرت ان اقاتل الناس حتى يقولوا لا اله الا الله فاذا قالوها عصموا منى دماءهم واموالهم فبِمَ تستحل دمى ولم آتِ شيئا من هذا يا امير المومنين اذكر وقوفك بين يدى الله عز وجل كوقوفى بين يديك يا امير المومنين راقب الله فلما راى المعتصم ثبوت ابى عبد الله وتصميمه لَانَ لابى عبد الله فخشِى ابن ابى دواد من رافته

number it is said, advanced in turn and each struck him two strokes and then went aside [1]). At first, with each stroke Aḥmed uttered a pious ejaculation, concerning the exact tenor of which the accounts vary [2]). There is an apocryphal story to the effect that, after he had been struck twenty-

عليه فقال يا امير المومنين ان تركته قيل انك تركت مذهب المامون وسخطت قوله وانه غلب خليفتين فهاجه ذلك وطلب كرسيا جلس عليه وقام ابن ابى دواد واصحابه على راسه ثم قال للجلادين الخ -

1) al-Subkî, p. 136, حدثنا ابو بكر السهروردى بمكة قال رايت ابا دن [Cod. ادر] بسهورد . . . . وكان ممن ضرب احمد [بن حنبل] بين يدى المعتصم قال دعينا فى تلك الليلة ونحن خمسون ومائة جلاد ان امرنا بضربه كنا نعدوا على ضربه ونَمُرُّ ثم يجى الاخر على اثره ثم يضرب [cf. Abû Nuʿaim, 150*b*, ثم دعا بجلّاد له يقال له ابو الدَّنِ فقال فى كم تقتله قال فى خمسة او عشرة او خمسةَ عشر او عشرين فقال اقتله]

2) al-Makrîzî, p. 8, فلما ضُرب سوطا قال بسم الله فلما ضرب الثانى قال لا حول ولا قوة الا بالله فلما ضُرب الثالث قال القران كلام الله غير مخلوق فلما ضرب الرابع قال قل لن يصيبنا الا ما كتب الله لنا فضربه تسعة وعشرين سوطا وكانت تكة سراويله حاشية ثوب فانقطعت فنزل السراويل الى عانته [read عورته?] فقلت الساعةَ ينهتك فرمى ابو عبد الله طَرْفه نحو السماء وحرك شفتيه فما كان باسرع من ان بقى السراويل لم ينزل قال ميمون فدخلت الى ابى عبد الله بعد سبعة ايام فقلت يابا عبد الله رايتك يوم ضربوك قد انحلّ سراويلك فرفعت طرفك نحو السماء ورايتك تحرك شفتيك فاىّ شىء قلتَ قال قلتُ اللهم انى اسالك باسمك الذى ملات بهِ العرش ان كنت تعلم

nine strokes, Aḥmed's nether garment threatened to fall to the ground, but that it was miraculously restored to its place and fastened securely, in answer to a prayer which

---

انى على الصواب فلا تهتك لى سترا وروى انه قال يا من لا يعلم العرش منه اين هو الا هُو ان كنتُ على الحق فلا تُبْدِ عَوْرتى انتهى وذكر البيهقى انه فى اول سوط قال بسم الله وفى الثانى قال توكلت على الله وهذا فى رضى الله وفى الثالث قال ما شآء الله كان وكل شىء عنده بمقدار وفى الرابع قال لا حول ولا قوة الا بالله وفى الخامس قال يا امير المومنين انك موقوف ومُسائَل عنى بين يدى رب لا يَظلم ويأخذ للمظلوم من الظالم وفى السادس قال يا امير المومنين سالتك بالله والدار الاخرة قال وهو لا يرفع راسه اليه وفى السابع قال يا امير المومنين اذكر الوقوف بين يدى الله كوقوفى بين يديك لا تستطيع مَنعا ولا عن نفسك دفعا فلما ضربه الثامن اضطرب المئزر فى وسطه قال المروزى وعباس بن مسكويه الهمذانى لقد راينا احمد رفع راسَه الى السماء وحرك شفتيه فما استتم الدعا حتى راينا كفا مِن ذهب قد خرج من تحت مئزره فردّ المئزر الى موضعه بقدرة الله تعالى فضجت العامة وهمّوا بالهجوم على دار السلطان فامَر بحَلّه قال المروزى وابن مسكويه فدخلنا على ابى عبد الله فقلنا اى شىء كان تحريك شفتيك عند اضطراب المئزر قال رفعت بصرى الى السماء وناديت يا غياث المستغيثين ويا رب العالمين ان كنت تعلمُ انى قائم بحق فلا تهتك عورتى فاستجاب الله دعائى قال فكان اسحق بن ابراهيم يقول انا والله رايت يوم ضُرب احمد وقد ارتفع السراويل من بعد انخفاضه وانعقد من بعد انحلاله وما رايت يوما كان اعظم على المعتصم من ذلك اليوم والله لو لم يرفع عنه الضرب لم يبرح من مكانه الا ميتا

he uttered. Some of the accounts go even so far as to say that a hand of gold was seen to go out from under his upper garment and adjust what was deranged [1]). As the flogging progressed Aḥmed lost consciousness under the blows, and was removed in an unconscious state into a room near by. Meanwhile, the crowd outside the Palace court became moved with anger at the Khalif's treatment of Aḥmed, perhaps, too, the report of his collapse had reached them; in any case, they were preparing to attack the Palace, when the Khalif ordered the suspension of the punishment. This order was due, it is likely, more to the fear of the multitude on the part of al-Muᶜtaṣim than to any other cause. One account relates that, even after Aḥmed was brought in unconsciousness to the room, his torturers continued their abuse by trampling upon him with their feet. When consciousness came back he was offered sawîḳ for the purpose of producing vomiting, but he refused to take it. Subsequent to this, he was removed to the house of Isḥâḳ ibn Ibrâhîm, where, after a short detention, he was set free, and went to his own dwelling. The date when all this occurred was within the last ten days of Ramaḍân 219 A. H., though the particular day is not known [2]). Aḥmed does not seem to have harbored blame against the Khalif for having done what he did, and, afterwards, declared that he had no ill-will against any of those who had taken part in his persecution.

Sequel to the Scourging. In his own dwelling he was visited by the prison physician and treated until he was cured of his wounds. The scars, however, remained on him to the day of his death; and he never ceased to suffer from the dislocation of his wrists, which was brought about by neglect to take hold, as he was advised to do, of the upper parts [lit. teeth] of the whipping posts. When he failed to do this the principal weight of his body was suspended from the wrists. After the scourging, al-Muᶜtaṣim brought

---

1) vid. foregoing note.

2) Ibn Chall. N°. 19.

out Isḥâḳ ibn Ḥanbal (Aḥmed's uncle) to the people, and asked them to witness that he would testify that he [the Khalif] gave over to them their Imâm without hurt or damage to his body. It is said that if the Khalif had not caused this deception to be practised, the people would have risen in insurrection. As it was however, they were calmed and evil consequences were averted. It was the wish of Ibn Abî Dowâd that Aḥmed should now be imprisoned; but al-Muᶜtaṣim was angry at the suggestion, and commanded his lieutenant Isḥâḳ to set Aḥmed free. It is probable, that in this instance, likewise, fear of a popular uprising deterred the Khalif from continuing to use severe measures against his prisoner. As matters stood al-Muᶜtaṣim gave him the gala dress, and as already related had him sent to his dwelling; and, as long as he was confined to his house, had his lieutenant Isḥâḳ enquire every day about his condition. The gala clothes, however, Aḥmed sold and distributed the price in alms [1]).

---

1) al-Maḳrîzî, p. 8, فصل فيما وقع له رضى الله عنه بعد انقضاء المحنة قال ابن ابى حاتم سمعت ابا زرعة يقول دعا المعتصم باسحق عمّ احمد بن حنبل ثم قل للناس تعرفونه قالوا نعم قال فانظروا اليه اليس هو صحيح البدن [i. e. 'Look ye at him. Thou, Isḥâḳ ibn Ḥanbal, Is he, Aḥmed ibn Ḥanbal, not sound in body?' Isḥâḳ, thereupon, nodded assent. Supply after اليه, ثم قال لاسحق and after البدن, فقال برأسه نعم]. ولو لا انه فعل ذلك لوقع شر لا يقدر على دفعه فلما قال قد سلمته اليكم صحيح البدن هدأ الناس وسكتوا وكان ابن ابى دواد يحاول الخليفة على حبس ابى عبد الله وعدم اطلاقه ويقول يا امير المؤمنين احبسه فانه فتنة فغضب المعتصم وقال لنائبه يا اسحق اطلقه قال ابو عبد الله فلا يجد بُدا من ان يخلى عنى ولو لا ذلك لكان قد حبسنى وقال المعتصم لهم ليس هذا كما وصفتم قال البيهقى وذلك انهم وضعوا من قدره وقللوه وصغروه عنده فلما شاهده ورأى ما عنده

It is related that he remained only sixteen days at the Camp, and during this period used altogether as food a rub[c] of sawîḳ (i. e. four handfuls of parched barley ground to meal). He took every night a dram of water and every third night a handful of sawîḳ. So much wasted was he by these experiences that it was a full six months after his return home before he seemed like himself again [1]).

Miḥna in Egypt in the Reign of al-Mu[c]*taṣim.*

During the short governorship of al-Muzaffar ibn Kaidar, who succeeded his father in Egypt, there came to him a letter from the Khalif al-Mu[c]taṣim ordering a renewal of the Miḥna. Al-Muzaffar tested the doctors in pursuance of the order he had

---

عرف له فضله وقل ميمون بن الاصبع أُخرج احمد بعد ان اجتمع الناس وضجوا حتى خاف السلطان فخرج قال البيهقى قال حنبل وخلع عليه المعتصم مُبَطَّنة وقميصا وطيلسانا وخُفّا وقلنسوة وأُخرج على دابة عند غروب الشمس فصار الى منزله ومعه الناس فدخل منزله ورَمَى بنفسه على وجهه وخلع ما كان خلّع عليه فامر به فبيع واخَذ ثمنه فتصدق به وبلغنا ان ابا اسحق يعنى المعتصم ندم وأُسقط فى يده وامَرَ اسحقَ نائبه ان لا يقطع عنه خبره قال فكان اسحق يأتينا كل يوم يتعرف خبره حتى صح وبَرَا بعد العِلاج وخرج للصلاة والحمد لله

1) Abû Nu[c]aim, 142*b* f. حدثنا ابى والحسين بن محمد قالا ثنا احمد ابن محمد بن عمر قال سمعت عبد الله بن احمد بن حنبل يقول * مكث ابى بالعسكر عند الخليفة ستة عشر يوما ما ذاق شيئا الا مقدار رُبْع سويقا كل ليلة كان يَشرب شربة ماء وفى كل ثلاث ليال ·يستَفّ حفنة من السويق فرجع الى البيت ولم ترجع اليه نفسُه 4· بعد ستة اشهر ورايت مُوْقَيْه دخلا فى حدقتيه

received, but it brought him only an increase of the troubles of his short term of authority, and of the success of the test we know nothing [1]. After him we have no specific record of trials for the Ḳorân in Egypt, but it is sure that al-Buwaiṭî underwent an examination in Egypt in the reign of al-Wâthiḳ. A little later on his case will be again noticed. In the year 231 A. H. al-Wâthiḳ sent a letter to his governors commanding the revival of the inquisition [2]. It must have been in the examinations which followed this command that al-Buwaiṭî was cited to answer for his faith [3].

Al-Muᶜtaṣim and the Miḥna.

Al-Subkî is, probably, right when he asserts that al-Muᶜtaṣim had not the learning which qualified him to decide whether the doctrine of the Ḳorân's creation was right or wrong, and that the prosecution of the Miḥna by him was due, in great part, to the charge which was left him in the testament of al-Maʾmûn, and to the moving spirit among those by whom he was surrounded [4]. We do not hear of any further action against Aḥmed on the part of this Khalif. He died in the year 227 A. H.

Al-Wâthiḳ and Aḥmed.

After the death of al-Muᶜtaṣim and the accession of his son Hârûn al-Wâthiḳ, Aḥmed became a very popular teacher, and was much resorted to. Al-Ḥasan ibn ᶜAlî the Ḳâḍî of Baghdâd noticing this wrote to Ibn Abî Dowâd of the circumstance. Aḥmed ibn Ḥanbal, however, heard of what had been done, and of his own will refrained from teaching, before any action was taken against him. Ibn Abî Dowâd once again tried to persuade al-Wâthiḳ to per-

1) Abu'l-Maḥ. I, 649.
2) Abu'l-Maḥ. I, 683; al-Sujûtî, Ṭarîkh al-Kholafâ, ٣٤٦.
3) Abu'l-Maḥ. I, 686.
4) al-Subkî, p. 145, قال المورخون ومع كونه كان لا يدرى شيئا من العلم حمل الناس على القول بخلق القران قلت لان اخاه المامون اوصى اليه بذلك وانضم الى ذلك القاضى احمد بن ابى دواد وامثاله من فقهاء السوء cf. Weil, Chalifen II, p. 334.

secute Aḥmed, but was unsuccessful. The Khalif let Aḥmed alone; whether he was moved at all by admiration for him, or by a superstitious fear that something might happen to him should he lay violent hands on so holy a man, does not clearly appear [1]). It is reported of al-Wâthiḳ in relation to the Miḥna that he did not personally wish it, but that the stimulus applied by his minister did not leave him much opportunity to escape from the work in which the latter was so zealous. The greater probability, as far as Aḥmed ibn Ḥanbal enters into consideration, is that al-Wâthiḳ, like his predecessor, feared a popular outbreak should anything further be visited upon the Imâm. And, for the reason that he wished to please all parties, he took the course of asking Aḥmed to leave Baghdâd, and dwell at a distance from him. Aḥmed, however, did not go away; he simply withdrew into a comparative seclusion, which he maintained for the greater part of his remaining life.

Al-Wâthiḳ Prosecutes the Miḥna. Al-Wâthiḳ did, nevertheless, carry on the policy of his predecessors. His command to all the governors of the provinces to apply again the Miḥna for the Ḳorân has been already mentioned [2]). It was issued

---

1) al-Maḳrîzî, p. 8 f. فلمّا مات المعتصم ووَلِى ابنه هرون الواثق اكثر الناسُ مِن الاخذ عن الامام* احمد فشق ذلك على اهل البدَع فكتب لحسَن بن على الجَعْد قاضى بغداد الى ابن ابى دُواد ان احمد قد انبسط فى الحديث فلما بلغ ابا عبد الله امسك عن الحديث من نفسه من غير ان يُمنع واستمر ابن ابى دُواد يُحسِّن للواثق امتحان الناس بخلق القران ففعل ذلك لكنه لم يتعرض للامام احمد قال الحافظ ابو الفرج اما لما عَلم من صبره او لانه خاف على نفسه ان يعرض له شىء ببركته يعنى كما عرض لابيه الا انه ارسل يقول له لا تُساكننى بارضى فاختفى الى ان مات الواثق vid. Weil, Chalifen II, 340; Abu'l-Maḥâsin I, 691.

2) vid. p. 114.

in 231 A. H. It is said that he gave this order, notwithstanding the fact that he had withheld his father al-Muʿtaṣim from the application of the Miḥna [1]). We have no record of those who were subjected to this examination, beyond the names and accounts of one or two who would not confess the doctrine of the Ḳorân's creation and suffered for their faith.

Aḥmed ibn Naṣr al-Khuzâʿî. The best known of those who suffered under this Khalif was Aḥmed ibn Naṣr ibn Mâlik al-Khuzâʿî [2]) from the city of Merv, who was of one of

1) Abu'l-Maḥ. I, 683; al-Sujûtî, Tarîkh al-Khol. 346.

2) v. Kremer, Herrsch. Ideen des Isl. 243; Weil, Chal. II, 341 f.; Dozy, Het Islamisme, 156; al-Sujûtî, Tarîkh al-Kholafâ, 346; al-Jaʿqûbî, II, 589; Ṭabarî, III, ١٣٤٣ ff.; De Goeje, Fragm. Hist. Arab., I, 529 f.; al-Maḳrîzî, 10 f. فامّا احمد بن نصر فكان من اهل الدين والصلاح والامارين بالمعروف سمع الحديث من مالك بن انس وغيره وروى عنه يحيى بن معين وغيره دعاه الواثق الى القول بخلق القران فابى فامَر بضرب عنقه فضُرب وحمل راسه الى بغداد فنُصب فى الجانب الشرقى اياما وفى الجانب الغربى اياما وأمّا جسده فصُلب بِسُرَّ مَن راى وروى الحافظ ابو الفرج بسنده الى ابراهيم بن اسمعيل قال كان احمد بن نصر خُلّى فلما قتل فى المحنة وصُلب راسُه أُخبِرتُ ان الراس يقرا القران فمضيت فبِتُّ بقرب من الراس وكان قد وُكل به مَن يحفظه فلما هدأت العيون سمعت الراس يقرا القران الٓمٓ أَحَسِبَ النَّاسُ أَنْ يُتْرَكُوا أَنْ يَقُولُوا آمَنَّا وَهُمْ لَا يُفْتَنُونَ [Ḳor. 29. 1] فاقشعر جلدى ثم رايته بعد ذلك فى المنام وعليه السندس والاستبرق وعلى راسه تاج فقلت ما فعل الله بك قال غفر لى وادخلنى الجنة قال المروزى * سمعت ابا عبد الله احمد بن حنبل وذكر احمد بن نصر فقال رحمه الله ما كان اسخاه لقد جاد بنفسه

the leading families of his tribe. One of his teachers was Mâlik ibn Anas and of his pupils one was Yaḥya ibn Maᶜin. Ibn Naṣr was, at first, left unmolested, but afterwards was apprehended for a cause that will be presently shewn. He was, according to Aḥmed ibn Ḥanbal, a man of noble spirit, and we know from other sources that he was of distinguished ancestry, both his father and grandfather having held high places under the Abbâside khalifs. At the same time, he had a great name among the orthodox traditionists and was himself a man of staunch orthodox belief. For this reason, he had a deep hatred toward the Khalif and Ibn Abî Dowâd, and openly defied both by his bold profession that the Ḳorân was the uncreated Word of God. When the people of the quarter of Baghdâd known as ᶜAmr ibn ᶜAṭâ saw his temper and considered his rank, they induced him to lend his moral and, it may be, also his material support to a conspiracy against the Khalifate. It was all arranged that the city of Baghdâd was to be taken on a certain night, when the drunkenness of some of the conspirators on the night previous to that which had been appointed led them to give the signal for the attack on that night, with the result that the mass of the confederates did not respond, and the leaders of the conspiracy were at once arrested by order of the acting-governor, Moḥammed ibn Ibrâhîm, their arrest being due to the turning State's-evidence of one of the subordinate plotters. Strangely enough, when brought before al-Wâthiḳ, the latter asked Ibn Naṣr nothing about his part in the incipient insurrection, but began, instead, to question him about the Ḳorân and the actual seeing of God on the day of Resurrection [1]); perhaps, because the case against him on this count was much stronger than it would have been on that of sedition. When al-Wâthiḳ questioned him about his belief relative to the Ḳorân, he, however, in reply, would give nothing but that he believed it to be the Word of God.

1) al-Wâthiḳ had forbidden his subjects to profess either of these beliefs, Houtsma, De Strijd over het Dogma, 109.

One rather inflated tradition represents that Ibn Abî Dowâd urged the Khalif to give his prisoner a delay, as he was an old man temporarily out of his senses and would come to a better mind if allowed time. Al-Wâthiḳ in the tradition appears as rejecting this view, and as declaring that Ibn Naṣr's unbelief had disciplined him to the view he had expressed. Whatever may be the truth of this story, the trial had not proceeded far when the Khalif called for the execution carpet and the sword Samsama; and, desiring to be allowed to personally strike off the obstinate infidel's head, as he expected to be rewarded by Heaven for disposing of him, he was allowed to try to despatch the martyr. He could not accomplish it, however, and Sîma al-Dimashkî had to come to his aid and dispose of the man. The head was then ordered to be sent to Baghdâd; where for some days it was exposed to view in the eastern part of the city, and then for some days in the western part, after which it was fixed up permanently in the eastern portion. The execution occurred on the second last day of Shaᶜbân, 231 A. H., and the trunk and head remained exposed to public view for six years, until the Khalif al-Mutawakkil ordered them to be taken down, and handed over for burial to Aḥmed ibn Naṣr's relations [1]).

A fabulous story, to the effect that the head, after being exposed, recited the Ḳorân until it was buried, is equalled by another which relates that, long years afterwards, a hunting party found the body and head of Aḥmed ibn Naṣr buried in the desert sand, and that there was not the slightest indication of decay upon them [2]).

---

1) Abu'l-Maḥ. I, 719.

2) al-Subkî, p. 142 f. قلت وبلغنى وما اراه الا فى تاريخ للحاكم ان بعض الامراء خرج يتصيد فالقاه السير على ارض نزل بها فعبث بعض غلمانه فى التراب فحضر [Read فحفر?] حتى راى ميتا فى قبره طريا وهو فى ناحية وراسه فى ناحية وفى اذنه رقعة عليها شىء مكتوب

Nuʿaim ibn Ḥammâd. Nuʿaim ibn Ḥammâd was another who held out. He was the fourth of a quartette who came from Merv and endured with steadfastness the Miḥna; the first was Aḥmed ibn Ḥanbal and the others, Moḥammed ibn Nûḥ al-Maḍrûb and Aḥmed ibn Naṣr. Nuʿaim ibn Ḥammâd studied Tradition a great deal in the Hijâz and ʿIrâḳ and went, afterwards, to Egypt. In the Khalifate of al-Wâthiḳ, he was brought from Egypt and examined; and, not satisfying the demand made upon him to confess the Ḳorân to be created, he was thrown into prison where he died [1]).

Abû Yaʿḳûb al-Buwaiṭî. Abû Yaʿḳûb, Yûsuf ibn Yaḥya al-Buwaiṭî, the pupil of al-Shâfiʿî to whom he entrusted his circle of scholars at his death, was imprisoned for his refusal to acknowledge that the Ḳorân was created, and died in prison 232 A. H. One of his fellow Shâfiʿites, al-Rabîʿ ibn Suleimân, relates that he saw al-Buwaiṭî in his chains, and heard him saying, 'God created the creation by 'Kun' [Be!], but, if 'Kun' be created, then it is as if a created thing created what was created [2]). By God! I will die in these thy chains, that

---

فاحضر من قراه ذاذا هو بسم * الله الرحمن الرحيم هذا راس احمد بن
نصر هذه الكلمات السابقة فعلموا انه راس احمد الخزاعى فدفن ورفع
سنام قبره وكان هذا فى زمن الحاكم ابى عبد الله الحافظ وهو على
طراوته وكيف لا وهو شهيد رحمه الله ورضى عنه

1) al-Maḳrîzî, p. 11, واما نعيم بن حماد فكان من اهل مرو طلب
الكثير من الحديث بالحجاز والعراق ثم نزل مصر ثم اشخص منها فى
خلافة الواثق وسئل عن القران فلم يوافقهم على ما ارادوه منه يعنى
القول بخلقه فحبس حتى مات

2) 'Kun' is here employed as synonymous with a manifestation of the Heavenly Word of God (as explained later in the present work). Al-Buwaiṭî seems to have been in full agreement with his master al-Shâfiʿî, and the latter in turn with Aḥmed, as far at least as the Ḳorân was concerned (cf. p. 49 and Abu'l-Maḥ. I, 686). The discussion of 'Kun' in Houtsma, De Strijd etc., 129, seems to look toward other views than those held by the orthodox at the time of the Miḥna.

those coming after us may know that men have died in their bonds for this cause; and, if I go in to him [al-Wâthiḳ], I will declare the truth before him'. From prison he wrote to al-Rabî^c ibn Suleimân entrusting him with the care of his circle of pupils, and bidding him be faithful to them [1]).

The remaining history of the Miḥna in the reign of al-Wâthiḳ is shortly told. There is one incident which is in keeping with the fanatical bigotry shewn by Aḥmed ibn Abî Dowâd in his efforts to establish the doctrine that the Ḳorân was created. In the year 231 A. H., it was proposed to ransom 4600 prisoners from the Greeks, when Ibn Abî Dowâd suggested that they should ransom only such as admitted the creation of the Ḳorân, and that these should each receive two dinârs on their release. This was actually done, and a small number of prisoners, who could not bring their consciences up to the point of meeting the test, were left unredeemed in the hands of the Greeks [2]).

Ransom of Prisoners from the Greeks.

---

1) Hammer-Purgstall, Lit. Gesch. III, p. 200, N°. 1050; al-Sujûtî, Tarîkh al-Khol. 350; Abu'l-Feda Ann. II, 132; Fihrist I, 212; Abu'l-Maḥâsin, I, 686; al-Maḳrîzî, p. 11, واما ابو يعقوب يوسف بن يحيى البويطى فاريد منه القول بخلق القران فامتنع فحُبس الى ان مات سنة اثنتين وثلاثين ومائتين قال الربيع بن سليمن صاحب الشافعى رايت البُويطى على بغل فى عنقه غُل وفى رجليه قيد وبين الغل والقيد سلسلة حديد فيها طُوبة وزنها اربعون رطلا وهو يقول انما خلق الله الخلق بكُن [cf. Ḳor. 6, 72] فاذا كانت كُن مخلوقة فكأنّ مخلوقا خَلَق مخلوقا والله لاموتنّ فى حديدك هذا حتى ياتى مِنْ بعدى قوم يعلمون انه قد مات فى هذا الشان قوم فى حديدهم ولئن دخلت عليه يعنى الواثق لَأُصْدُقنّه

2) Ṭabarî III, ١٣٥١ ff.; De Goeje, Fragm. Hist. Arab. II, 531; Abu'l-Maḥ. I, 684; al-Subkî, p. 146.

Al-Wâthiḳ Surrenders the Doctrine of the Korân's Creation.

Al-Wâthiḳ is generally considered to have given up the doctrine of the Miḥna before his death, and an incident [1]) which we may accept as fundamentally true, accounts for its

Alleged Cause.

surrender. Ibn Abî Dowâd caused to be brought before the Khalif a sheikh of Adhana on the charge of heresy. The Khalif bade him discuss the question of the creation of the Ḳorân with Ibn Abî Dowâd, but the old man objected on the ground that Aḥmed ibn Abî Dowâd was a Sabaean and was too unsound in his views to spend words upon. At this al-Wâthiḳ began to be very angry, but the sheikh promised to prove his points, if the Khalif would but give close attention to the discussion which was to take place between them.

To begin with, the sheikh asked Ibn Abî Dowâd if his view were to be looked upon as an essential of the believer's creed. The latter answered that it was to be so regarded. Then the sheikh pointed out that God, having sent Moḥammed with a revelation to his people, the Messenger of God did not leave unpublished any part of the Divine Message. Ibn Abî Dowâd allowed that Moḥammed had fully delivered the Message. His opponent then asked, if (on the basis of the revelation made through him) the Prophet had called upon men to accept the doctrine of the Ḳoran's created existence. Ibn Abî Dowâd gave to this no answer, and the sheikh claimed from al-Wâthiḳ one point established in proof of his charges. The Khalif allowed the point.

The second step was the quotation of Ḳorân 5 . 5, 'This day have I completed for you your religion and perfected my grace upon you'; and the sheikh asked how any new doctrine could be justifiable in view of such a passage. Ibn Abî Dowâd did not attempt a defence of his position against this assault upon it, and the sheikh claimed his second point, which al-Wâthiḳ conceded him.

---

1) v. Kremer, Herrsch. Ideen, 243 ff.; al-Sujûtî, Tarîkh al-Kholafâ, 347 f.; Abu'l-Maḥ. I, 691 f.; al-Maḳrîzî, p. 9 f.; al-Subkî, p. 143.

In the third place, the old man asked if the Prophet had known the doctrine now propounded, and if he had ever invited men to accept it. Ibn Abî Dowâd claimed that Moḥammed knew the doctrine, but he would not answer the question as to whether the Prophet had made its profession obligatory upon the believer or not. Here the sheikh claimed his third and final point. But he did not stop here. He argued that, allowing Moḥammed to have known the doctrine in point and the early Khalifs to have known it; seeing that both he and they had been satisfied to refrain from obliging men to confess the tenet of the Ḳorân's creation, was it the part of a modern zealot to do what they had not done? Supposing they did believe as he did, was it not his part to keep his belief a mere private opinion as they had done, instead of forcing people to think as himself? A companion of the Khalif al-Muhtadî who tells this story says that al-Muhtadî, who was present on the occasion, gave up the doctrine of the creation of the Ḳorân from this time, and that al-Wâthiḳ ordered the sheikh to be at once set free, and, apparently, himself believed no longer as he had believed relative to the Ḳorân. Other accounts say that al-Wâthiḳ changed his view before he died, and, in the connection where it occurs in the Arabic record, the testimony of al-Muhtadî is cited to shew that the incident above given occurred toward the end of al-Wâthiḳ's Khalifate [1]).

Al-Mutawakkil Abrogates the Miḥna.

Al-Mutawakkil began to reign in 232, and the Miḥna continued to exist for two years in his reign, being brought to a close in the year 234. The whole term of its duration was, thus, from the last year of al-Ma'mûn, 218 A. H., to the second or third year of al-Mutawakkil, 234 A. H. In the latter year, al-Mutawakkil stopped the application of the test, and by public proclamation throughout the Empire forbade men on

1) Steiner, 78, says al-Wâthiḳ brought the Miḥna to a close. But the truth is that he went no further than to change his view in relation to the Ḳorân and to purpose abrogating the test. His death prevented him from actually carrying his purpose into effect.

pain of death [1]) to profess the creation of the Ḳorân. At this there was great rejoicing everywhere. Men praised the virtues of the Khalif, and forgot his vices; prayers for blessing upon him were heard on all sides and his name was mentioned with those of the good Khalifs Abû Bekr and ʿOmar ibn Abd al-Azîz. Two things alone were remembered against him by his Muslim subjects, both of which occurred in the year 236 A. H. The one was the permission granted for the sack of Damascus to the Turkish soldiery (the event however did not happen); and the other, the destruction of the tomb of al-Ḥosain together with the buildings round about it, and the conversion of the land into fields [2]).

---

1) On death penalty for heresy cf. Goldziher, Moh. Stud. II, 216.

2) cf. v. Kremer, Herrsch. Ideen d. Isl. 245 ff.; cf. Dozy, Het Islam. 163; cf. Ibn Chall. N°. 133; Abu'l-Maḥ. I, 691, 695, 702; al-Sujûtî, Tar. al-Khol. 352; al-Jaʿqûbî II, 592; al-Subkî, p. 143, وقد طال امر هذه الفتنة وطال شرّها واستمر من هذه السنة التى هى سنة ثمان عشرة ومائتين الى سنة اربع وثلاثين ومائتين فرفعها المتوكل فى مجلسه ونهى عن القول بخلق القران وكتب بذلك الى الافاق وتوفّر دعآء الخلق له وبالغوا فى الثناء عليه والتعظيم له حتى قال قائلهم الخلفاء ثلاثة ابو بكر الصديق يوم الردة وعمر بن عبد العزيز فى رده المظالم والمتوكل فى احيآء السنّة وسكت الناس عن ذنوب المتوكل وقد كانت العامة تنقم عليه شيئين احدهما [Abu'l-Maḥ. I, 714] انه ندب لدمشق افريدون التركى احد مماليكه وصيره والـيًا عليها وكان ظالمًا فاتكا فقدم فى سبعة الاف فارس واباح لهم المتوكل القتل والنَهب على ما نقل الينا ثلاث ساعات فنزل ببيت لهيا واراد ان يصبح البلد فلما اصبح نظر الى البلد وقال يا يوم يصبحك منى فقدمت له بغلة فضربته بالزوج فقتلته وقبره ببيت لهيا ورد الجيش الذى معه خائبين وبلغ المتوكل فصلحت نيته لاهل دمشق والثانى [Abu'l-Maḥ. I, 712; Fragm. Hist. Arab. II, 546.]

General Survey of the Miḥna. Taking a general survey of the inquisition [1]) inaugurated by al-Ma'mûn, and carried on by the two succeeding Khalifs, we can say that as an attempt to stamp out by force moral convictions it was a failure from the start; for, in the Muslim world as everywhere else, there was an admiration and a moral support accorded by the great body of the people to those who suffered persecution, such as might have led men far less sincere than Aḥmed ibn Ḥanbal to stand out against a tyrannous crusade of repression [2]). That the principles of the strictest orthodox

---

انه امر بهدم قبر الحسين وهدم ما حوله من الدور وان يعمل مزارع ومنع الناس من زيارته وحُرث وبقى صحْراء فتألم المسلمون لذلك وكتب اهل بغداد شتمه على الحيطان والمساجد

al-Maḳrîzî, p. 10, وقال الحافظ ابو الفرج وَلِىَ المتوكل على الله سنة اثنتين وثلاثين ومائتين فاظهر الله به السُّنة وكشف تلك الغمة فشكره الناس على ما فعل ثم ذكر بسنده الى محمد بن خلف قل كان ابراهيم بن محمد التيْمىّ قاضى البصرة يقول الخُلفاء ثلاثة ابو بكر قاتل اهل الرِدّة حتى استجابوا له وعمر بن عبد العزيز رَدّ مظالم بنى امية والمتوكل مَحى البدَع واظهر السّنة

1) A short account of the Miḥna and its issues is to be found, Dozy, Het Islamisme, 154 ff.

2) Houtsma (De Strijd etc. 106 f.) appears to make the motive for the resistance of the orthodox theologians to their rationalistic opponents one of religious policy. If they surrendered the doctrine of the uncreated nature of the Ḳorân, the hope of the universal spread of Islâm would have to be given up. I have not found this motive alleged in any of my sources, but can well believe that it may have been a secondary, though not a primary one. The primary motive was altogether personal. Aḥmed and those who stood with him had a simple belief, incapable of analysis, in the eternity and unoriginateness of the Ḳorân; they hoped, too, for a reward if they maintained their faith at all costs, and feared grave spiritual consequences should the doctrine be given up. The honor of God, the Divine Legation of the Prophet, the unique and ineffable dignity of the Ḳorân, and, finally, the everlasting well-

as bla of which Aḥmed was the leading representative, wou not win their way in the following generations of Islâm was not because they had been killed out by persecution, ut because a more liberal and enlightened sentiment had been introduced into the Muslim commonwealth; because the yoke this Puritanism would have imposed was one which people could not bear amid the practical concerns of every-day life; and because the system rested upon casuistries, which, though deductively perfect, were false in their premises and could never have satisfied the untrammeled common sense of men. The inquisition only retarded the development of freer and purer conceptions among the adherents of the religion of the Prophet. But the retardation was not an unmixed evil. It checked, for a time, a philosophical movement, to give it a theological and religious concern, without which the Muslim people would have had for their teachers men indifferent to practical questions of religious life and observance, and unsympathetic in their attitude toward popular theological conceptions.

Of the men, persecuting and persecuted, connected with the Miḥna, Aḥmed ibn Ḥanbal comes out with the greatest credit to himself. Bishr ibn al-Ḥârith al-Hâfî had a saying that God had cast Aḥmed ibn Ḥanbal into the crucible and he had come out pure gold. Aḥmed's method of argument was no more unsound than that of his opponents [1]).

---

being of their own souls and the souls of those who looked to them for an example — these are expressed motives for the orthodox apologetic, which in some cases became a defence of conviction even unto death. The faith in the Divine and uncreated nature of the Ḳorân lay at the root of all their arguments and actions in this defence. In the historical instances of such a resistance as this the personal element of conviction, rather than any considerations of religious policy, has been the moving principle of the defence which has been put forward.

1) The statement of Houtsma (De Strijd etc. 106) would give the impression that the orthodox when in disputation with their opponents had no arguments worth mentioning to offer, and were quite incapable of dealing with those who stood against them. Judging from a modern point of view neither side had very strong points; but, judged from a Muslim standpoint, the

They had, on philosophical grounds, declared the ⁾ in- as well as the attributes of God, to be created; but, w.e they opposed him, they sought to convict him of error on his own ground, and by his own method of proof, and he seems to have had the better of them in most of their word passages. The arguments used were childish enough, but not more so for him than for them. The fact that he had earnest convictions to defend, and that many of those who stood against him had been either frightened or bribed into taking their present stand, stood him in good stead, and must command our respect as we, to-day, review the whole historical scene in which he is a figure.

As to al-Ma'mûn, he evidently disliked the slavishness of orthodoxy, and was impatient at its many absurdities; but he shewed at the same time how easy it is for a learned man to display a disdainful and narrow spirit toward the unlearned, for a philosopher to become a dogmatist, and for an advocate of liberal views to become a tyrant toward those of stricter beliefs.

Aḥmed ibn Abî Dowâd was a man whom one finds it difficult to credit with earnest convictions. His first master, al-Ma'mûn, may be credited with acting in the belief that he was right and in the consequent wish to secure the general adoption of his opinions; but his minister will not be misjudged if we look upon him as actuated by contempt and violent hatred toward men of strict life and toward zealous advocates of religious duties, whose puritanism appeared in his eyes to be but pharisaic hypocrisy. He is not

---

disputations which are recorded in these pages shew that the orthodox had the great arguments of the Word of God and the Tradition, and could wield these as well or better than their opponents. Isḥâḳ ibn Ibrâhîm the governor, Abd-al-Raḥmân ibn Isḥâḳ, and al-Muᶜtaṣim are all said to have been impressed by the force of what Aḥmed ibn Ḥanbal said and the way in which he said it. Steiner (Die Muᶜtaziliten, 8) says that the Muᶜtazila used the Ḳorân interpreting it allegorically and giving their reasonings a philosophical cast. Houtsma, (De Strijd etc. 80) speaks of the Muᶜtazila as being, in general, men lacking in earnestness and given to dialectic trifling in disputation.

as black a character as the partisans of Aḥmed ibn Ḥanbal would represent him to be, but I have met no record of his connection with the Miḥna which shews him as other than arbitrary and unfeeling, except the isolated reference in the trial of Aḥmed ibn Naṣr the conspirator whom al-Wâthiḳ put to death. There, as we have already seen, Ibn Abî Dowâd suggests, when al-Wâthiḳ grows angry with Ibn Naṣr for persisting in his belief, that the prisoner is an old man whose mind is deranged, but who will see differently when he has had time to come to himself. This account, be it remarked, occurs in al-Subkî's Ṭabaḳât (life of Aḥmed ibn Ḥanbal), where Ibn Abî Dowâd finds from the author an apology for his acts in more than one instance, but in each case the apology is a personal opinion of the author of the book, rather than well supported historical tradition. In earlier accounts, and in later as well, Ibn Abî Dowâd is put before us as an able man, with eminent social qualities, but with a persecuting spirit in administration; and, though we have said that al-Maʾmûn wished to enforce the Miḥna before he really did so, we must remember that he actually did not do so of his own motion, but that it was Ibn Abî Dowâd alone who turned the scale which brought about the long tyranny of sixteen years ending shortly after al-Mutawakkil's accession. We can believe too, that had it not been for him the Miḥna would have lapsed for want of interest or from positive distaste on the part of al-Muʿtaṣim or al-Wâthiḳ.

For al-Muʿtaṣim's part in this movement we have not much to say. He found no pleasure in the wretched business of persecuting men's convictions, and clearly shewed Aḥmed's case that, had it not been for obligations which he held to be inviolable, he would have had nothing to do with the enforcement of the test as to the Ḳorân.

Al-Wâthiḳ, as to his part in the Miḥna, is in somewhat greater degree a return to al-Maʾmûn. Like his predecessors he, too, was dominated by Ibn Abî Dowâd. The recorded cases, very few in number, of those whom he tried for the Ḳorân evince cruelty as a feature of this Khalif's character, and that of Aḥmed ibn Naṣr, in particular, is positively brutal [1]).

Not much can be said in favor of those who yielded in the Miḥna. The assent of the first seven who were summoned to the Khalif's presence was the fatal factor which led to the following up of the persecution. Still, it was not the less weakness in those who recanted afterwards that they should have been terrified into submission. The doctrine of the Taḳîa was generously applied to them by their friends and companions, and, no doubt, saved them a great deal in the estimation of the public; but their course was not felt by themselves to have been creditable, and bitter was the regret of men like Yaḥya ibn Maᶜîn that the sword should have frightened them into surrender of a doctrine which was felt to be the truth. It is the fault of an age of controversy that theological opinions are based too much on the logic of words, and not upon verities from which the moral and intellectual judgment cannot separate itself. This was the case with the doctrine of the unoriginate nature of the Ḳorân. Its evidences were simply words, and it was only an exceptional character like Aḥmed ibn Ḥanbal, who had seen the purely speculative question of the Ḳorân's origin in relations, the maintenance of which seemed to him to involve the very existence of his religious life and faith, to whom a surrender of his opinion became of transcendent moment. Others had not the same great conception of the question that he had, they knew it only as one of the controverted points in the polemic which was going on abo[illegible] them. The surrender of it might be a victory for an [illegible] nent, but it was worth making for the sake of one's [illegible] Those who yielded took, at a later date, a more serious view of what they had done, but, at the time when they

1) In the account of Aḥmed ibn Naṣr's execution, p. 118, we have suppressed the more harrowing features.

committed the act of denying their own confession, it appeared as simply a question of yielding an unessential point and acknowledging themselves beaten. Even their plea of the Taḳîa cannot be taken as rendering this explanation nugatory; though it might seem to suggest that they looked upon their act as one involving the cardinal sin of apostasy, to which sin the Taḳîa stood specially related. This plea was but an excuse used for effect upon the people, and was not, of course, an explanation of how they came to do what they had done. Aḥmed ibn Ḥanbal excused them on this ground, but his excuse contemplates the act after its commission and finds grounds of pardon for it. It does not offer any exposition of its inward cause and significance. The Taḳîa itself might render impossible the proving of an act to be apostasy, for it could often be urged that a man's apostasy was but in word, while in heart he was sound in the faith.

Notwithstanding the testimony of historians to al-Mutawakkil's cruelty, it cannot be said that he ever shewed any unkindness or impatience with Aḥmed ibn Ḥanbal. He might have been provoked to acts of harshness by Aḥmed's peevishness had he allowed himself to yield to the provocation, but he was, instead, constantly kind and thoughtful of the old man's comfort and welfare. He does not appear to have been as intolerant in matters of religion as his predecessors, unless his hostility to ʿAlyite movements be counted as of a religious character [1]). We are justified, in my judgment, in assuming that the interest in religion and theology which he shewed was not that of a persecuting partisan of a political faction, but of a sincere though fanatical religious bigot [2]). His connection with orthodoxy was, because free from any immediate and violent display of persecuting spirit [3]), hardly from a political motive. Counter persecution

1) On this hostility cf. pp. 140, 152; Abu'l-Maḥ. I, 712.

2) For a different view cf. Goldziher, Moh. Stud. II, 57, 66; Dozy, Het Islamisme, 163.

3) Houtsma, De Strijd etc. 113 infra.

would surely have followed the persecution already past, had al-Mutawakkil desired to make capital out of his connection with orthodoxy. It is more likely that his relation to theology and religion is to be explained by temperament and revulsion of feeling from the course of his predecessors. The latter, indeed, had already shewn strong signs that, personally, they were weary of the inquisition. They, however, still accorded in their theological views with the persecuting party and were subject to their influence. Al-Mutawakkil was, apparently, a Shâfiᶜite [1]). None will deny that his theological position made him friends as a result, but, however black his record may be, and whatever there may be to blame in his narrow bigotry, we think that his intention was only to reform abuses in religion as he saw them [2]).

III.

Al-Mutawakkil and Aḥmed ibn Ḥanbal.

In the early years of al-Mutawakkil's reign there were those who sought to injure Aḥmed with the Khalif [3]). One report, in particular, was

---

1) al-Sujûtî, Tarîkh al-Khol. 359.

2) Nearly all European writers impute political motives to this Khalif, as well as to al-Maʾmûn when he inaugurated the persecution. It may be admitted that al-Mutawakkil recognized the futility of persecution as long as the great mass of his subjects were of orthodox sympathies (Houtsma, 112); but the fact, which appears to be well established, that al-Mutawakkil was personally orthodox in his theological convictions, as well as the other facts which have been noticed in the text, would seem to fully account for what he did. It is nowhere stated in the original sources which I have consulted that he had any other motive than that of personal religious preference. Out of this personal ground sprang his intention to bring about a restoration of orthodoxy. His antagonism to ᶜAlyites, too, was more that of a fanatical representative of certain *views* than that of a man who hoped to make himself more popular with the majority by the step he took. The public feeling when he destroyed the tomb of al-Ḥusain shews this.

3) Abû Nuᶜaim, 150 *b* ff. (This source is now followed with a few exceptions which are noted). ذكر ورود كتاب المتوكل بمحنته اولا ثم

that he had charged with Atheism the predecessors of

بجائزة له واشخاصه الى العَسكر ثانيا رحمه الله حدثنا محمد بن جعفر
والحُسين بن محمد وعلى بن احمد قالوا ثنا محمد بن اسمعيل بن
احمد ثنا ابو الفضل صالح بن احمد بن حنبل قال لما توفى اسحاقُ بنُ
ابرهيم ومحمد ابنه وولّى عبدُ الله بن اسحاق كتب المتوكل اليه ان
وَجِّهْ الى احمد بن حنبل ان عنْدَك طَلِبَةَ امير المومنين فوجّه بحاجبه
مظفر وحضر معه صاحب البريد. وكان يعرف بابن الكلبى وكتَب له
ايضا فقال له مظفر يقول لك الامير قد كتَبَ انىّ امير المومنين انّ
عِنْدك [Cod. عَبْدك] طِلبَتَه [Cod. طَلِبْته] وقال له ابن الكلبى مثلَ ذلك
وكان قد نام الناس فدفَع الباب وكان عَلى ابى رحمه الله ازار [Cod. ازارًا]
ففتح لهم الباب وقعدوا على بارِيّة ومعهم نسآء فلما قرئَ عليه الكتاب*
قال لهم ابى ما اعرف هذا وانى لأَرى طاعتَه فى العُسر واليُسر والمَنشط
والمكره والاثرة وانى اتاسّف عن تخلّفى عن الصلاة وعن حضور الجماعة
ودَعوة المسلمين وقد كان اسحاق بن ابرهيم وجّه الى ابى ان الزم
بيتك ولا تخرج الى جمعة ولا جماعة والا نـزَل بك ما نزل فى ايام ابى
اسحاق ثم قال ابن الكلبى قد امرَنى امير المومنين ان أُحَلِّفَك ما
عندك طلِبتُه فتحلف فقال ان استحلفتنى حلفتُ فأَحْلَفَه [Cod. فأُحَلِّفُه]
بالله وبالطلاق ما عِندَك [Read ما عِنْدهُ ?] طَلِبةٌ [Cod. طلبته] امير
المومنين فكانهم اوموا الى ان عَنْده [Cod. عبْده] علويًّا· ثم قال اريد ان
أُفتِّشَ مَنزِلك قال ابو الفضل وكنت حاضرا فقال ومنزل ابنك فقام مظفر
وابن الكَلبى وامرأتان معهما فدخلا ففتّشا البيت ثم فَتشت الامرأتان
النساء والصبيان قال ابو الفضل ثم دخلوا مَنزِلى ففتّشوه ودلّوا شمعة
فى البئر فنظروا ووَجّهوا بالنسوة ففتشوا الحرم وخَرجوا فلما كان بعد

the Khalif — a report which the latter did not appear to con-

---

يومين ورد كتابُ على بن الجَهْم انّ امير المومنين قد صَحّ عنده
براءتك مما قُرِفتَ به وقد كان اهلُ البدع قدّموا اعناقهم فالحمد لله
الذى لم يشمتهم بك وقد وَجّه اليك امير المومنين يعقوبَ [Cod. يعقوبُ]
المعروف بقَوصَرَّةَ ومعه جائزة ويامرك بالخروج فالله اللهَ ان تستعفى او
تَرُدَّ الجائزة، قال ابو الفضل ثم ورد من الغد يعقوب فدخل الى ابى
فقال له يابا عبد الله اميرُ المومنين يَقْرأ عليك السلام ويقول قد صَحّ
نقاء ساحتك وقد احبَبتُ ان آنس بقربك واتبرك بدعائك وقد
وجهت اليك عشرة آلاف درهم معونة على سفرك واخرج بدرة فيها صرة
نحو من مائتى دينار والباقى دراهم صحاح فلم ينظر اليها ثم شدّها
يعقوب وقال له اعودُ غدًا حتى انظر على ما تعزم عليه وقال له يابا
عبد الله الحمد لله الذى لم يُشَمّت بك اهل البدع وانصرف فجئتُ
باجّانة [Cod. باجّانة] خَضْراء كَبَبتُها على البدرة فلما كان عِنْد المغرب
قال يا صالح خذ هذه صيّرها عندك فصَيّرتها عند راسى فوق البيت
فلمّا كان سَحَر اذ هو ينادى يا صالح فقمت وصَعدتُ اليه فقال يا صالح
ما نمتُ ليلتى هذه فقلت له لِمَه فجعل يبكى وهو يقول سلمت مِن
هولاء حتّى اذا كان فى آخر عمرى بُليتُ بهم قد عَزمت على انْ افرّق
هذا الشيء اذا اصبحتُ فقلتُ ذاك اليك فلمّا اصبح جاءه الحسن
ابن البَزّار والمشايخ فقال جئنى يا صالح بالميزان فقال وجّهوا الى ابناء
المهاجرين والانصار ثم قال وَجّه الى فلان حتى يفرّق فى ناحيته والى
فلان فلم يزل حتى فرقها كُلّها ونفض الكيس ونحن فى حالة الله بها
عليمٌ فجاء بُنى له فقال يا ابه اعطنى درهما فنظر الى فاخرجتُ قِطعة
اعطيتُه وكتب صاحب البريد انّه تصدق بالدراهم من يومه حتى

sider very seriously, for he is said to have ordered the man

تَصَدَّقَ بالكيس قال على بنُ الجَهْم فقلتُ يا امير المومنين قد تَصدّق بها وعلم الناسُ انه قد قَبِل منك ما يصنعُ احمد بالمال وانما قوته رَغيف قال فقال لى صدقت يا على، قال ابو الفضل ثم أُخرج ابى ليْلا ومعنا حُرّاسٌ معهم النفاطات فلمّا اضآء الفجر قال يا صالح معك دَراهم قلت نعم قال اعْطهم فاعطيتُهم درهما درهما. . . . . .قال ابو الفضل وقصّر ابى * فى خروجه الى العسكر وقال تُقصَّر الصلاة فى اربعة برد وهى ستّة عشر فرسخا وصليتُ به يوما العصر فقال لى طوّلتَ بنا العصر تقرأ فى الركعة مقدار خمس عشرة آية وكنتُ اصلى به فى العسكر فلما صِرْنا بين الحائطين قال لنا يعقوب اقيموا ثم وجّه الى المتوكل بما عَمِل فدخلنا العسكر وابى مُنكَّسُ الراس وراسه مغطّى فقال له يَعقوب اكْشفْ راسَك يابا عبد الله فكشف ثم جآء وصيفٌ يُريد الدار فلما نظر الى الناس وجمعهم قال ما هولآء قالوا احمد بن حنبل فوجّه اليه بعد ما جاز بيحيى بن هَرثَمة فقال يقرئك السلام ويقول الحمد لله الذى لم يُشَمِّت بك اهل البدع قد علمتَ ما كان حالُ ابن ابى دواد فينبغى ان نتَكلّم بما يجب لله ومضى يحيى قال ابو الفضل انزل ابى دار ايتاخ فجآء على بن الجهم فقال قد امر لكم امير المومنين بعشرة آلاف مكانَ التى فرّقها [scil. ابوكم] وامركم ان لا يُعلَم بذلك فيَغتم ثم جآءه محمد بن معاوية فقال ان امير المومنين يُكثِر ذكرَك ويقول تقيم هاهنا تُحدِّثُ فقال انا ضعيف ثم وضَع اصبعه على بعض اسنانه فقال انّ بعضَ اسنانى يتَحرك وما أَخبرتُ بذلك ولَدى ثم وجه اليه ما تقول فى بهيمتين انتطحَتا فعقرت احداهما الاخرى فسقطت فذُبح فقال انْ كان اطّرف بعَينه ومصع بذنبه وسال دَمُه يُوكل

who made it to be flogged for trying to injure a good subject.

قال ابو الفضل ثم صار اليه يحيى بن خاقان فقال يابا عبد الله قد امرنى اميرُ المومنين ان أُصير اليك لتركبَ الى ابى عبد الله [المعتزّ .i. e] ثم قال لى قد امرنى ان اقطع له سوادًا وطّيلسانا وقلنسوة فاى قلنسوة يلبس فقلت له ما رايته لبس قلنسوة قط فقال له انّ امير المومنين قد امرنى ان تَصير لك مرتبة فى اعلا المَرَاتب [Cod. omits] ويَصير ابو عبد الله فى حجرك ثم قال لى انّ امير المومنين قد امر ان يُجْرَى عليكم وعلى قراباته اربعةُ الاف درهم ففرقها عليهم ثم عاد يحيى من الغد فقال يابا عبد الله تركب فقال ذاك اليكم فقال استخير الله فلبس ازاره وخُفَّيه وقد كان خُفُّه قد اتى له عنده نحو من خمسة عشر سنة مرقوع برقاع عدة فاشار يحيى الىّ يلبَس [تلبَس .Cod] قلنْسُوة فقلت له ما له قلنسوة قال كيف يدخل عليه حاسرا ويحيى قائم فطلبْنا له دابة يركبها فقال يحيى تُصَلّى [نُصَلّى .Cod] فجلس على التراب وقال منْهَا خَلَقْنَاكُمْ وَفِيهَا نُعِيدُكُمْ [Kor. 20. 57] ثم ركب بَغْل بعضِ [بعضَ .Cod] التجار فمَضينا معه حتى ادخِل دار المُعْتَزّ فاجلس فى بيت الدهليز ثم جآء يحيى فاخذ بيده حتى ادخله ورفع الستر ونحن ننظر وكان المعتز قاعدا على دُكان فى الدار وقد كان يحيى تقدّم اليه فقال لا تمدّ يدك اليه فلما صَعد الدُكَّان جلس فقال له يحيى يابا عبد الله ان امير المومنين جآء بك ليُسَرّ بقُربك ويَصير ابو عبد الله فى حجرك . . . .

وقد كانوا حدّثوا انه يخلع عليه سوادًا ثم انصرف فلما صار الى الدار نَزَع الثياب عنه ثم جَعل يبكى ثم قال قد سَلِمتُ من هولآء منذ

ستين سنة حتّى اذا كان فى آخر عمرى بُليتُ بهم ما احْسبنى سلمت من دخولى على هذا الغلام فكيف بمن يجب علىّ نُصْحه من وقت تقع عينى عليه الى انْ اخرُج من عنده ثم قال يا صالح وَجّه بهذه الثياب الى بغداد تُباع ويتصدق بثمنها ولا يشترى احد منكم شيئا قال ابو الفضل فوجّهْت بها الى يعقوب بن البختُمان فباعها وفرق ثمنها وبقيت عندى القلنسوة ثم اخبرناه ان الدار التى هو فيها كانت لايتاخ فقال اكتُب رُقعةً الى محمد بن الجراح ليَستعفى لى من هذه الدار فكتبنا رقعة فامر المتوكل ان يُعفا منها ووجّه الى قوم ليخرجوا من منازلهم فسال ان يُعفا من ذلك فاكتُريت له دار بمائتَى درهم فصار اليها وأُجرى لنا مآئدة وثلج وضرب الخيش وفرش الطبرى فلما رأى الخيْش والطّبرى نحى نفسه عن ذلك الموضع والقى نفسه على مضرّبة له . . . .

. . . . وجعل يُواصل يُفطر كل ثلاث على ثُمن سَويق فمكث خمس عشرة يُفطر فى كل ثلاث ثم جعل بعد ذلك يُفطر ليلة ليلة لا يفطر الا على رغيف فكان اذا جئ بالمآئدة تُوضع فى الدهليز لكى لا يراها فياكل من حضر فكان اذا جهده الحر تُبلّ له خِرقة فيضعها على صَدره وفى كل يوم يُوجه اليه بابن ماسُويهْ فينظر اليه ويقول يابا عبد الله انما اميل اليك والى اصحابك وما بك علة الا الضّعف وقلة الرزْء فقال له ابن مَاسُويهْ انا رُبّما امرنا عُبادنا باكل دُهن الخَل [Cod. الخل] فانه يلين وجعل يجيئه بالشيء ليشربه فيَصبه وقطع له يحيى دراعة وطيلسانا سوادا . . . .

. . . . وكان ربّما صار اليه يحيى وهو يصلى فيجلس فى الدهليز

حتى يفرُغ ويجىء على بن الجهم فينزع سيفه وَقلنسُوته ويدخل عليه وامر المتوكل ان تُشترَى [يُشترى .Cod] لنا دارٌ فقال يا صالح قلت لبّيك قال لئن اقْررْتَ لهم بشرَى ذلك لتكونن القطيعةُ بينى وبينكم انما يريدون ان يُصَيّروا هذا البلد لى ماوى ومَسْكنا فلم يزل يدفع شرى الدار حتى اندفع وصار الىّ صاحبُ المنزل فقال اعطيك كل شهر ثلاثة الاف مكان المائدة فقلت لا افعل وجعلَتْ رُسُل المتوكل تاتيه يسئلونه عن خبره فَينصرفون [فيصيرون .Cod] اليه ويقولون هو ضعيف وفى خلال ذلك يقولون يابا عبد الله لا بد له من ان يراك فسكت فاذا خرجوا قال الا تعجب من قولهم لا بد له من ان يراك وما عِلمُهم انه لا بد له من ان يرانى وكان فى هذه دار حجرةٌ صغيرة [الصغيرة .Cod] فيها بيتان فقال لى ادخلونى تلك الحجرة ولا تُسرجوا لى سراجا فادخلناه اليها فجاءه يعقوب فقال يابا عبد الله امير المومنين مشتاق اليك ويقول * انظر اليوم الذى تصير الى فيه اى يوم هو حتى اعرفه فقال ذاك اليكم فقال يوم الاربعاء يومٌ خال وخرج يعقوب فلما كان من الغد جاء فقال البشرى يابا عبد الله امير المومنين يقرأ عليك السلام ويقول قد اعفيتك عن لُبْس السواد والركوب الىّ والى ولاة العهود والى الدار فانْ شئت فالبس القطن وانْ شِئت فالبس الصوف فجعل يحمد الله على ذلك . . . .

. . . . قال انى أعطى اللهَ عهدا انّ ٱلْعَهْدَ كَانَ مَسْـُٔولًا [Kor. 17. 36] وقد قال الله تعالى يَـٰٓأَيُّهَا ٱلَّذِينَ ءَامَنُوا أَوْفُوا بِٱلْعُقُودِ [Kor. 5. 1] انى لا أُحدّث حديثا تماما ابدا حتّى القى الله ولا أَستثنى منكم احدا فخَرَجنا وجاء على بن الجهم فقلنا له فقال انّا للّه وَانّا اليه راجعون واخبر المتوكل بذلك وقال انما يُريدون

ان أُحدِث فيكون هذا البلدُ حَبْسى وانما كان سبَبُ الذين اقاموا بهذا البلد لَمّا أُعطوا وأُمِروا فحَدَّثوا وكانوا يدخلون عليه فيتكلمون وهو مُغَمِّض العينِ يتعلّل وضَعُف ضَعفا شديدا فقلوا يخبرونه فيتوجّع لذلك وجعل يقول والله لقد تمنيت الموت فى الامر الذى كان وانى لاتمنى الموت فى هذا وذاك انّ هذا فتنة الدنيا وكان ذاك فتنة الدين ثم جعل يَضم اصابع يده ويقول لو كانت نفسى فى يدى لأرْسلتها ثم يفتح اصابعه وكان المتوكل يُوجه اليه فى كل وقت يَسئله عن حاله وكان فى خلال ذلك يومَر لنا بالمال فيقول يُوصَل اليهم ولا يَعلَمْ شيخهم فيغتَم ما يُريد منهم انْ كان هولآء يريدون [Cod. يريد] الدنيا فما يمنعهم وقالوا للمتوكل انه كان لا ياكل من طعامك ولا يجلس على فراشك ويُحرِم الذى تشرب فقال لهم لو نُشِر المعتصم لم اقبَلْ منه قال ابو الفضل ثم انى انحدَرت الى بغداد وخلّفتُ عبد الله عنده فاذا عبدُ الله قد قدم وجآء بثيابى التى كانت عنده فقلت ما جاء بك قال قال لى انحدِر وقل لصالح لا تخرج [Cod. يخرج] فانتم كنتم آفتى واللّٰه لو استقبَلْت من امرى ما استدبرتُ ما اخرجت واحدا منكم معى لولا مكانكم لِمَن كان توضع هذه المآئدة ولمن كان يُفرش هذا الفرش ويجرى الاجراء قال ابو الفضل فكتبتُ اليه اعلمه ما قال لى عبد الله فكتب الىّ بخطه بسم الله الرحمن الرحيم احسن الله عاقبتك ودفع عنك كُلّ مَكروه ومَحذور الذى حملنى على الكتاب اليك والذى [Cod. اللذى] قلت لعبد الله لا يأتينى احد منكم رجآء ان ينقطعَ ذكرى ويخمل فانكم اذا كُنتم هاهنا فشا ذكرى وكان يجتمع اليك قوم ينقلون اخبارنا ولم يَكُن الا خيرا واعْلَم يابنى انّك ان اقمتَ [Cod. اقمتُ] فلا تاتينى انت ولا اخوك فهو رضآءى فلا

تجعل فى نفسك الا خيرا والسّلام عليك ورحمة الله وبركاته، قال ابو الفضل ثمّ ورد الىّ كتابٌ اخر بخطه يذكر فيه بسم الله الرحمن الرحيم احسن الله عاقبتك [Cod. عافيتك] ودفع عنك السوء برحمته كتابى اليك وانا فى نعم الله متظاهرة واسئله اتمامها والعونَ على أداء شكرها قد انفكّت عنّا عقد انما كان حُبس مَن هاهنا لما أُعطوا فقبلوا وأُجرى عليهم فصاروا فى المحدّ الذى صاروا اليه وحدثوا ودخلوا عليهم فهذه كانت قيودهم فنسئل الله ان يُعيذنا من شرهم ويخلصنا فقد كان ينبغى لكم لو قد فديتمونى باموالكم واهاليكم لهان ذلك عليكم للذى انا فيه فلا يَكبرُ عليكم ما اكتب به اليكم فالزموا بيوتكم فلعل الله ان يخلصنى والسلام عليكم ورحمة الله ثم ورد غيرُ كتاب الىّ بخطه بنحو من هذا فلما خرجْنا من العَسْكر رفعت المائدة والفرش وكل ما اقيم لنا قال ابو الفضل واوصى وصية بسم الله الرحمن الرحيم * هذا ما اوصى به احمد بن حنبل اوصَى انه يشهد ان لا اله الا الله وحده لا شريك له وانّ محمدا عبده ورسوله ارسله بِٱلْهُدَى وَدِينِ ٱلْحَقِّ لِيُظْهِرَهُ عَلَى ٱلدِّينِ كُلِّهِ وَلَوْ كَرِهَ ٱلْمُشْرِكُونَ [Kor. 9. 33; 61. 9] وأَوْصَى مَن اطاعه مِن اهله وقَرابَتِه ان يَعبُدوا الله فى العَابدين ويَحمدوه فى الحامدين وان ينصحوا لجماعة المسلمين واوصَى أنّى قد رضيت بالله ربا وبالاسلام دينا وبمحمد صلى الله عليه وسلم نبيًّا واوصى انّ لعبد الله بن محمد المعروف ببُوران علىّ نحوا من خمسين دينارا وَهو مصدق فيما قال فيُقْضَى ما له علىّ من غَلة الدار ان شآء الله فاذا استوفى أُعطى ولدُ صالح وعبدِ الله ابنىْ [Cod. ابن] احمد بن حنبل كل

First Invitation to Visit al-Mutawakkil

An invitation from the Khalif to Aḥmed to visit him was brought to him before the end of the year 235 A. H. by Isḥâḳ ibn Ibrâhîm [1]), who on this occasion asked Aḥmed's forgiveness for the part which he had taken in the scourging under al-Muᶜtaṣim. Aḥmed, in reply, assured him that he had fully forgiven all who had sought his hurt, or participated, in any way, on that occasion.

and Conversation with Isḥâḳ ibn Ibrâhîm on the Subject of the Ḳorân.

Isḥâḳ then proceeded to ask Aḥmed for his own private satisfaction about the Ḳorân, and the latter expressed himself, as he uniformly did, to the effect that it was the uncreated Word of God. Isḥâḳ then asked for the proofs of the statement, and Aḥmed, in answer, cited Ḳorân 7.52, 'Are not the Creation and the Command his?' and pointed out that in the passage a distinction was made between the Creation and the Command. The 'Command' الامر, in controversies of this kind refers to the eternal and heavenly Word of God, just as does 'Kun', on page 119. Isḥâḳ said, 'The Command is created'. 'What!' exclaimed Aḥmed, 'the Command created! Nay, it creates that which is created'. Isḥâḳ then asked, 'Who has handed down in Tradition the view that it is not created'? Aḥmed answered, "Jaᶜfar ibn Moḥammed, who said, 'It is neither a creator nor a created thing" [2]). Then, this conversation being ended and Isḥâḳ having secured Aḥmed's agreement to go to the camp, it was not long before he was on the way thither; but, for some unexplained cause, orders came while the

---

ذكر وانثى عشرة دراهم بعد وفاة مال ابى محمد شهد ابو يوسف
وصالح وعبد الله ابنا احمد بن محمد بن حنبل،

1) Isḥâḳ ibn Ibrâhîm, the governor of ᶜIrâḳ, as well as Isḥâḳ ibn Ibrâhîm al-Mausîlî, the favorite of the Khalifs, died in 235 A. H. The one referred to in the text is, of course, the former.

2) This appears to be not only an authentic tradition, but, as well, the clearest and most direct which was offered by the orthodox in support of their view.

journey was in progress for him to be returned to his home. It is altogether likely that a suspicion of ʿAlyite leanings in Aḥmed ibn Ḥanbal afford an explanation of this fact. As will presently appear, Aḥmed was two or three times accused of such leanings to this Khalif.

Aḥmed Accused of ʿAlyite Intrigues. In the year 237 A. H., information was given to the Khalif charging Aḥmed with having sent one of his companions to meet an ʿAlyite who was coming to him from Khorasân. On hearing this, the Khalif wrote a letter to Abdallah ibn Isḥâḳ, governor of Baghdâd, (who had succeeded his brother Moḥammed and his father Isḥâḳ ibn Ibrâhîm in the office) asking him to inquire of Aḥmed as to the truth of the charge laid against him, and, also, to search his premises and make sure in the matter. In pursuance of these directions, Abdallah sent his chamberlain Muẓaffar and the postmaster Ibn al-Kalbî [1]), together with women who were to examine the women's apartments, to carry out the orders which had come to hand. When they were come and had read to Aḥmed the Khalif's letter, he protested that the report was without foundation, and that he was in all respects a loyal subject [2]). The searching of the premises, too, revealed nothing to substantiate the charge against him.

The result was reported to the Khalif, and a day or two later, there came a letter from ʿAlî ibn al-Jahm [3]) to Aḥmed saying that the Khalif was fully satisfied of the groundlessness of the report, and that it had been fabricated by heretics with the design of injuring him. The letter of ʿAlî intimated, likewise, the Khalif's wish that Aḥmed should

---

1) For employment of postmasters in this sort of detective service vid. Houtsma, 71.

2) Aḥmed had been keeping to his house up to this time, following the orders of Isḥâḳ the former governor. On theologians keeping to their houses cf. Goldziher, Moh. Stud. II, 94. On the similar practice by the so-called Ḳaʿada (still-sitters) cf. Houtsma, De Strijd etc., 26 f.

3) ʿAlî ibn al-Jahm banished to Khorasân and killed there by al-Mutawakkil's directions, 239 A. H., vid. Ibn Chall. Nº. 473; Abu 'l-Maḥ. I, 730; Abu 'l-Feda Ann. II, 190.

Second Invitation from al-Mutawakkil.

visit him, and advised that a messenger was on the way with a gift of money from the Khalif. The day following the arrival of the letter the messenger, Yaᶜkûb Ḳausarra, arrived bringing, in official form, the invitation already alluded to, and handing over the sum of 10,000 dirhems as the royal gift (جائزة). Yaᶜkûb then went away, telling Aḥmed that he would return next morning for an answer to his message. That night was a sleepless one for Aḥmed. The gift of al-Mutawakkil, which he had given into the charge of Ṣâliḥ his son, troubled him greatly. Finally, he made up his mind to be rid of the money altogether, and, rising betimes in the morning, he summoned persons whom he ordered to take portions to the descendants of the Muhajirûn and Anṣâr and to the genetal poor, until the whole sum received had been paid out. It was a great grief to him that now at the end of his life, after he had successfully resisted anything of the kind for so long a time, he was to be forced to be a compromised pensioner on the bounty of the Khalif, a relationship which he with all his might sought to avoid, and from which after this he succeeded in keeping himself almost entirely free to the very end of his days. When word came to the Khalif of Aḥmed's action, ᶜAlî ibn al-Jahm prevented his master's displeasure by the explanation that such a man as Aḥmed had no need of money, for his living consisted but of a crust of bread.

In a short time, Aḥmed was on his way to the Khalif. Of the journey nothing of special interest is recorded, save that he availed himself of the legal provision that the prayers might be shortened while travelling, and that he, interpreting the provision as positive and not merely permissive, on one occasion complained that Ṣâliḥ his son had made the prayers too long. Arrived at the camp, he was first lodged in the house of Îtâkh [1]), and word was sent to his sons from the Court that an allowance of 10,000 dirhems had been appointed

1) v. p. 144, note 2.

to be given them, in place of the money which had been given away by their father. It was, at the same time, specially ordered that their father should not be told of the matter. Al-Mutawakkil now sent his greeting to Aḥmed, and congratulated him on his escape from the attempts of his enemies to involve him in suspicions. If we may believe the record, and we probably may, al-Mutawakkil also expressed his pleasure at Aḥmed's presence, as he wished to consult him in the matter of Ibn Abî Dowâd, who had just fallen into disgrace [1]). Very soon a wish of the Khalif was made known to Aḥmed that he should remain with him to teach Tradition and give up the idea of returning to Baghdâd. Especially did the Khalif desire him to undertake the teaching of al-Muᶜtazz, his favorite son [2]). From all this Aḥmed tried to excuse himself on the ground of physical infirmity, pointing to his loose teeth and other evidences of age and weakness. He declared his belief to be that the invitation and entertainment were, together, parts of a conspiracy to keep him in restraint — to make him a prisoner while yet the guest of his Sovereign. And he vowed a vow that he would never as long as he lived tell another complete tradition. Some say that this vow extended over the last eight years of his life; but if he came to the Khalif in 237 A. H., and took upon him the vow in order to escape detention where he was, the duration of its binding force was a little over four years. It may be that the vow was taken when al-Wâthiḳ requested him to leave Baghdâd, for we know that he ceased to teach during the latter months of that Khalif's reign; still, as a matter of fact, we have in this case more than eight years, and, on the whole, it seems desirable to date his final cessation of teaching from the time of this visit to al-Mutawakkil, when he was 73 years of age and, as we really know, a man much weakened in his physical constitution.

Aḥmed Objects to Remain at the Camp

and Virtually Gives up Teaching.

---

1) vid. note 2, p. 56.
2) al-Sujûtî, Tarîkh al-Khol. 357.

The Interest of al-Mutawakkil in Aḥmed. It appears to have been some time before Aḥmed was summoned to the Palace; but, in the meantime, the Khalif shewed a friendly interest in him and evinced a respect for his learning by submitting to him questions for his judgment upon them. One of these was the following: Supposing two animals to be fighting with their horns, and the one mortally wound the other; may the wounded animal if slaughtered be used for food? Aḥmed's answer was that, if the animal shewed signs of life by moving its eyelids and by switching its tail, and if its blood was still flowing and not congealed, it might be slaughtered and eaten.

His Visit to the Palace. At last, he was ordered to appear in the presence of the Khalif's son al-Muᶜtazz. It was a sore affliction to Aḥmed when Yaḥya ibn Khaḳân came to fit on him the Court costume, but he was induced to allow it to be put upon him, though put it on himself he would not. On this occasion, Yaḥya ibn Khaḳân told the sons of Aḥmed that a stipend of 4000 dirhems per month had been ordered to be paid to them, but that their father was not to know of it. On arriving at the Palace, Aḥmed was well received, though there is but a very scant notice of the audience. After his return to his lodgings from this first visit to his new protégé, he felt badly over the sin he thought he had committed in wearing the fine clothes he had been obliged to put on; and, at once removing them, he ordered his son Ṣâliḥ to send them to Baghdâd, where they were to be sold and their price given to the poor. His own family he forbade to reserve any of the garments for their personal use; but, notwithstanding, Ṣâliḥ kept the bonnet. Aḥmed's peace of mind was much disturbed at this time, also, over his prospective visits to the Sovereign himself, and the charge he should have as tutor to the Khalif's son; for it seems that al-Mutawakkil did not, at first, take into consideration the vow which Aḥmed had taken not to tell Tradition perfectly.

It is not likely that he really appeared before al-Mutawakkil at all; at least, we have nothing to shew that he did, nor have we any evidence that he actually had the charge of the Khalif's son. Al-Muʿtazz, at the time of Aḥmed's arrival at Surramanra, was not more than six years of age, if as old as that [1]).

Asks a Change of Residence Aḥmed's next grievance arose when he learned that the house in which he was lodged had belonged to Îtâkh [2]). On hearing this, he had a letter written to Moḥammed ibn al-Jarrâḥ, seeking that al-Mutawakkil would release him from the obligation to remain there. The Khalif granted this request, and then sought to engage another home for him, by asking some people to move out of the house which they were occupying. This Aḥmed did not wish and it was given up. Finally, a suitable *and is Offended at the Luxurious Provision Made for Him.* place was hired for him at a rent of 200 dirhems. Here he was grieved at the luxury with which the house was furnished, and, leaving the finely furnished apartments, contented himself with a humble mattress which he had brought with him. The bountiful table which was placed at his disposal was, likewise, a great offence to him; a fact which we can readily believe, when we are informed that the landlord of the house offered Ṣâliḥ ibn Aḥmed a sum of 3000 dirhems a month for it, and was refused. Those of his family who were desirous of retaining the table were obliged to have it set *Fasting and Sickness.* down in the vestibule of the house, where he might not see it. He himself fasted most of the time, partaking only of a little sawîḳ and bread, until, at last, he was taken sick and the well-known physician Ibn Masûyah had to be sent to prescribe for him. He examined Aḥmed, assured him that his trouble was not really a disease, but simply weakness and wasting of the body from lack of nourishment, and prescribed for him sesame oil, which he declared that he, as a Christian, was accustomed to give to the ascetics of his own faith when they had brought

---

1) He was born 232 A. H., Abu'l-Maḥ. II, 24.

2) Îtâkh the Turk killed 234 A. H., Abu'l-Maḥ. I, 702.

themselves to a similar condition. Aḥmed at this time seems to have received every attention at the hands of al-Mutawakkil and those about him; though, it does not surprise us to find him sometimes refusing kindnesses which were proffered.

Consulted about Ibn Abî Dowâd. At different times, attempts were made to draw from Aḥmed an expression of opinion regarding Aḥmed ibn Abî Dowâd his former persecutor, who had now fallen from favor. But neither about the man, nor about his estates and their disposition would he express himself at all. Nor was he any more willing to hear reports of the public gossip about his old adversary and the course of action which had been adopted towards him [1]).

Proposal to Buy a House for Him. After a time al-Mutawakkil proposed that he should buy a house for Aḥmed, but the latter obstinately refused his consent to the proposal, and ordered his son Ṣâliḥ to be no party to such a project. In the end the idea was given up.

Aḥmed again Urged to Attend on the Khalif The Khalif now began to urge that Aḥmed should attend continuously on him, as had been his intention in bringing him from Baghdâd. The day that he should begin had actually been agreed upon. Aḥmed, however, never concealed from anyone how extremely distasteful to him the obligation was. His uncle Isḥâḳ ibn Ḥanbal also urged him to go in to the Khalif and offer him direction and cited the example of Isḥâḳ ibn Râhawaih, who had done this with Ibn Ṭâhir (with advantage to himself). Aḥmed replied that he did not approve of Ibn Râhawaih or his course, and that in his conviction to be near persons in authority or to keep company with them was to imperil faith and violate conscience. Even as it was, he did not feel himself safe from guilt. After *but is Released.* all this a message came from the Khalif releasing him from all obligation to appear before either himself or his successors, and from the wearing of the black

1) vid. note 2, p. 56; Abu'l-Maḥ. I, 719.

Court costume. He might wear cotton or wool just as pleased him. It appears, in fact, to have been a general dispensation from fulfilling any requests from persons in authority which might be distasteful to him [1]). Now, at last, he was released from his fear that they were going to make of him an attaché of the Court, and on this point had ease of mind. For his fellow-traditionists who remained at Court his feeling appears to have been one of censuring contempt. They were afraid to do that which would deprive them of their stipends from the Khalif, and, possibly, bring upon them much worse consequences. Aḥmed had accomplished his end in securing his exemption from attendance at Court; not, however, by a direct refusal of the Khalif's mandate, but by persistent excuses; by shewing a dislike to what he was expected to do; and by his discontent with the general arrangements which were made for him by al-Mutawakkil's orders. He obstructed as far as possible the royal wishes, but did not deny them.

Correspondence with his Sons. His two sons, Ṣâliḥ and Abdallah, now returned to Baghdâd, and, after they had gone away, the fine furnishings of the house were removed, and the Khalif's daily provision ceased to be provided. By Abdallah, who left him later than his brother, he sent word to Ṣâliḥ, telling him that both he and his brother were not desired to attend on him any further, for he regarded most of the

---

1) al-Maḳrîzî, p. 10, قال المروزى سمعت اسحق بن حنبل عم احمد ونحن بالعسكر يُناشده ويساله الدخول على الخليفة ليامره وينهاه وقال انه يَقبل كلامك هذا اسحق بن راهويه يدخل على ابن طاهر فيامره وينهاه فقال له ابو عبد الله تحتجّ علىّ باسحق وأنا غير راضٍ بفعله ما له فى رؤيتى خير ولا لى فى رؤيته خير يجب علىّ اذا رايته ان آمره وانهاه الدنوّ منهم فتنة والجلوس معهم فتنة نحن متباعدون منهم ما أرانا نسْلم فكيف لو قرُبْنا منهم

unpleasant experiences through which he had passed as due to their not supporting him in the stand he had taken and their want of active sympathy with his principles. Their acceptance of the Khalif's fine provision, if they came back, would bring him only into ill-favor with the public; and their acceptance of the Khalif's stipend, against his known wish and sense of duty, he considered a grave breach of filial piety. They both might go where they would with his prayers following them, but he desired that they should not cumber him further by their presence. Such was the tenor of his first two letters to his son Ṣâliḥ. In a third he reproaches his sons for not taking steps to secure his release from his unwilling detention. But he advises them to keep to their dwellings [1]), and expresses the hope that God, by some means will open up his way.

Aḥmed's Testament. While at the camp, Aḥmed made his testament, which was as follows: In the name of God, the Merciful, the Gracious. This is the testament of Aḥmed ibn Ḥanbal. He testifies that there is no God but Allah, alone and without fellow, and that Moḥammed is his Servant and his Messenger whom He sent with the right guidance and the true religion, that he might make it known as the perfect religion, though the idolaters be displeased. He, further, testifies that those who obey his family and his relatives worship God among those who worship, praise him among those who offer praise and do good service to the Community of the Muslims. I, also, testify that I am satisfied with Allah as Lord, with Islâm as a religion, and with Moḥammed as Prophet. I, further, testify that Abdallah ibn Moḥammed, known as Bûrân, has a claim against me for about fifty dinârs, and that he is to be credited in whatever he may say. Let what is due to him be paid from the rent of the house, if God will, and after he has been paid, the children of Ṣâliḥ and Abdallah, sons of Aḥmed ibn Ḥanbal, are to receive, each male and female, ten dirhems,

---

1) p. 140, note 2.

after the payment of the money to Abû Moḥammed. Witnessed by Abû Yûsuf and Ṣâliḥ and Abdallah the two sons of Aḥmed ibn Moḥammed ibn Ḥanbal.

Permission Granted to Return to Baghdâd.

It was not a great while before Aḥmed again requested a change of residence[1]), and the Khalif, with great kindness, acceded to his request and, not only allowed him to engage another dwelling, but sent to him one thousand dinârs that he might

1) Abû Nuʿaim, 153*a*, (The narrative now follows this source for a time.)
قال ابو الفضل ثم سال ابی رحمه الله ان يتحوَّل من الدار التی اكتريَت
له فاكتری هو دارا وتحوَّل اليها فسال المتوكل عنه فقيل انه عليل فقال
كنتُ احب ان يكون فی قربی فقد اذِنت له يا عبَيدَ الله احمل اليه
الف دينار يَقسِمُها وقال لسعيد تُهيّیء له حَرَّاقة ينحدر فيها فجآءه
علی بن الجهم فی جوف الليل فاخبره ثم جآء عُبَيد الله ومعه الف
دينار فقال ان امير المومنين قد اذن لك وقد امر لك بهذه الالف
دينار فقال قد اعْفانی امير المومنين مما اكره فردَّها وقال انا رقيق
علی البَرِد [so Cod.] والظهرُ ارْفق بی فكُتب له جواز فكتب الی
محمد بن عبد الله فی بره وتعاهده فقدم علينا فيما بين الظهر
والعصر فلما انحدر الی بَغداد ومكث قليلا قال لی يا صَالح قلت
لبيك قال احب ان تَدَعَ [Cod. تَدْعُ] هذا الرزق فلا تاخذه ولا تُوكِل
فيه احدا فقد علمت انكم انما تاخذونه بسببی فسكتُّ فقل
ما لَك فقلتُ أكره انْ اعطيَك شيئا بلسانی واخالف الی غيره فاكونَ قد
كذبتك ونافقتك وليس فی القَوم اكثرُ عِيالا مِنی ولا أعذَرُ وقد كُنتُ
اشكو اليك فتقول امرُك منُعقَد بامری ولعل الله ان تُنحل عنی عن [del.?]
هذه العقدة ثم قُلتُ له وقد كنتَ تَدْعو لی فارجو ان يكونَ الله
استجاب لك قال ولا تفعل قلتُ لا فقال قم فعل الله بك وفعل

distribute it in alms. At the same time, he gave him leave to return home and ordered a pleasure barge to be

---

فامر بسدّ الباب بينى وبينه فتلقانى عبدُ الله فسألنى فاخبرته فقال ما
اقولُ انا قلت ذاك اليك فقال له مثل ما قال لى فقال لا افعل فكان منه
اليه نحوُ ما كان منه الىّ فلقينا عَمُه فقال لو اردتم ان تقولوا له
وما علمه اذا اخذتم شيئا فدخل عليه فقال يابا عبد الله لستُ اخذ
شيئا من هذا فقال الحمد لله وهَجَرنا وسَدّ الابواب بيننا وبينه وتحامى
منزلنا ان يَدخل منها الى منزله شىء . . . .
قال ابو الفضل فلما مَضى نحوٌ من شهرين كُتِبَ لنا بشىء فجىء
به الينا فاولُ من جآء عَمه فاخذ فاخبر فجآء الى الباب الذى كان
سَدّه بينى وبينه وقد فتح الصبيان كوة فقال ادعو لى صالحا فجآء
الرسول وقلتُ له قل له لستُ اجىء فوجّه الىّ لِمَ قال [؟ قلتَ] لا
تجىء فقلت قُل له هذا الرزق تَرتَزِقه جماعة كثيرة وانما انا واحد
منهم وليس فيهم اعذر منى واذا كان توبيخ خُصِصتُ به انا فلما نادى
عمه بالاذان خرَج فلما خَرج قيل لى انه قد خرج الى المسجد
فجئتُ حتى صِرتُ فى موضع اسْمع فيه كلامه فلما فرغ
التفت الى عمه ثم قال له نافقْتَنى وكذبتنى وكان غيرك اع
زعمت انك لا تاخذ من هذا شيئا ثم اخذته وانت تستغل ...ى
درهم وعمدت الى طريق المسلمين تَستغله انما اشفق عليك ان تُطوّق*
يوم القيامة سبع ارضين اخذت هذا الشىء بغير حقه فقال قد
تصدقتُ فقال تصدقتَ بنصف درهم ثم هجره وترك الصلاة فى المسجد
وخرج الى مسجد خارج يصلى فيه . The account of his difficulties with the members of his family over the Khalif's allowances is in the Ms. considerably extended, but the rest of it has no special interest, and varies but slightly from the extract here given.

made ready to take him to Baghdâd; this last favor however, Aḥmed declined, preferring to travel by land on account of risk to his health from the coldness of the river journey. When he left for home, al-Mutawakkil had a letter written to Moḥammed ibn Abdallah, the governor of Baghdâd, ordering him to deal kindly with Aḥmed and take good care of him.

Objects to his Family Receiving Stipends.

From the time of his return to Baghdâd, the story of Aḥmed's life is little more than a record of his differences with his family — in particular, with his sons Ṣâliḥ and Abdallah, and his paternal uncle Isḥâḳ ibn Ḥanbal, — about the receiving of the Khalif's stipends and gifts which came to them from time to time. He would block up the doorways between his sons' houses and his own, when they expressed determination to accept the moneys, which they needed for the support of their families, and vigorously dissented from his view that their position was the same as his own, and that what was good for him was, likewise, good for them. For as long as two or three months together he would have nothing to do with his sons; and it was, apparently, only as their children in playing made their way into their grandfather's house and touched a more sympathetic chord of his nature, or as the offices of his good friend Bûrân (Abdallah ibn Moḥammed) were called in that reconciliation was brought about. His uncle Isḥâḳ certainly played a worthy part toward him. He pretended great friendship and complete deference to his wishes as to the receiving of money, and at the same time accepted it with the rest. When Aḥmed discovered the dissimulation, he was very angry; and it was all to no purpose that Isḥâḳ tried to excuse himself on the ground that he had used the money in giving alms, for he knew, and Aḥmed knew, that he had not done so. Aḥmed then ceased to worship in the mosque where his sons and uncle worshipped, and for the necessary prayers went to a mosque outside the city quarter in which he lived.

Harassed as they were by him, the members of Aḥmed's

family agreed once or twice to receive no more money; but, after a period of abstinence, the urgent needs of their families forced them to give up the self-denial and again claim their stipends. At last, Aḥmed went so far as to write to Yaḥya ibn Khaḳân, telling him that he had made up his mind to request the withdrawal of the regular aid which was granted to his family. Ṣâliḥ anticipated his father, however, by informing the officer who was over that part of Baghdâd in which they resided, and he succeeded in preventing Aḥmed's letter from accomplishing its object. The aid was continued and, not only that, but all that was due to the family, 40,000 dirhems, being the undrawn stipend for ten months, was paid over to his sons. And, though the Khalif had ordered his officers not to inform Aḥmed of the payment, Ṣâliḥ himself sent word of it to his father. The old man, when he heard the message, exclaimed after a meditative silence, 'What can I do when I desire one thing and God orders another!' [1])

---

1) Abû Nu^caim, 153*b*, قال ابو الفضل ثم كتب ابى رحمه الله الى يحيى ابن خاقان يسئله ويعزم عليه ان لا يعيننا على شىء من ارزاقنا ولا يتكلم فيها فبلغنى فوجهت الى القيم لنا وهو ابو غالب بن بنت معاويَة بن عَمرو وقد كنت قلت له يا ابه انه يكبُر عليك وقد عزمتُ اذا حدث امر اخبرتك به فلما وصل رسوله بالكتاب الى يحيى اخذه صاحب الخَبَر فاخذ نسخته ووصلت الى المتوكل فقال لعبيد الله كم من شهر لولد احمد بن حنبل فقال عشرة اشهر قال يُحمَل اليهم الساعة اربعون الف درهم من بيت المال صحاح ولا يُعلم هو بها قال فقال يحيى للقيم انا اكتب الى صالح واعلمه فورَدَ علىّ كتابُه فوجهت الى ابى أُعلمه فقال الذى اخبرَه انه سكت قليلا وضرب بذَقْنه [Cod. بذقْنه] ساعة ثم رفع راسه فقال ما حِيلتى اذا اردتُ امرًا

Again Suspected of ᶜAlyite Intrigues.

After Aḥmed's return to Baghdâd (the date of which we do not know) some talebearer reported to al-Mutawakkil the old slander that Aḥmed was harboring an ᶜAlyite. The Khalif sent word to Aḥmed of the report, and told him that he had imprisoned the man who made it until he should advise him as to what truth there was in the report, and direct him what to do to the man. Aḥmed answered asserting his ignorance of the whole matter, but advised that the man should be set free, as to visit him with death might bring affliction to many others who were no sharers in his crime.

A man whose name is given as Abû Jaᶜfar ibn Dharîḥ al-ᶜUkbarî relates that, in the year 236, (which appears to be a mistake, for the circumstances point to the time of the second accusation of harboring an ᶜAlyite, and this was after Aḥmed's return to Baghdâd from his visit to the camp in 237 A. H.) he sought Aḥmed to ask him some doctrinal question, but was told at his house that he had gone outside that quarter of the city to prayers. So Abû Jaᶜfar sat down at the gate of the street to wait for his return. Presently, an old man, tall, with dyed hair and beard, and of a dark brown complexion, came up and entered the street, the visitor entering with him. At the end of the street, Aḥmed, for such it was, opened a gate and entered it, closing it after him and at the same time bidding his companion go his way. Just then, the latter noticed at the gate a mosque, in which an old man, also with dyed hair, was leading the prayers. When he had finished, Abû Jaᶜfar asked a man who was at the prayers about Aḥmed ibn Ḥanbal and why he had refused to answer him. The man re-

---

واراد الله امرا، قال ابو الفضل وجآء رسول المتوكل الى ابى يقول لو سَلِم احدٌ من الناس سلمتَ رفع رجُل الىّ فى وقت كذا انّ عَلويا قدم من خراسان وانك وجهت اليه بمن يلقاه وقد حَبَستُ الرجل واردتُ ضربَه وكرِهتُ ان تغتمّ فمُر فيه فقال هذا باطل ويُخلى سبيله

plied that Aḥmed had been suspected of harboring an ᶜAlyite; that, on this account, the prefect of police had surrounded his dwelling with a cordon of police and then had proceeded to search it. For this reason he avoided speaking to people. The police had, however, found nothing to give substance to the suspicion which had been raised. Abû Jaᶜfar, then, enquired who it was whom he had seen leading the prayers, and, on learning that it was Aḥmed's uncle Isḥâḳ, he asked why Aḥmed ibn Ḥanbal did not pray behind his uncle in this mosque which was near his own door. The man answered that he did not worship with his uncle, nor even his own sons, nor speak with any of them, because they had accepted the stipends and gifts of the Khalif [1]).

---

1) Abû Nuᶜaim, 142 *a*, حدثنا ابو بكر احمد بن جعفر بن مالك ثنا ابو جعفر بن ذريح العُكبرى قال طلبت احمد بن حنبل فى سنة ست وثلاثين لاسئله عن مسئلة فسألتُ عنه فقالوا خرج يصلى خارجا فجلَسْتُ له على باب الدرب [so marg.; text الدار] حتى جآء فقمت فسلمت عليه فردّ علىّ السلام وكان شيخًا مَخْضُوبًا طوالا اسْمَر شديدَ السُمرة فدخل الزقاق وانا معه اماشيه خطوةً بخَطوة فلما بلغْنا آخرَ الدرب اذا باب يفرج دفعه وصار خلفه وقال اذهَبْ عافاك الله فثنيتُ عليه فقال اذْهَبْ عافاك الله قال فالتفتُّ فاذا مسجد على الباب وشيخ مخضوب قائم يصلى بالناس فجلسْت حتى سَلم الامام فخرج رجل فسالته عن احمد بن حنبل وعن تخلفه عن كلامى فقال أُدّعى عليه عند السلطان انّ عنده علويا فجاء محمد ابن نصر فاحاط بالمَحلة ففُتِشَتْ فلم يوجد فيها شىء مما ذكر فاعْجَم عن كلام العامة فقلت هذا الشيخ من هو قال عَمُّه اسحاق قلت فما له لا يُصَلى خلفه قال ليس يكلم ذا ولا بنيه لانّهم اخذوا جآئزة السلطان،

Al-Mutawakkil never ceased to shew his interest in Aḥmed's welfare, and to make frequent inquiries about him. This was, for some reason which is hard to divine, most disagreeable to Aḥmed; and he professed himself as preferring to die rather than have to live through such incessant attentions [1]).

The Khalif Asks for Aḥmed's View as to the Ḳorân.

Among the evidences of the Khalif's interest was a letter written by ʿObaidallah ibn Yaḥya on his account, asking Aḥmed to write him his views on the Ḳorân, not by way of assurance of his accordance with the opinion of the Sovereign, but merely for the information of the Commander of the Faithful. In reply Aḥmed dictated to his son a letter to ʿObaidallah, in which he said [2]): —

---

1) Abû Nuʿaim, 153*b*, قال وكان رسولُ المتوكل ياتى ابى يُبلغه السلام ويسئله عن حاله فنُسَرُّ نحن بذاك فياخذه نغضة [Cod. نَعضه] حتى تُدَثِّره [Cod. no points] يقول والله لو ان نفسى فى يدى لارسلتُها وبضُم اصابعه ثم يفتحها

2) Abû Nuʿaim, 153*b* ff. حدثنا سليمان بن احمد ثنا عبد الله ابن احمد بن حنبل ح وحدثنا محمد وعلى والحسين قالوا ثنا محمد ابن اسمعيل ثنا صالح بن احمد بن حنبل قال كتبَ عُبَيد الله بن يحيى الى ابى رحمه الله يُخبره ان امير المومنين امرَنى ان اكتبَ اليك اسالك عن امر القران لا مسئلة امتحان ولكن مسئلة معرفةٍ وبَصيرة فاملّى علىّ ابى رحمه الله الى عُبَيدِ الله بن يحيى وحدى ما معى احد بسم الله الرحمن الرحيم احسن الله عاقبتك ابا الحسن فى الامور كلها ودفع عنك مكاره الدنيا والاخِرة برحمته قد كتبتُ اليك رضى الله عنك بالذى سال عنه امير المومنين بامر القران بما حضرنى وانى اسئل الله تعالى ان يديم توفيقَ امير المومنين فقد كان الناس فى خوض من الباطل* واختلاف شديد يغتمسون فيه حتى افضَت الخلافة الى

Ahmed's Letter in Reply. I ask God to continue his aid to the Commander of the Faithful, for men were in the depth of falsehood and immersed in violent differences of opinion until the Khalifate came to the Commander of the Faithful, and God banished by means of the Commander

---

امير المومنين فنفى الله بامير المومنين كلّ بدعة وانجلى عن الناس ما كانوا فيه من الذل وضيق المحابس [Cod. المجالس] فصرّف الله ذلك كله وذهب به بامير المومنين وَقع ذلك من المسلمين موقعا عظيما ودعوا الله لامير المومنين فاسئل الله ان يستجيب فى امير المومنين صالحَ الدعآء وان يُتمّ ذلك لامير المومنين وان يزيد فى نيته ويُعينه على ما هو عليه فقد ذكر عن عبد الله بن عباس رضى الله عنه انه قال لا تضرِبوا كِتاب الله بعضَه ببعض فانّ ذلك يُوقع الشك فى قلوبكم وذُكر عن عَبد الله بن عمر [Cod. عمرو] رَضى الله عنه ان نفرًا كانوا جلوسا بباب النبى صلى الله عليه وسلم فقال بعضهم الم يقُل الله كذا وقال بعضهم الم يقل الله كذا قال فسَمع ذلك رسول الله صلى الله عليه وسلم فخرج كانما فُقِئَ فى وجهه حَبُّ الرمّان فقال افبهذا أُمرتم ان تضربوا كتاب الله بعضَه ببعض انما ضلّت الامم قبلكم فى مثل هذا انّكم لستم مما هاهنا فى شىء انظروا الذى أُمرتم به فاعملوا به وانظروا الذى نُهيتم عنه فانتهوا عنه، وروى عن ابى هريرة رضى الله عَنْهُ [Cod omits] عن النبى صلى الله عليه وسلم انه قال مرآء فى القران كفر وروى عن ابى جهيم رجلٍ من اصحاب النبى صلى الله عليه وسلم عن النبى صلعم قال لا تماروا فى القران فانّ مرآءً فيه كفر، وقال عبد الله بن عباس رضى الله عنه قدم على عمر بن الخطاب رضى الله عنه رَجُل فجعل عمر يسئله عن الناس فقال يا امير المومنين قد قرأ القرانَ منهم كذا وكذا فقال ابنُ عباس فقلت والله

of the Faithful every heresy, and took away from men the straitness and humiliation of the prisons. God has, thus, changed all that, and removed it through the Commander of the Faithful, [all of] which has made a great impression upon the Muslims; hence, they pray God to bless the Commander of the Faithful, and I ask God to hearken to all

---

ما أُحِب ان يتسارعوا يومهم هذا فى القران هذه المسارعة قال فزبرنى عمر وقال مَه فانطلقتُ الى منزلى مُكتئبا حزينا فبينّا انا كذلك اذ [Cod. اذا] اتانى رجل فقال اجبْ امير المومنين فخرجْتُ فاذا هو بالباب ينتظرنى فاخذ بيدى فخلا بى وقال ما الذى كرهتَ مما قال الرجلُ آنفا فقلت يا امير المومنين متى يتسارعوا هذه المسارعة يحتقوا ومتى ما يحتقوا يَختصموا ومتى ما [Cod. لا] يَختصموا يختلفوا ومتى ما يختلفوا يقتتلوا قال لِلّهِ ابوك والله انْ كنت لاكتمها الناس حتى جئتَ بها، وروى عن جابر بن عبد الله رضى الله عنه قال كان النبى صلعم يَعرِضُ نفسَه على الناس بالموقف فيقول هل من رجل يحملنى الى قَومه فانّ قريشا قد منعونى ان ابلغ كلام ربى، وروى عن جُبَيْر بن نُفَيْر قال قال رسول الله صلعم انكم لن تَرجعوا الى الله بشىء افضلَ مما خرج منه يعنى القرآن، وروى عن عبد الله بن مسعود رضى الله عنه انه قال جَرِّدوا القران ولا تكتُبوا فيه شيئا الا كلام الله، وروى عن عمر بن الخطاب رضى الله عنه [Cod. omits] انه قال هذا القرانُ كلامُ الله فضَعُوه مواضِعَه، قال رجل للحسن البصرى يابا سعيد انى اذا قرأْتُ كتابَ الله وتدبرته كِدتُ ان آيَس وينقطع رجاءى قال فقال الحسن انّ القران كلام الله اعمال بنى آدم الى الضعف والتقصير فاعمل وابشر، وقال فروة بن نوفل الاشجعى كنت جار الخبّاب وهو من اصحاب النبى صلى الله عليه

good petitions for the Commander of the Faithful and to perfect [all] that for the Commander of the Faithful, that he may go on in his design; [I ask God] to help him, also, in that in which he is engaged. Now, it is related from Ibn ᶜAbbâs

---

وسلم فخرجت معه يوما من المسجد وهو آخذ بيدى فقال يا هناه تَقَرَّب الى الله بما استطعت فانك لن تُقَرِّبَ الله بشىء احبَّ اليه من كلامه، وقال رجل للحكم بن عيينة ما حمل اهلَ [Cod. اهلُ] الاهوآء على هذا قال الخصومات، وقال معاوية بن قُرّة * وكان ابوه ممن اتى النبى صلعم اياكم وهذه الخصومات فانها تحبط الاعمال، وقال ابو قِلابَةَ وكان قد ادرك غير واحد من اصحاب رسول الله صلعم لا تجالسوا اصحاب الاهوآء او قال اصحاب الخصومات فانى لا آمن ان يَغمسوكم فى ضلالتهم ويلبِسوا عليكم بعض ما تعرفون، ودخل رجلان من اصحاب الاهوآء على محمد بن سيرِين فقالا يابا بكر نُحدّثك بحديث فقال لا فقالا فنَقْرأ عليك آية من كتاب الله قال لا لتَقومان عنى او لأقومَنّه قال فقام الرجلان فخرجا فقال بعض القوم يابا بكر وما عليك ان تُقرأ عليك آية من كتاب الله فقال له ابنُ سيرين انى خشيت ان يقرأا [Cod. يقرءا] علىّ اية فيُحرفانها فيقر ذلك قلبى، وقال محمدٌ لو أعلم انى اكون مثلِى الساعة لتركتهما، وقال رجل من اهل البدع لايوب السختيانى يابا بكر اسألك عن كلمة فى فوَلّى وهو يقول بيَده ولا نصف كلمة، وقال طاووس بن طاوس لابن له وتكلم رجل من اهل البدع يَابنى أدخِل اصبعيك فى اذنيك حتى لا تسمع ما يقول ثم قال اشْدُد اشدد، وقال عمر بن عبد العزيز من جعل دينه غرضا للخصومات اكثر التنقّل، قال ابو الفضل وجدت فى كتاب ابى بخطه ثنا اسمعيل عن يونس قال نُبِّئْتُ ان

that he said, ‘Do not smite God’s Book one part of it with another part, for that casts doubt into your hearts’. And it is told from Abdallah ibn ʿOmar that he said, ‘Some persons were sitting at the Prophet’s door, and some of them

---

عمر بن عبد العزيز قال من جعل دينه غرضا للخُصومات اكثر
التنقّل، وقال ابرهيم النَخَعىّ ان القوم لم يُدَّخر عنهم شىء [Cod. شيا]
حتى لكم لفضل عندكم، وكان الحسن يقول شرّ دآء خالط قلبا يعنى
الاهوآء، وقال حُذَيْفَة بن اليمان رضى الله عنه وكان من اصحاب رسول
الله صلعم اتّقوا الله مَعشر القرآء وَخُذوا طريقَ من كان قبلكم والله
لئن اسْتَبَقْتُم لقد سُبقتم سبقا بعيدا ولَئن تركتموه يمينا وشمالا
لقد ضللتم ضلالا بعيدا او قال مُبينا قال ابى وانما تركتُ ذكر
الاسانيد لما تقدم من اليمين التى حلفتُ بها مما قد عَلمه اميرُ
المومنين لو لا ذاك ذكرتُها باسانيدها وقد قال الله تعالى وإنْ
أَحَدٌ مِنَ ٱلْمُشْرِكِينَ ٱسْتَجَارَكَ فَأَجِرْهُ حَتَّى يَسْمَعَ كَلَامَ ٱللَّهِ [Ḳor. 9. 6]
وقال أَلَا لَهُ ٱلْخَلْقُ وَٱلْأَمْرُ [Ḳor. 7. 52] فاخبرَ بالخلق ثم قال والامر
فاخبرَ ان الامر غيرُ الخلق وقال تعالى ٱلرَّحْمٰنُ عَلَّمَ ٱلْقُرْآنَ خَلَقَ
ٱلْإِنْسَانَ عَلَّمَهُ ٱلْبَيَانَ [Ḳor. 55. 1, 2, 3] فاخبر تعالى ان القُرآن من
علمه وقال وَلَنْ تَرْضَى عَنْكَ ٱلْيَهُودُ وَلَا ٱلنَّصَارَى حَتَّى تَتَّبِعَ مِلَّتَهُمْ
قُلْ إِنَّ هُدَى ٱللَّهِ هُوَ ٱلْهُدَى وَلَئِنِ ٱتَّبَعْتَ أَهْوَآءَهُمْ بَعْدَ ٱلَّذِى جَآءَكَ
مِنَ ٱلْعِلْمِ مَا لَكَ مِنَ ٱللَّهِ مِنْ وَلِيٍّ وَلَا نَصِيرٍ [Ḳor. 2. 114] وقال
وَلَئِنْ أَتَيْتَ ٱلَّذِينَ أُوتُوا ٱلْكِتَابَ بِكُلِّ آيَةٍ مَا تَبِعُوا قِبْلَتَكَ وَمَا أَنْتَ
بِتَابِعٍ قِبْلَتَهُمْ وَمَا بَعْضُهُمْ بِتَابِعٍ قِبْلَةَ بَعْضٍ وَلَئِنِ ٱتَّبَعْتَ أَهْوَآءَهُمْ مِنْ
بَعْدِ مَا جَآءَكَ مِنَ ٱلْعِلْمِ إِنَّكَ إِذًا لَمِنَ ٱلظَّالِمِينَ [Ḳor. 2. 140] وقال
وَكَذَلِكَ أَنْزَلْنَاهُ حُكْمًا عَرَبِيًّا وَلَئِنِ ٱتَّبَعْتَ أَهْوَآءَهُمْ بَعْدَ مَا جَآءَكَ مِنَ

were saying, Does not God say so and so? while others were saying, Nay! does not God say so and so? and the Messenger of God heard that, and went out — and it was as if pomegranates [1]) had been burst over his face — and he said, 'Was it this ye were commanded to observe, to smite God's Book one part of it with another? The peoples who were before you erred thus, but ye have nothing to do with this. Observe what ye are ordered to do and do it; and observe what ye are forbidden to do and abstain from it'. It is related from Abû Huraira from the Prophet that he said, 'Disputation about the Ḳorân is unbelief.' It is related from Abû Juhaim, one of the Companions of the Prophet, from the Prophet that he said, 'Do not dispute over the Ḳorân, for disputation over it is unbelief.' Abdallah ibn ʿAbbâs said, 'A man came to ʿOmâr ibn al-Khaṭṭâb, and ʿOmâr began to ask him about the people, and he said, 'O Commander of the Faithful, so and so many of them recite the Ḳorân (or, supply مرّةً: 'Some of them have read the Ḳorân so and so many times'?).' And Ibn ʿAbbâs said, 'So I said, By God, I do not like them to vie with each other in rapid reading of the Ḳorân, but ʿOmâr

---

ٱلْعِلْمِ مَا لَكَ مِنَ ٱللّٰهِ مِنْ وَلِيٍّ وَلَا وَاقٍ [Ḳor. 13. 37] فالقرآن من علم الله وفى هذه الايات دليل على انّ الذى جآءه صلعم هُوَ القرآن لِقوله ولئن اتبعت اهوآءهم بعد الذى جاءك من العلم، وقد رُوِى عن غَير واحد ممن مضى مِن سلفنا انهم كانوا يقولون القرآن كلام الله غير مخلوق وهو الذى اذهَب اليه لَسْتُ بصاحب كلام ولا ارى الكلام فى شىء من هذا الامر الا ما كان فى كتاب الله او فى حديث عن النبى صلعم اوْ عن اصحابه او عن التابعين فامّا غير ذلك فانّ الكلام فيه غير مَحمود،

1) حبّ الرمان "the seeds of the pomegranate", but often "the pomegranate" itself.

blamed me for saying this, and said, 'Stop! Hush!' I went down, then, to my dwelling afflicted and grieving [because he seemed to oppose my zeal for the Ḳorân]. And, while I was in this state of mind, a man came to me and said, 'Answer the summons of the Commander of the Faithful'. So I went out, and lo! he was at the door waiting for me, and he took me by the hand, went aside with me, and said, 'What was that with which you were displeased in what the man said a little while ago?' I said, 'O Commander of the Faithful, when they indulge in this rivalry to see who can read fastest, they read with mumbling voice; and if they read with mumbling voice, they dispute with one another; and if they dispute with one another, they fall into discord; and if they fall into discord they fight with one another. He said, 'Very good! Verily, by God, I was concealing it [the same opinion] from anyone until you said it'. It is related from Jâbir ibn Abdallah that he said, 'The Prophet was presenting himself to the men in the Mauḳif [at Arafât] and he said, Is there any man who will take me to his people? for the Ḳoreish have refused me the right to make known the Word of my Lord'. It is related from Jubair ibn Nufair that he said, 'The Messenger of God said, You cannot return unto God by means of anything more excellent than that which went out from him. He meant the Ḳorân'. It is related from Abdallah ibn Masᶜûd that he said, 'Write the bare Ḳorân, but do not write in it anything except the Word of God'. It is related from ᶜOmar ibn al-Khaṭṭâb that he said, 'This Ḳorân is the Word of God; give it, then, its proper place'. A man said to al-Ḥasan al-Baṣrî, 'O Abû Saᶜîd, when I read the Word of God, and think over it, I almost despair and give up hope'. And al-Ḥasan said, 'The Ḳorân is the Word of God; the works of the children of Adam incline toward weakness and insufficiency, but work and be of good cheer!' Farwa ibn Naufal al-Ashjaᶜî said, 'I was a neighbour of al-Khabbâb, who was one of the Companions of the Prophet, and I went out with him one day from the mosque, he holding me by the hand, and he said, O you! draw near to God by means of that which you are able to use as means, but you cannot draw near to God by means of anything dearer unto him than his Word'. A man said to al-Ḥakam ibn ʿUyaina, 'What leads the sceptics [1]) unto this [state of theirs]?' He said, 'Disputation'. Muʿâwia ibn Ḳurra, whose father was one of those who came to the Prophet said, 'Beware of these disputations, for they spoil good works'. Abû Ḳilâba said (and he had met more than one of the Companions of the Messenger of God), 'Do not keep company with sceptics, (or he said, 'With disputatious people') for I do not feel secure that they will not plunge you in their error, and make obscure unto you a part of what ye know'. There entered two sceptics unto Moḥammed ibn Sîrîn, and they said, 'O Abû Bekr, let us tell thee a tradition'. He said, 'Nay'. Then they said, 'Then let us recite unto thee a verse from the Ḳorân'. He said, 'Nay; ye surely shall go away from me, or else I shall go away'. So the two men arose and went out, and one of those present said, 'O Abû Bekr, what was the matter, that a verse from the Ḳorân might not be recited unto thee?' and Ibn Sîrîn said to him, 'I was afraid that they would recite a verse unto me and would pervert it and that that should become fixed in my heart'. Moḥammed however, added, 'Had I known that I should be as I am now, I would certainly have allowed them'. A sceptic once asked Ayûb al-Sakhtiyânî, 'O Abû Bekr, I would ask thee just a word'; but he turned his back, and motioned with his hand, 'Nay; not half a word'. Ṭâûs ibn Ṭâûs said to a son of his, when a sceptic was speaking, 'O my son, put your fingers in your ears so that you shall

1) This word does not quite represent the idea of the original اهل الأهواء. These were a class of men who were not prepared to accept the religious systems of other persons, except as their own reasoning confirmed their positions. They were thus in the first instance sceptical and then eclectic, taking from different systems such views as they approved or 'desired' to take. The name Ahluʾl-ʾAhwâ 'men of desires', is thus appropriate. v. Shahrastânî, Haarbrücker's transl'n I, p. 1 and note; Steiner, Die Muʿtaziliten, 6.

not hear what he says'. Then he said, 'Run! Run!' ᶜOmar ibn Abd al-ᶜAzîz said, 'He who makes his religion a butt for disputations is the most unsettled of men'. (*Abû'l Faḍl* said, 'I found it in a book of my father's in his own handwriting, 'Ismaᶜîl told us from Yûnus saying, I was told that ᶜOmar ibn Abd al-ᶜAzîz said, 'He who makes his religion a butt for disputations is the most unsettled of men'). Ibrâhîm al-Nakha'î said, 'These people shall have nothing laid up in store for them until there is with you an excellent provision'. Al-Ḥasan used to say, 'The worst diseased person is the man diseased at heart'; he meant the desires [i. e. men of desires — sceptics]. Hudhaifa ibn al-Yamân said, 'Fear God, O ye Reciters of the Ḳorân, and go in the way of those who were before you; for, if ye strive for precedence, ye have yet been preceded by a great distance, and if ye leave this way to the right or left ye have clearly committed error'. The letter went on to say: 'I have omitted the mention of the Isnâds because of the oath that I previously swore, of which the Commander of the Faithful is cognizant. If it were not for that, I should have mentioned them [the traditions] with their Isnâds. The Ḳorân, too, has said, 'And, if one of the idolaters seek protection of thee, grant him protection that he may hear the Word of God (Ḳorân 9. 6). 'Do not the Creation and the Command belong to him?' (Ḳorân 7.52). So he tells about 'the Creation', and then he says, 'and the Command', thus he tells us that the 'Command' is something else than 'the Creation' [1]). Also, 'The Merciful taught (عَلَّمَ) the Ḳorân, he created man, he taught him the explanation' (Ḳorân 55. 1, 2, 3). Thus God tells that the Ḳorân is from his Knowledge (عِلْم). He, also, says, 'And the Jews will not be content with thee, nor the Christians, until thou dost follow their religion. Say, 'Verily the direction of God is the right direction; but, surely, if thou dost follow their passions and their desires, after that which has come to thee

1) cf. p. 119 and, also, p. 139.

of knowledge (عِلْم) there is for thee from God neither friend nor helper' (Ḳorân 2 . 114). He says also, 'Even if thou dost give to those to whom the Book has been given every sign, they will not follow thy ḳibla, and thou wilt not follow their ḳibla, and one part of them will not follow the ḳibla of the other part. And, surely, if thou dost follow their passions, after what has come to thee of knowledge (عِلْم), in that case, thou art, verily, one of those who do evil' (Ḳorân 2 . 140). And also, 'And, thus, we have sent it down as a decision in the Arabic language; and, surely, if thou dost follow their passions, after what has come to thee of knowledge (عِلْم), there shall be for thee from God neither friend nor helper' (Ḳorân 13 . 37). Now, the Ḳorân is from the Knowledge of God; and in these verses is a proof that that which came to him [the Messenger of God] is the Ḳorân, according to his [God's] saying, 'And, surely, if thou dost follow their passions, after what has come to thee of knowledge (عِلْم)'.1)

It has been related, moreover, from more than one of those who went before us that they used to say, 'the Ḳorân is the Word of God uncreated', and that is what I believe. I am no dialectical theologian; I approve of argument in a matter of this kind only by means of what is in God's Book or a tradition from the Prophet, or from his Companions, or from those who followed them (Tâbᶜiûn), but, as for anything else, argument by means of it is not to be commended.

On one occasion, when al-Mutawakkil came to al-Shamasîya on his way to al-Madâ'in, it was expected that Aḥmed and his family would come, or send, to pay their respects to him, but Aḥmed would neither go himself nor would he

---

1) "Passions" in these passages represents the word 'ʾAhwâ' found in the name Ahlu'l-ʾAhwâ, so that the passages must be taken as condemning rationalism in theological matters.

Visit of Yaḥya ibn Khaḳân to Aḥmed.

allow Ṣâliḥ to go, for fear he should call attention to himself. The result of this was that the next day Yaḥya ibn Khaḳân came with a great retinue to visit Aḥmed, bringing him greeting and many friendly enquiries from the Khalif, who, at the same time, besought the prayers of the Imâm. These last Aḥmed assured Yaḥya were offered up every day for his master. Yaḥya then offered him a thousand dinârs for distribution among the poor. These, however, Aḥmed would not accept, pleading exemption, as he did on other occasions, on the ground that the Khalif had agreed to excuse him from obligation to do anything that might be distasteful to him. The money was finally given to Aḥmed's sons.

Invitation from Moḥammed ibn Abdallah ibn Ṭâhir.

On another occasion, Moḥammed ibn Abdallah ibn Ṭâhir besought Aḥmed to pay him a visit and strongly urged his request. This invitation, however, Aḥmed also declined, offering as an excuse the Khalif's dispensation. After these incidents he took upon himself a rigid fast, abstaining from all fat and, apparently, from meat, for the record states that *before* this time he had been provided with a dirhem's worth of meat, from which he ate for a month![1])

---

1) Abû Nu'aim, 155*a*, قال ابو الفضل وقدم المتوكل فنزل الشماسيّة يريد المدائن فقال لى ابى يا صالح احبُّ ان لا تذهب اليهم ولا تُنَبِّهَ [Cod. without points] علىّ فلما كان بعد يوم وانا قاعد خارجا وكان يومُ مَطَرٍ اذا يحيى بن خاقان قد جآء والمَمْطَر [Cod. المطر] عليه فى موكب عظيم فقال سُبحان الله لم تصر الينا حتى تُبلِغ امير المومنين السلام عن شيخك حتّى وجّه بى ثم نزل خارج الزقاق فجهدت به ان يدخل على الدابة فلم يفعل فجعل يخوض المطر فلما صار الى الباب نزع جُرموقه وكان على خفه ودخل وابى فى الزاوية* قاعد عليه كسآء مربع وعمامة والستر الذى على الباب خَيش فسلم

Aḥmed's Sickness and Death. In the course of events we have been brought now to the year 241 A. H. On the first day of Rabîʿ I of this year [1]), Aḥmed was taken with a

---

عليه وقبّل جبهته وسائله عن حاله وقال امير المومنين يقرئك السلام
ويقول كيف انت فى نفسك وكيف حالك وقد آنست بقربك
وَيَسئَلك ان تدعو له فقال ما ياتى علىّ يوم الا وانا ادعو له ثم قال
قد وجه معى الف دينار لك تفرقها على اهل الحاجة فقال له يابا
زكريّاء انا فى البيت منقطع عن الناس وقد اعفانى من كل ما اكرّه
وهذا مما اكره فقال يابا عبد الله الخلفاء لا يحتملون هذا فقال يابا
زكرياء تَلَطَّف فى ذلك فدعا له ثم قام فلما صار الى الدّار رجع وقال
هكذا لَو وَجَّه اليك بعضُ اخوانك كنتَ تفعل قال نعم فلما صِرْنا الى
الدهليز قال قد امرنى امير المومنين ان ادفعها اليك وتفرقها فقلت
تَكُونُ عندك الى ان تمضى هذه الايام، قال ابو الفضل وقد كان وجه
محمد بن عبد الله بن طاهر الى ابى فى وقت قدومه مع العسكر
احب ان تصير [Cod. تصبّر] الىّ وتعلمنى اليوم الذى تعزم عليه حتى
لا يَكُونَ عندى احد فوجّه اليه انا رجل لم اخالط السلطان
وقَد اعفانى امير المومنين مما أكره وهذا مما اكرَه فجهد ان يصير
اليه فابى وكان قَد ادمن الصوم لما قَدم وجَعل لا ياكل الدّسم
وكان قَبلَ ذلك يُشْتَرَى له لحم بدرهم وَياكل منه شَهرا فترك اكل الشحم
وادامَ الصوم والعمل فتَوهّمت انه كان قد جعل على نفسه ان سَلِم
ان يفعل ذلك وكان حُمل الى المتوكل سنة سبع وثلاثين ومائتين ثم
مَكث الى سنة احدى واربعين وكان قلّ يوم يمضى الا ورَسُول المتوكل
ياتيه

Moḥammed ibn Abdallah ibn Ṭâhir came from Khorasân, and was appointed over ʿIrâḳ in 237 A. H. Abu'l-Maḥ. I, 719.

1) The sources now used are the following extracts; al-Maḳrîzî, p. 15,
فصل فى ذكر مرضه ووفاته قال صالح لما كان فى اول يوم من شهر ربيع

fever attended with difficulty in breathing, and became so weak that his limbs would not support him. A physician came to see him, and prescribed for his sickness roast

---

الاول سنة احدى واربعين ومائتين حُمّ ابى فدخلت عليه وهو محموم فتنفس نفسا شديدا فقلت على ما افطرت البارحة فقال على ماء باقلا ثم اراد القيام فقال خذ بيدى فاخذت بيده فلما صار الى الخلا ضعفت رجلاه حتى توكا علىّ وكان يختلف اليه غيرُ متطبب كلهم مسلمون فوصف له متطبب قرعة تشوى ويُسقى ماءها فقال يا صالح قلت لبيك قال لا تشوى فى منزلك ولا فى منزل عبد الله اخيك وأتَى الفتح بن سَهل وعلى بن الجَعْد فحجبتهما وكثر الناسُ قال فاىّ شىء ترى قلت تاذن لهم فيدعون لك فاذنّا لهم فجعلوا يدخلون عليه افواجا حتى تمتلئَ الدار وكثر الناس وامتلأ الشارع واغلقنا باب الزقاق وجاء رجل من جيراننا قد خَضَبَ فقال انى لارى الرجل يُحيى شيئا من السنّة فأفرح به فجعل الرجل يدعو له فيقول ابى ولجميع المسلمين ثم قال لى اقبض من السكّان دراهم واشتر تمرًا وكفّر عنى كفارة يمين فاشتريت وكفّرت واخبرته فقال الحمد لله قلت وزاد الدينورى فى كتاب المجالسة ان الامام احمد قال فانى حنثت فى دهرى فى يمين واحدة ثم قال لى أحضِر الوصية واقراها وكان كتبها قبل ذلك فقراتها فاقرّها على ما هى عليه . . . .

قال واشتدت به العلة يوم الخميس فلما كان يوم الجمعة اجتمع الناس حتى ملئوا السّكك والشوارع قال حنبل وكان عنده ثلاث شعرات من شعر النبى صلعم فاوصى عند موته ان يجعل على لسانه شعرة وعلى كل عين شعرة ففعل به ذلك عند موته قال ولده عبد الله قال لى ابى فى مرضه الذى توفى فيه اخرِج لى كتاب عبد الله بن ادريس فاخرجت الكتاب فقال لى اخرج احاديث ليث بن ابى سُليم

pumpkin, with the liquor of the pumpkin to be taken as a drink. Aḥmed asked particularly that this might not be prepared in the houses of either of his sons. As soon as it was learned that he was sick, people began to come in crowds to visit him, until it became necessary to close the door of the street; and the governor, hearing of the crowds,

---

فاخرجتها فقال لى اقرا علىّ حديث [Cod. repeats حديث] ليث قلت لطلحة ان طاوسًا كان يكره الانين فى المرض فما سُمع له انين حتى مات رحمه الله فقرات ذلك على ابى فما سمعته أَنَّ فى مرضه الى ان توفى . . . . وسُئِل عبد الله هل عقل ابوك عند الموت المعاينة قال نعم كنا نوضئه [Cod. نوصيه] فجعل يشير بيده فقال لى صالح اىّ شىء يقول فقلت هو يقول خلِلوا اصابعى فخللنا اصابعه ثم ترك الاشارة فمات من ساعته تغمده الله برحمته وذلك لاثنتى عشرة ليلة خلت من ربيع الاول سنة احدى واربعين ومائتين وهو ابن سبع وسبعين سنة فصل فى غسله وتكفينه والصلاة عليه وعدد مَن اسلم يوم موته قال ولده صالح لما توفى ابى كان المتوكل غائبا فوجّه الامير ابن طاهر حاجبه ومعه غلامان معهما مناديل فيها ثياب وطِيب وقالوا الامير * يقرئك السلام ويقول لك قد فعلتُ ما لو كان امير المومنين حاضرا لَفعله فقلت له اقرئه منى السلام وقل له ان امير المومنين قد كان اعفاه فى حياته مما كان يَكره ولا أُحب ان اتبعه بعد موته بما كان يكرهه فى حياته فعاد وقال يكون شعارَه ولا يكون دِثاره فاعَدت عليه مثل ذلك ورَددته عليه وكفّناه فى ثلاث لفائف قال المروزى لما اردت ان اغسله جاء بنو هاشم واجتمع فى الدار خلق كثير فادخلته البيت وغطيته بثوب وارخيت السِتر حتى فرغت من امره فلما اردت تكفينه غلبَنا عليه بنو هاشم واخذوا فى البكاء عليه

consideratcly placed guards before the street door, while the family also placed guards before the door of the house. Only his physicians and such as he himself desired to see were then admitted. Among those who were thus allowed to see him was a neighbor, an elderly man with dyed hair and beard, on seeing whom Aḥmed became greatly excited, and called the attention of those about him to this man as one ‘who

---

وجعل اولادهم ينكبّون عليه ويقبلونه قال صالح وارسل الىّ ابن طاهر يقول مَن يصلى على ابيك قلت انا فلما صرْنا الى الصحراء وجدْنا ابن طاهر فخَطا الينا خطوات وعَزّانا فلما وُضع السرير تقدمت للصلاة فجاءنى ابن طالوت ومحمد بن نصر وقبضا على يدىّ وقالا الاميرُ فمانَعْتهم فغلبوا علىّ وصَلى ولم يعلم اكثر الناس بتقدمه فلما كان من الغد وعلموا بذلك صاروا ياتون القبر افواجا فيصلون عليه ومكثوا على ذلك اياما قال ولده عبد الله وكُنا نحن والهاشميون صلينا عليه داخل الدار قال الخلال سمعت عبد الوهاب الورّاق يقول ما بلغنا انّ جمعا كان فى الجاهلية والاسلام مثله حتى ان المواضع التى وقف الناس فيها مُسحت وحُزرت فاذا هى نحو من الف الف وحزرنا على السور نحوًا من ستين الف امراة وقال ابو زرعة بلغنى ان المتوكل امَر ان يمسح الموضع الذى وقف الناسُ فيه للصلاة على احمد بن حنبل فبلغ مقام الفى الف وخمس مائة الف وفتح الناس ابواب المنازل فى الشوارع والبيوت والدروب وصاروا ينادُون من اراد الوضوء وقال احمد بن الحسن المقانعى كنت ببغداد وانا فى بستان لصديق لى فاذا بشيخ وشابّ وعليهما طمران فسلمت عليهما وقلت اراكما من غير هذا البلد قالا نعم نحن من جبل اللُكام [اللِكام .Cod] حضرنا جنازة احمد بن حنبل وما بقى احد من الاولياء

was keeping alive the good rule of the Prophet'. Daily reports of the sick man's condition were now sent from Baghdâd to the Khalif at the camp. These were never very encouraging, however, as Aḥmed sank gradually day by day until he died. He seems to have borne his sickness with great fortitude, in which he was supported by a tradition of Ṭâûs,

---

لا حضرها وقال عبد الوهاب الوراق اظهر الناس فى جنازة احمد بن حنبل السنة والطعن على اهل البدع قال جعفر بن محمد النسوى شهدت الناس فى جنازة احمد بن حنبل يلعنون بشرا المريسى والكرابيسى باصوات عالية واقام الناس اياما يزدحمون على القبر حتى قال ابو الحسن التميمى مكثت اياما رجاء ان اصل الى القبر فلم اصل اليه الا بعد اسبوع

Al-Subkî, p. 134 f. قال المروزى رضى الله عنه مرض ابو عبد الله ليلة الاربعاء لليلتين خلتا من ربيع الاول ومرض تسعة ايام وكان ربما اذن للناس فيدخلون عليه افواجا يسلمون عليه ويرد عليهم وتسامع الناس وكثروا وسمع السلطان بكثرة الناس فوكل ببابه وبباب الزقاق الرابطة واصحاب الاخبار ثم اغلق باب الزقاق فكان الناس فى الشوارع والمساجد حتى تعطل بعض الباعة وحيل بينهم وبين البيع والشراء وكان الرجل* اذا اراد ان يدخل اليه ربما تخلل من بعض الدور وطور الحالة ربما تسلق وجآء اصحاب الاخبار فقعدوا على الابواب وجاء حاجب ابن طاهر فقال ان الامير يقرئك السلام وهو يشتهى ان يراك فقال هذا مما اكره وامير المومنين اعفانى مما اكره واصحاب الخبر يكتبون بخبره الى العسكر والبرد تختلف كل يوم وجآء بنو هاشم فدخلوا عليه وجعلوا يبكون عليه وجآء قوم من القضاة وغيرهم فلم يوذن لهم ودخل عليه شيخ فقال اذكر وقوفك بين يدى

who is reported to have 'disliked groaning in sickness', on the ground that it was tantamount to complaining against God. Aḥmed, therefore, was never heard to groan, except on the day in which he died. Two or three days before his death, he enquired for his purse, and asked his son Ṣâliḥ to look what was in it. Ṣâliḥ did so and found a solitary

---

الله فشهق ابو عبد الله وسالت الدموع على خديه فلما كان قبل وفاته بيوم او يومين قال ادعوا لى الصبيان بلسانٍ ثقيل فجعلوا ينضمون اليه وجعل يشمهم ويمسح بيده على رؤسهم وعينه تدمع وادخلت الطشت تحته فرايت بوله دمًا عبيطا ليس فيه بول فقلت للطبيب فقال هذا رجل قد فتت الحزن والغم جوفه . . . .

. . . . قال موسى بن هرون الحافظ يقال ان احمد لما مات مسحت الارض المبسوطة التى وقف الناس للصلاة عليها فحصر مقادير الناس بالمساحة ستمائة الف واكثر سوى ما كان فى الاطراف والاماكن المتفرقة قلت وقيل فى عدد المصلين عليه كثير قيل كانوا الف الف وثلاثمائة الف سوى من كان فى السُّفن فى الماء كذا رواه خشنار بن سعيد وقال ابن ابى حاتم سمعت ابا زرعة يقول بلغنى ان المتوكل امر ان يمسح الموضع الذى وقف عليه الناس حيث صُلّىَ على احمد فبلغ المقام الفى الف وخمسمائة وعن الوركانى وهو رجل كان يسكن الى جوار الامام احمد قال اسلم يوم مات احمد من اليهود والنصارى والمجوس عشرون الفا وفى لفظ عشرة الاف قال شيخنا الذهبى وهى حكاية منكرة تفرد بها الوركانى والراوى عنه قال والعقل يحيل ان يقع مثل هذا الحادث فى بغداد ولا يرويه جماعة تتوفر دواعيهم على نقل ما هو دونه بكثير وكيف يقع مثل هذا الامر ولا يذكره المروزى ولا صالح بن احمد

dirhem. This his father directed him to use, together with some of the rent to be collected from the lodgers in his house, in buying dates to discharge an oath of almsgiving which he had taken upon himself. Ṣâliḥ carried out the order he had received, and returned to his father one-third of a dirhem, on receiving which Aḥmed rejoiced at the prospect of dying as poor as he had lived.

The duration of his sickness was not long. The physician declared that grief and the hard ascetic character of his life had ruptured the internal organs of his body and could give the family little hope of his recovery. A characteristic incident occurred when he was being washed preparatory to the performance of the last devotions in which he took part. He was unable to speak, but, strong in the ruling passion of scrupulousness in the law, he made a sign that his sons who were washing him should wash *between* his fingers as well as on the back and front of them. When this was done, it is said that he rested quietly until he passed away. His prayers he performed to the very last, his sons assisting him in the rakᶜas. One of his last charges was that three hairs of the Prophet which he had in his possession should at his death be placed, one on each eye and one on his lips, and this was actually done [1]). So he died. The date of the

---

ولا عبد الله ولا حنبل الذين حكوا من اخبار ابى عبد الله جزئيّات كثيرة قال قالوا فوالله لو اسلم يوم موته عشرة انفس لكان عظيما ينبغى ان يرويه نحو من عشرة انفس

Abû Nuᶜaim, 155 *a*, وكنتُ انام بالليل الى جَنبه فاذا اراد حاجَةً حرّكنى فاناوله وجعل يُحرك لِسانه ولم يَئنّ الا فى الليلة التى توفى فيها ولم يَزل يُصلى قائما أُمسكه فيركع ويَسجد وارفعه فى ركوعه واجتمعَتْ عليه اوجَاعُ الحُصر وغير ذلك ولم يزل عقله ثابتا فلما كان يوم الجمعة لاثنتى عشرة ليلة خلت من شهر ربيع الاول لساعتَين من النهار توفى رحمة الله عليه ومغفرته ورضوانه ،

1) cf. Goldziher. Moh. Stud. II, 358 and note 5.

event was Friday, the twelfth of Rabî^{c} I, 241 A. H., his age being a few days, or it may be hours, more or less than seventy-seven years.

His Funeral. There was the most wonderful scene of grief all over the city of Baghdâd, and even in distant places, when the news of his death became known. The scene at the funeral, on the afternoon of the day of his death, was one such as must have been seldom witnessed anywhere. The estimates of the number of those who attended are very discrepant. Some say 600,000 were present on the spot where the prayers were held over him; others say 2,500,000, and other figures fall between these two [1]). It is said that there were 10,000, and some say even 20,000, converts to Islâm from the other religions on the occasion of Aḥmed's death; but inasmuch as the family and others specially interested in him knew nothing of any such number, al-Subkî's teacher Dhahabî thought such figures to be absurd and that ten converts would be nearer the truth. The Emîr Ibn Ṭâhir wished to furnish the burial suit of Aḥmed but Ṣâliḥ refused to accept it, as he knew that his father when living would have been unwilling to accept any gift from the Emîr. The filial respect of Ṣâliḥ for his dead father's wishes in regard to receiving gifts or attentions from persons of state now took very decided form. It was only by main force that his friends withheld him from displacing Ibn Ṭâhir in the official conduct of the prayers at the funeral [2]). Indeed, it was not known by the people that Ibn Ṭâhir had prayed over Aḥmed, until the day after he was buried. When they knew they flocked in crowds to his grave in the cemetery of the Bâb-Ḥarb [3]); so much so, that one man who attended the funeral, declared that it was a week before he was able to come near the tomb. His own family and the Hâshimites also conducted prayers for him inside their own quarters on the evening of the day of his death [4]). In the time of Ibn Challikân the

1) cf. Ibn Chall. N°. 19.
2) Maçoudî VII, 229.
3) cf. Ibn Chall. N°. 19.
4) Ibn Chall. N°. 19.

tomb of Aḥmed in the cemetery of the Bâb-Ḥarb was known far and wide and was much visited [1]). At a later time, the raised work of the tomb was destroyed and the grave made level with the surface of the ground because of the undue reverence which was being shewn to it [2]).

His Biographers. Among those who are said to have written of the Manâḳib of Aḥmed are Abu'l-Ḥasan ibn al-Munâdî [3]), the Ḥâfiẓ al-Manda [4]), al-Baihaḳî [5]), Abû Ismâ'îl al-Anṣârî, the Faḳîh Abû 'Alî ibn al-Bannâ, commentator of al-Khurkî, the Ḥâfiẓ Ibn Nâṣir, the Ḥâfiẓ Abu'l-Faraj ibn al-Jauzî [6]), Abd al-Raḥmân ibn Abî Hâtim al-Râzî and al-Ḥasan ibn Moḥammed al-Khallâl [7]) [8]).

IV.

His Family. The immediate descendants of Aḥmed ibn Ḥanbal [9]), except his two sons Ṣâliḥ and Abdallah, both of whom

---

1) Ibn Chall. N°. 19; vid. also al-Nawawî, p. 146.

2) Goldziher, Moh. Stud. I, 257.

3) al-Fihrist I, 38 f.; Dhahabî Ṭabaḳât 11, N°. 55.

4) Dhahabî, Ṭabaḳât 13, N°. 29.

5) Ibn Chall. N°. 27; Dhahabî Ṭabaḳât 14, N°. 13.

6) In his book الجرح والتعديل, Chapter on the Manâḳib of Aḥmed ibn Ḥanbal. v. al-Nawawî Biog. Dict. 143; cf. on Ibn al-Jauzî, Goldziher, Moh. Stud. II, 186 and note 2.

7) Dhahabî, Ṭabaḳât 13, N°. 68. The others I have not been able to trace in the authorities at command.

8) al-Maḳrîzî, p. 18, وقد افرد جماعة من الائمة مناقبه بالتصنيف كالامام ابى حسن بن المنادى والحافظ ابن منده والبيهقى وشيخ الاسلام الانصارى والفقيه ابى على بن البنّا شارح الخُرقى والحافظ ابن ناصر والحافظ ابى الفرج بن الجوزى وعبد الرحمن بن ابى حاتم الرازى والحسن بن محمد الخلال وغيرهم رضى الله عنهم اجمعين انتهى

9) al-Maḳrîzî, p. 2, واما اولاده فاكبرهم صالح وكنيته ابو الفضل وُلد

were men of eminence, were not remarkable in their time. His eldest son was Ṣâliḥ, surnamed Abu'l Faḍl, who was born in the year 203. He related Tradition from his father and from Abu'l Walîd al-Ṭayâlisî and ʿAlî ibn al-Madînî, and had as pupils his own son Zuhair, who died in 303, al-Baghawî and Moḥammed ibn Makhlad. Ṣâliḥ occupied the office of Ḳâḍî of Ispahân. His mother was ʿAbbâsa bint al-Faḍl. His death occurred in the year 265 1). The second son was Abdallah Abû Abd al-Raḥmân 2). He studied a great deal with his father, and studied, also, with Abd al-Aʿlâ ibn Ḥammâd, Yaḥya ibn Maʿîn, Abû Bekr ibn Abî Shaiba, and many others. He was a man thoroughly conversant with

---

سنة ثلاث ومائتين وروى عن ابيه وابى الوليد الطيالسى وعلىّ بن المدينى وروَى عنه ابنه زُهير والبغوى ومحمد بن مخلد وولى قضاء اصبهان وهو من زوجته عبّاسة بنت الفضل توفى سنة خمس وستين ومائتين وعبد الله وكنيته ابو عبد الرحمن سمع من ابيه واكثر عنه ومن عبد الاعلى بن حماد ويحيى بن معين ومِن ابى بكر بن ابى شيبة وخلق كثير قال الذهبى كان اماما خبيرا بالحديث وعِلله مقدّما فيه ولما مرض قال ادفنونى بالقطيعة فقيل لهُ الا تُدفن عند ابيك يعنى بمقبرة باب حرب فقال صَحّ عندى ان بالقطيعة نبيا مدفونا ولَأن اكون فى جوار نبى احب الىّ مِن ان اكون فى جوار ابى وكانت وفاته فى سنة تسعين ومائتين وسِنّه سبع وسبعون سنة كأبيه وللامام احمد ولد اسمه سعِيد من سُرّية يقال لها [Cod. له] حِسْن ولِىَ قضاء الكوفة ولهُ منها ولدٌ اسمُه محمد واخَرُ اسمه الحَسَن ولهُ منها بنت اسمها زينب وله منها ولدان توءمان احدهما الحسن والاخرُ الحسين وماتا بالقرب مِن ولادتهما وله بنتٌ اسمها فاطمة والله اعلم

1) Ibn Chall. N°. 19, says 'Ramaḍân 266 A. H.'

2) Abu 'l-Maḥ. II, 136. cf. his relation to the Musnad of his father, p. 24.

Tradition and the arguments for it. The special distinction which he enjoyed, however, was that of being the greatest authority on the traditions of his father. It is related of him that, when he was on his death-bed, he asked to be buried in the quarter called commonly al-Ḥarbîya [or القطيعة = the quarter of the city or the plot of ground in which his house stood?]. Those present asked him if he would not rather be buried with his father in the cemetery at the Bâb-Ḥarb, but he said he preferred to be under the protection of a prophet whom he knew by trustworthy reports to have been buried in al-Ḥarbîya to being under the protection of his father. He died at the age of 77 in the year 290 A. H. [1]) By a concubine named Ḥisn Aḥmed had a third son, who was named Saᶜîd and who became in time Ḳâḍî of Kûfa. By the same mother he had, further, two sons Moḥammed and al-Ḥasan and a daughter Zainab, and, likewise, by the same mother, twin sons al-Ḥasan and al-Ḥusain, who died soon after their birth. Finally, he had another daughter whose name was Fâṭima. [2]) This is all that is known of his family.

Testimonies of Esteem. A few evidences of the esteem in which Aḥmed was held will assist us to place him in the position which he really occupied in the estimation of his own and of following generations. His pupil Abû Zurᶜa said he had never met with any one in whom learning (عِلْم), selfdenial, knowledge of the law and general knowledge (معرفة) were so combined as in his master [3]). This is one opinion out of a host of similar ones, all of which are ex-

---

1) Ibn Chall. N°. 19 says, '8th day remaining of Jumâdâ I, some say Jumâdâ II'.

2) cf. Abû Nuᶜaim, 153 *b*, قال ابو الفضل صالح ثم كُتِبَ لنا بشىء الى بادُورَيّا فبلغه فجآء الى الكوة التى فى الباب فقال يا صالح انظر ما كان للحسن وأُم على فاذهب به الخ The ʾUmm ᶜAlî here referred to may be the Zainab or Fâṭima named above.

3) Abû Nuᶜaim, 139 *a*, اخبرنا ابو بكر محمد بن احمد بن محمد

ceedingly fulsome in expression, but still afford us the substantial truth of his high worth in the view of the men among whom he moved. By many testimonies he is placed at the side of the greatest doctors of Islâm in the ages which had preceded him, — Sofyân al-Thaurî, Mâlik ibn Anas, Abd al-Raḥmân ibn Amr al-Auzâᶜî, al-Laith ibn Saᶜd and Ibn ᶜAbbâs. The regard in which Aḥmed ibn Ḥanbal was held is also seen in the way in which he is cited as giving an opinion on the doctors of his time; as, for example, by al-Nawawî, biographies of ᶜAlî ibn al-Madînî, Yazîd ibn Hârûn, Yaḥya ibn Saᶜîd al-Kaṭṭân, Yaḥya ibn Maᶜîn; also Ibn Challikân on Abû Thaur and Isḥâḳ ibn Râhawaih. Al-Dhahabî, too, in his Ṭabaḳât adduces Aḥmed's opinion in regard to the men of his time with great frequency and with evidence of much respect. It used to be held that, if Aḥmed discredited anybody, he could not fail to suffer for it in the eyes of people generally [1]). A noteworthy testimony is that of al-Ḥusain ibn ᶜAlî ibn Yazîd al-Karâbîsî, a man with whose theological views Aḥmed had little sympathy. He said that those who spoke evil of Aḥmed were

---

ثنا عبد الله بن محمد بن عبد الكريم قال سمعت ابا زرعة يقول ما رأتْ عينى مثلَ احمد بن حنبل فقلت له فى العلم فقال فى العلم والزهد والفقه والمعرفة وكلّ خير ما رأتْ عينى مثله

1) Abû Nuᶜaim, 140 *a*, قال (عمر بن الحسن القاضى) سمعت ابا يحيى الناقد يقول كنا عند ابراهيم بن عَرْعَرة فذكروا على بن عاصم فقال رجلٌ احمدُ بن حنبل يُضَعّفه فقال رجل وما يضرّه من ذاك اذا كان ثِقة فقال ابراهيمُ بن عَرْعَرة والله لو تكلم احمدُ بن حنبل فى عَلْقمة والاسود لضَرّهما The force of the passage is clear. For ᶜAlḳama and al-Aswad cf. Dhahabî علقمة بن قيس Ṭabaḳ. 2, 1; الاسود النخعى ib. 6; Abu'l-Maḥ. I, 280, l. 2.

like people who tried to kick over the mountain Abû Ḳubais with their feet [1]).

Aḥmed as a Faḳîh. As a faḳîh he bore a great reputation among his companions, as well as with others in his own generation and the generations following. The reputation of Aḥmed in Baghdâd at the time of Abû Jaʿfar Moḥammed ibn Jarîr al-Ṭabarî († 310 A. H.) is shewn by the anger of the Baghdâd people that al-Ṭabarî should have omitted reference to Aḥmed in his book upon 'the Faḳîhs and their distinctive doctrines'. His reason was that Aḥmed was no faḳîh but rather a traditionist [2]). The opinion was given out in his own day that he was a greater faḳîh than ʿAlî ibn al-Madînî [3]). One traditionist in speaking of Aḥmed's authority on the subject of Tradition said that when Aḥmed supported him in a tradition he was indifferent as to who might differ from him in relation to it [4]). He was credited with extraordinary power of discrimination in the judging of sound and unsound traditions [5]). The general impression that one gets from the biographical details which we have brought together in the present work, and from less important notices which could not with propriety be introduced into the narrative, is that Aḥmed's judgment on points of Fiḳh was seriously reached and often shrewd, but always shewed narrowness. His general reliance upon the Ḳorân and the Tradition cannot be discredited from a Muslim standpoint, and was a safer course, ewed from that point of view, than any setting aside of such idences in favor of individual judgment could have been [6]). it his principle of slavish literalness and his incorrigible ar- rariness in the interpretation of his evidences was that

1) Abû Nuʿaim, 141 a, يقول (الكرابيسى) مثل الذين يذكر احمد بن حنبل مثل قوم يجيئون الى ابى قبيس يريدون ان يهد بنعالهم

2) cf. Goldziher, Ẓahiriten, p. 4 (from Abu'l-Feda Ann. II, p. 344).

3) al-Nawawî, p. ۱۴۴.

4) al-Nawawî, p. ۱۴۴.

5) cf. p. 28.

6) cf. Houtsma, De Strijd etc. 95.

which vitiated his claim to direct men to sound and permanent positions in theology. Such was impossible with his method. Belief founded on the letter of any standard of faith will always be narrow, dogmatic and polemical. Life founded on the letter of any rule of conduct can be only hard and exclusive in character. Just but not genial; irreproachable, but unattractive — such is the life. Sincere and earnest and, with its own postulates, correct, but, still, wrong at its foundation and unsightly in its superstructure — such is the opinion.

We subjoin a few remarks about the traits of character and habits of life of Aḥmed ibn Ḥanbal, with a passing notice of his personal appearance. He was abstemious in the extreme, so much so, in fact, that his life might be termed a continuous fast. He is reported never to have bought a pomegranate, quince or any other kind of fruit, unless it might be a melon or grapes, which he ate with bread. In eating his bread he frequently dispensed with the use of vinegar. It was often the case that his sons bought things which they deemed permissible or even necessary, but which were luxuries in his eyes; and to escape in such a case his strictures they hid the things from him altogether [1]). It is said that when he appeared before Isḥâḳ ibn Ibrâhîm after his long imprisonment in 219 A. H., Isḥâḳ looked in the little basket which Aḥmed had with him and found his store of food to consist of two pieces of bread, a piece of cucumber and some salt [2]).

Habits of Life.

He had a profound dislike to the receiving of money assistance from others, and took very little pains to secure a

1) al-Nawawî, p. ١٤٥.

2) al-Maḳrîzî, p. 5, بعث اسحاق بن ابراهيم فاخذ الزنبيل الذى فيه افطار ابى عبد الله فنظر اليه فاذا فيه رغيفان وشىء من قثاء وملح فعجب اسحاق من ذلك

money for himself. His happiest moments were those when he was left without a coin in his purse [1]). His needs were few and his expenses next to nothing [2]). We have had in the course of the narrative abundant illustration of his selfdenial and his preference for poverty, and, were it desirable to do so, much more of the same kind of incident could be furnished.

Characteristics. His demeanor was that of a man abstracted from the common concerns of life, though in questions of learning he always shewed the liveliest interest [3]). He was a man of gentle nature, but capable of being roused to vehemence at the sight of injustice or wrong done to men or of impiety shewn toward God [4]). That he was looked upon as a scrupulously just man, even among those who were not Muslims, is shewn in many ways. One incident may be mentioned. It is related that two Magian women had a dispute about an inheritance before a Muslim Ḳâḍî, and when judgment had been rendered, the woman against whom the judge had decided said to him, 'If thou hast decided against me according to the decision of Aḥmed ibn Ḥanbal, I am content; if not, I will not acquiesce in it'. The narrator of the story thought it such a strong testimony to Aḥmed's character that he told it far and near to those whom he met [5]). Aḥmed's aversion toward lightness,

---

1) al-Nawawî, p. ١٤٥.

2) al-Nawawî, ١٤٤, cf. pp. 141, 164.

3) Abû Nuᶜaim, 138 *b*, حدثنا سليمان بن احمد ثنا احمد بن محمد القاضى قال سمعت ابا داود السجستانى يقول لقيت مائتين من مشايخ العلم فما رايت مثل احمد بن حنبل لم يكُن يخوض فى شىء مما يخوض فيه الناس من امر الدنيا فإذا ذُكِرَ العِلم تكلَّم

4) cf. pp. 73, 150.

5) Abû Nuᶜaim, 141 *a*, حدثنا ابى ثنا ابو الحسن ثنا عبد الله بن احمد بن حنبل حدثنى نوح بن حبيب القُومسى قال كان عندنا

particularly in men of learning, was pronounced. On a certain occasion Yazîd ibn Hârûn was indulging in pleasant badinage with his amanuensis, when some one in the room gave a slight cough. Yazîd enquired who it might be that had given the apparent sign of disapproval, and, on being told that it was Aḥmed, he smote his forehead, and, turning to those nearest to him, asked them reproachfully why they had not told him of Aḥmed's presence that he might have observed becoming gravity before him [1]).

People used to say that Aḥmed himself was a touchstone or Miḥna. A versifier, Ibn A^{c}yan, has the lines, 'Ibn Ḥanbal is a safe test (Miḥna): By the love borne to Aḥmed the pious man is known; But when one is seen who defames him, Then be sure that his true character will be disclosed' [2]).

يعنى بلدهم امرأتان مَجوسيّتان فاختصمتا [Cod. فاختصما] فى مواريث
لهن الى رجل من المسلمين فقضى لواحدة منهنّ على الاخرى
فقالت له ان كنتَ قضيتَ علىّ بقضاء احمد بن حنبل رضيتُ
والّا فانى لا ارضى قال نوح فحدثت به اهلَ طرسُوس والشامات

1) Abû Nu^{c}aim, 140 *a*, حدثنا سليمان بن احمد ثنا الحسن بن
على المعمرى قال سمعت خلف بنَ سالم يقول قل كنّا فى مجلس يزيدَ
ابن هرون فمَزَح يزيد مع مُستمليه فتنَحْنح احمد بن حنبل وكان
فى المجلس فقال يزيد من المتنَحْنح فقيل له احمد بن حنبل فضرب
يزيدُ بيده على جَبينه وقال الّا اعلمتونى انّ احمد هاهنا حتى
لا امْزح

2) al-Subkî, p. 134, قال (ابو جعفر محمد بن دينار الموصلى)
انشدنى ابن اعين فى الامام احمد بن حنبل رضى الله عنه

'اضحى ابن حنبل محنةً مأمونةً
'وبِحُبّ احمد يعرف المُتنَسّك

Religious Character. An indication of Aḥmed's character from the religious point of view is found in the following verses, which are said to be of his composition and furnish the only discoverable trace of his poetic talent. 'Whenever thou art alone at any time, do not say I am alone, but say over me is a Watcher; And do not think that God is indifferent to what has passed by, and that what thou hidest from him is out of his sight. We give ourselves no care until sins follow upon the track of sins; But then! would that God would grant us repentance, and we would repent! [1])

It is said that he was wont to pray every day 300 rakᶜas, and that, even after he was scourged and his bodily weakness was extreme, he reached the number of 150 daily. He completed a recitation of the Ḳorân once in every seven days. It was his custom at night after the last prayer of the day, to sleep for a short time, and then to arise and pray formal or extemporized prayers until the morning [2]).

'واذا رايتَ لاحمد متنقصًا

'فاعلم بان ستوره سَتُهَتَّك

1) Abû Nuᶜaim, 155 *a*, حدثنا ابو على عيسى بن محمد الخريجى [Cod. الجرىحى] ثنا احمد بن يحيى ثَعْلَب النَحوى قال كنت احب ان ارى احمد بن حنبل فدخلت عليه فقال لى فيم تنظر فقلت له فى النحو والعربية والشعر فانشدنى احمد بن حنبل

'اذاما خلوتَ الدهر يوما فلا تَقُل، خَلوتُ ولكن قُل علىَّ رَقيبُ،

ولا تَحسبنَّ الله يُغفِل مَا مَضَى، وأنَّ الذى تُخفِي عليه يغيبُ،

'لَهَونَا عن الايام حتى تَتابَعَتْ، ذُنوب على اثارهن ذنوبُ،

'فيَا لَيْتَ أنّ الله يَغفِر مَا مضى، ويأذَن لنا فى توبة فنَتُوبُ،

2) Abû Nuᶜaim, 143 *a* ., حدثنا سليمان بن احمد ثنا عبد الله ابن احمد بن حنبل قال كان ابى يصلى فى كل يوم وليلة ثلثمائة

When at home in Baghdâd he is said to have perseveringly kept to his house, so that none ever saw him, unless it were at public worship, at a funeral, or visiting the sick [1]). He was scrupulous in his adherence to Tradition and to the ritual observances. We have already cited the incident of the ritual ablutions performed on him by his sons just before his death, when, though unable to speak, he made signs that they should wash between, as well as upon the front and back of his fingers [2]).

Personal Appearance. In personal appearance, Aḥmed was of beautiful countenance and of medium height. He used to dye his hair and beard with henna and katam, but not a

---

ركعة فلما مرِض من تِلك الاسواط اضْعَفَتْه* وكان يصلى فى كل يوم وليلة مائة وخمسين ركعة وقد كان قرب من الثمانين، حدثنا سليمان بن احمد ثنا عبد الله بن احمد بن حنبل قال كان ابى يَقرأ فى كل يوم سُبعا يختم فى كل سبعة ايام وكانت له خَتْمَة فى كل سبع ليال سِوَى صلاة النهار وكان ساعةَ يُصَلّى عشآء الاخرة ينام نومة خفيفة ثم يقوم الى الصباح يصلى ويدعو

1) Abû Nuʿaim, 143 *b*, قال عبد الله وكان ابى اصبر الناس على الوحدة لم يره احد الا فى مسجد او حضور جنازة او عيادة مريض وكان يكره المشى فى الاسواق، . . . . حدثنا ابى ثنا احمد ثنا عبد الله بن احمد بن حنبل قال خرج ابى الى طرسوس ماشيا وخرج الى اليمن ماشيا وحج خمس حجج ثلاثا منها ماشيا ولا يمكن لاحد ان يقول راى ابى* فى هذه النواحى يوما الا اذا خرج الى الجمعة وكان اصبر الناس على الوحدة وبِشْر رحمه الله فيما كان فيه لم يكن يصبر على الوحدة فكان يخرج الى ذا ساعة والى ذا ساعة

2) vid. p. 171.

deep red, for in his beard were seen black hairs. He began the practice of dyeing his hair and beard when in his sixty-third year, and then wholly out of regard for the practice of the Prophet [1]).

V.

His Views. Aḥmed ibn Ḥanbal was a man whose peculiar temperament disposed him not only to the kind of life which he lived — intense, ascetic, and fierce in its protest against liberalism, — but also to those views and beliefs which were, to a certain extent, the springs of such a life [2]). His beliefs were not entirely free from adjustment to the circumstances of his age, but the measure of accommodation was the least that could be made. In fact, look where we will in Aḥmed's life, and the elements of concession and compromise are never found to be present by his own wish, and, when found, their degree is the minimum possible.

Sources. We propose to generalize on the basis of the narrative already furnished and the few other sources of information accessible, in order to reach, if we can, a fair notion of the leading theological opinions or principles by which Aḥmed ibn Ḥanbal directed his life. His testament, which has been given in the foregoing pages [3]), is a very colorless document, and affords no view of his characteristic beliefs. The confession it contains comprises stock phrases, which might come from a Muslim of any kind or character. The letter to ʿObaidallah ibn Yaḥya, in an-

1) Ibn Chall. N°. 19; Abû Nuʿaim, 138 *b*, قال عبد الله وخضب ابى راسَه ولِحيتَه بالحنّاء والكَتم وهو ابن ثلاث وستّين سنة

2) Abû Nuʿaim, 153 *b*, فدخلتُ اليه فاكبَبْتُ عليه وقلت له يا ابةِ تُدخِلُ على نفسك الغَم فقال يابنى ياتينى ما لا املكه

3) p. 147.

swer to the Khalif's enquiry relative to the Ḳorân, has so much that is characteristic that we may credit it with representing accurately Aḥmed's belief [1]). The conversation on the Korân with Isḥâḳ ibn Ibrâhîm is fully in the spirit of Aḥmed's life, and lends us an interesting view of his faith as touching the Ḳorân [2]). The trials before Isḥâḳ ibn Ibrâhîm and al-Muᶜtaṣim, with the conversations connected with them, furnish much light on Aḥmed's opinions and the individual element which they contain [3]).

The Ḳorân. First, Aḥmed ibn Ḥanbal's doctrine of the Ḳorân [4]). The Ḳorân he asserted to be the Word of God, by which he meant the expression of God's Knowledge, as such expression must be thought to be eternally present to God's Being. Or, if we must modify this at all, it would be to say, that, as long as there has been present to God that which is objective to Himself, so long has there been a Word of God as the expression of his Knowledge. Before the Objective came into existence, the Word of God was potential in Him and not actual. This gives us the Eternity of the Word of God. Then, as the Divine Knowledge cannot be conceived to be without the eternal adjunct of symbolic expression, and as speech is to be looked upon as a faculty expressing itself in energy and not a creation, the Word of God is not only eternal but uncreated as well. It may be objected that *a* Word of God is not the point in question, but the Ḳorân, *the* Word of God as known to men. Be it noted, however, that the distinction between the written or otherwise presented Ḳorân and the heavenly and essential Word of God is clearly drawn [5]). This, too, is

---

1) p. 155. 2) p. 139. 3) p. 93 ff.

4) p. 101. cf. Goldziher, Ẓahiriten, p. 138 ff. The Word of God was said by some of the orthodox to be an attribute of God, Houtsma, De Strijd etc. 103 f. cf. Shahrastânî. All the evidence at command, however, shews that Aḥmed ibn Ḥanbal's belief was as I have set it forth.

5) cf. von Kremer, Herrsch. Ideen d. Isl. 227; Steiner, Die Muᶜtaziliten, 38 f. The accounts given of the orthodox view as to the Ḳorân differ from that which I have inferred Aḥmed ibn Ḥanbal to have held. Nor does he

not drawn for the purposes of mere controversy, but represents, as we take it, a belief in the difference of extent between the visible and invisible Word of God. All the words spoken to Moses are the Word of God [1]); certainly, not as belonging to the visible Ḳorân, but as belonging to the one eternal Word of God. All God's words to Moḥammed and to the prophets are the Word of God; all those which were spoken to ʿIsâ ibn Maryam are equally the Word of God. And, in controversy, the words spoken to these various persons are used to prove the uncreated and eternal nature of the *visible* Ḳorân, though they form no part of the Book. Why? Because they, with the substance of the Ḳorân, are the revelations of the Eternal Word, not revelations coextensive with it but partial revelations. This leads to the doctrine that the Word of God is one as well as eternal and uncreated [2]). It could not be one if the visible words were taken in evidence, but regarded as a faculty of expression, latent or energizing, belonging to a Being, we

---

seem to have been alone in his idea of the Ḳorân, but had both among the learned and unlearned a large number who sympathized with his opinions. Most of those who have expounded the orthodox view make the distinction between the visible and invisible *Ḳorân* and go no further, thus making the Book as known to men the equivalent of that preserved in Heaven. The great distinction to be drawn is between the visible *Ḳorân* and the invisible *Word of God*, the latter being not an equivalent but infinitely more extensive than the former. The connection with the doctrine of the Logos as held by Syrian Christians (Houtsma 101, note 1) confirms the presentation of the Ḳorân doctrine which is given in the text. The manifestation of the Logos in Jesus Christ is to be set over against the Heavenly and Uncreated Logos which is in the bosom of the Father. As for the 'Well-guarded Table' of the Ḳorân, Sura 85, 22, (cf. Steiner 39 and note 5, also in the preceding account in these pages, p. 67) this, it is true, was an archetype of the visible Ḳorân kept in Heaven, but, still, even this celestial archetype was not coextensive with the eternal and uncreated Word of God of which it was one manifestation. We thus think that the orthodox in Aḥmed's day held to three elements in their doctrine of the Ḳorân: 1st, the Visible Ḳorân; 2nd, the Heavenly Ḳorân; 3rd, the Eternal Word of God.

1) p. 38.

2) cf. Goldziher, Ẓahiriten, p. 138 ff.; Houtsma, De Strijd etc. 129.

may see how the Word of God came to be looked upon as a continuous unity; or, as we may better express a fact in relation to a Being not knowing any succession of time, as a unity in an eternal present. Such a Word of God, considered both as to its thoughts and words, is necessarily without fault and infallible [1]). The Word of God is, thus, Eternal, Uncreated, One and Infallible. This we conceive to have been the doctrine of the Ḳorân held by Aḥmed ibn Ḥanbal and the theologians of his type. We have used modern expression to voice his ideas; the ideas, however, are not ours but his.

The Ḳorân, in terrestrial relations [2]), is to be regarded as a manifestation of the One Word of God such as constitutes a revelation of the perfect religion, a means of salvation and a right guidance for men. In all the forms of its existence among men, written, recited or committed to memory, the substance and the unexpressed words in which the substance is embodied in God's thought are eternal, uncreated, infallible [3]). The human acts in relation to the substance and the words as found in connection with these human acts are temporal, created, fallible. This is the doctrine of the so-called Lafẓ al-Ḳorân.

This Ḳorân doctrine [4]) is strongly suggestive of Pantheism, for the Word of God as spoken to Moses, to Moḥammed and as found in the Ḳorân is the One Word — not parts of it — coming to manifestation; just as the moon at its quarter may be called a particular manifestation of the moon, but not a part of the moon. The Pantheistic suggestion is much the same as that found in the Christian doctrine of the Logos, from Eternity resident in God, inseparable from a true conception of Deity, and proceeding to manifestation at the coming into being of Objective Existence.

---

1) cf. Houtsma, De Strijd etc. 101.

2) Ẓahiriten, as in note 2, p. 185, especially p. 141, l. 18 ff.; cf. present work, pp. 32 ff.

3) cf. Houtsma, De Strijd etc. 117 f.

4) cf. von Kremer, Herrsch. Id. d. Isl., 41. On the whole much like the doctrine of al-Ashʿarî, Houtsma, De Strijd etc. 118.

The Divine Unity. We are now prepared to consider the doctrine of the Divine Unity. Aḥmed ibn Ḥanbal was firm in his belief in the unity of God [1]), and, when we keep in view the doctrine of the Ḳorân which we believe him to have adopted, it is easy to understand with what vigor and conviction he would resist the charge of polytheistic heresy which his opponents sought to fasten upon him. We may, by the way, notice his belief in the eternity of the Divine attributes [2]). His view, except in the case of the Divine Sovereignty and Knowledge, the attributes formally connected with the origin of the Ḳorân, is stated but not elaborated in the sources to which I have had access. We have, however, in the case of the two attributes named sufficient data to enable us to arrive at his opinions. He stated, with all emphasis, that God could not exist without his Knowledge. And, though his adversaries declared that to make eternal and uncreated anything which was in thought separated from the bare idea of Deity was to make as many more deities as there were things so thought of [3]), Aḥmed, taking the concrete view of an unphilosophical mind, could not think of Absolute Being, except as involving all the fulness of a perfect, or yet to be perfected, finite creature, and a finite creature he could not think of except as having attributes. The Absolute was the infinite correspondent and correlate of the perfect finite.

The Anthropomorphic Attributes. The same conviction evidently lay at the basis of Aḥmed ibn Ḥanbal's faith in the anthropomorphic attributes given to Deity in the Ḳorân [4]).

---

1) p. 106 infra. For the Muᶜtazilite doctrine of the Divine Unity, vid. Steiner, Die Muᶜtaziliten, 50.

2) pp. 90, 101 f., 139; cf. a slightly different view, von Kremer, Herrsch. Id. d. Isl., 40 f.

3) For the Muᶜtazilite view of the attributes of God, vid. Steiner, Die Muᶜtaziliten 50, 52, 59; Houtsma, De Strijd etc. 103, 124; Shahrastânî, Haarbrücker's transl'n I, 71.

4) p. 72; cf. Goldziher, Moh. Stud. II, 186; von Kremer, Herrsch. Id. d. Isl. 41 f. (a more positive view).

Puzzled by philosophical arguments the untrained mind, though resting on the analogy of perfect human being, and holding fast to this as the undoubted ground and explanation of the Ḳorân's anthropomorphisms, asserted its impotence to answer philosophizing objections by saying, 'He is even as he has described himself, I will say no more than this' [1]. There was a much less arbitrary answer, which may not have been fully formulated in Aḥmed ibn Ḥanbal's mind any more than it was in that of Moḥammed himself, but which, had it been clear to the mind of either, would have seemed a blasphemy in its utterance, and would have involved inevitably a proof of the charge made by those who were arguing on the other side. This answer would have been to assert the literal truth of the Ḳorân's anthropomorphisms. Aḥmed's belief was anthropomorphic. That was the simple fact [2]. And the Prophet's was not the less so. The principle on which Aḥmed formed his notion of Deity was essentially right, 'the absolute is the perfection and infinitude of the perfect finite'; but his opponents properly objected to the giving of accidents of human nature, which may or may not be found when the human creature is in other environments, to the Being in connection with whom to speak of accidents and environments would be paradoxical and contradictory.

The fact of the matter in relation to these anthropomorphic attributes is that Aḥmed ibn Ḥanbal had to set himself up not only, as his own apologist, but, also, as the apologist of the Ḳorân and the Prophet, and he knew that — at least, so it

1) cf. Dozy, Het Islamisme, 136; an argument of the Ṣifatîya, Shahrastânî, Haarbrücker's transl'n, I, 95.

2) cf. Goldziher, Ẓahiriten, p. 133, l. 24 ff. The so-called negative position of Mâlik ibn Anas and Aḥmed ibn Ḥanbal in this connection is hard to understand (vid. Shahrastânî, Haarbrücker's transl'n, I, 97, 114 f.). Refusing to accept the figurative meaning of the anthropomorphic expressions, and yet insisting on the real force of these same expressions, as Aḥmed certainly did, how can passivity be conceived to exist in such minds? Insistence on the positive meaning, and yet not stating what the specific meaning was, though denying it to be figurative, leaves only anthropomorphism over.

seems to us. If Aḥmed had believed differently from the Ḳorân and Moḥammed, its human author, the case would have been a hard one for him; but anthropomorphism existed in higher quarters. Aḥmed had the Word of God to uphold, as well as his own theological character and he made the best defence that could be made under the circumstances. He asserted that God was describing himself, and who knew about himself more or better than he did? To such an argument there is no direct answer. One must follow the much more circuitous route of proving the apologist's conception of the Ḳorân revelation to be wrong, and once this is done the controversy on minor points would be time lost. The allegorical interpretation of the anthropomorphic expressions appears to be justly repudiated by any man who wishes to expound the Ḳorân according to the temper of the man who composed it, the temper of the men to whom it was first addressed, and the special intention actually present in the mind of Moḥammed, as far as this can be learned.

Ḳorân Interpretation. The step to the consideration of Aḥmed ibn Ḥanbal's principle in the interpretation of the Ḳorân is not a great one [1]). He believed that the Ḳorân was to be explained literally, except in cases where the Book itself indicated a limitation or modification of this method to be necessary, and in cases where a practical impossibility was involved. We say practical impossibility, for purely abstract necessity he was loth to admit as a regulating principle. There are so few ascertainable instances of allegorical interpretation on his part, that one can say that his general principle of hermeneutics governed him in dealing with the portions of the Ḳorân which might seem to some to be figurative. The indications of the Book itself and practical necessity would determine for him the application of the literal or some other method to such passages. In all cases

---

1) cf. his use of texts pp. 72, 90 f., 101 ff., 106, 139, 162 f. For the freer method of the Muʿtazila, v. Steiner, Die Muʿtaziliten, 79.

where the literal method had to he given up the interpretation handed down in Tradition ever found favor with Aḥmed.

Extra-Ḳorân Sources of Doctrine. Closely allied with the interpretation of the Ḳorân is the question as to the authoritative source of doctrine and rules of conduct, where the Ḳorân fails to give sufficiently explicit directions. For Aḥmed ibn Ḥanbal this lay in the Tradition. What had the Prophet said? What had the Prophet done? What had the Companions of the Prophet reported from him? Or, their Followers? Or, the second generation of Followers? What was the consensus of opinion and practice in the Muslim Communion? The admission of the Ḳiyâs or of Raʾy was generally opposed, but admitted where there was no better help to be found [1]). His monumental work, the great collection of traditions called the Musnad, had for its declared purpose the furnishing, in all conceivable instances, of sound traditional arguments to those who might resort to it [2]). Its composition and the importance Aḥmed attached to it shew that Tradition next to the Word of God itself was the great rock on which he stood. Many testimonies go to prove that he was more tenacious of Tradition than any of the other doctors of his age [3]). We find that when he forgave his persecutors it was because of a traditional interpretation of a Ḳorân verse [4]).

1) Goldziher, Moh. Stud. II, 217, note 4; Sachau, Zur Aeltesten Gesch. d. Moh. Rechts, 17; Houtsma, De Strijd etc. 91 f.; cf. Goldziher, Ẓahiriten, 20, note 1. Houtsma's words p. 92, l. 16 ff. seem to be too favorable to the Muʿtazila. Their interpretation of the Ḳorân as far as the attributes of God, the anthropomorphic expressions regarding God, and the predestination passages are concerned was wholly figurative, and we know how large a part of the polemic which they waged was over these points. The name Rationalists, or Freethinkers, is justly applied to the Muʿtazila and implies that the Ḳorân with them was authoritative, not absolutely or as far as practical necessity would admit, but only as far as the rational demands of human life and comfort and the fair requirements of human thought allowed.

2) p. 19.

3) Ibn Khaldûn, Proleg. III, 6; Goldziher, Ẓahiriten, 23, l. 25; Sachau, Zur Aeltesten Gesch. d. Moh. Rechts 15; cf. present work p. 16 f.

4) Abû Nuʿaim, 150 *a*, قال ابو الفضل دخلت على ابى يوما فقلت

When the author of the Ḥilya relates that Aḥmed was angry [غضبة لله] with those who weakened under the test in the days of al-Ma'mûn, he follows up the incident with a tradition of some of the Prophet's Companions having been very angry when they were called upon to give up any part of their religion [1]. The author's purpose in introducing the tradition where it stands, is to point out the analogy between Aḥmed's case and that cited, and to justify Aḥmed in view of what the Prophet's Companions had done. He may wish to intimate, also, that Aḥmed acted knowing this precedent, and being stimulated by it to feel as he did.

The Interpretation of Tradition. His interpretation of Tradition also leaned to the most rigorous view. A provision for relief in exceptional cases he often made imperative in such

---

له بلغنى ان رجلا جاء الى فَضْل الانماطى فقال له اجعلنى فى حل اذ لم اقم بنُصرتك فقال فضل لا جعلتُ احدا فى حل فتبسم ابى وسكت فلما كان بعد ايام قال لى مَرَرْتُ بهذه الآية فَمَنْ عَفَا وَأَصْلَحَ فَأَجْرُهُ عَلَى ٱللَّهِ [Kor. 42. 38] فنَظرتُ فى تفسيرها فاذا هُوَ ما حدثنى به هاشم بن القاسم ثنا ابن المبارك حدثنى من سمع الحسن يقول اذا جَثَتِ الامم بَيْن يدى رب العالمين يوم القيامة نودُوا لَيقُم من اجْرُه على الله فلا يقوم الا من عفا فى الدنيا قال ابى فجعلت المَيّتَ فى حِل من ضَربه اياى ثم جعل يقول وما على رجل الا يعذب الله بسببه احدا

1) Abû Nu'aim, 147 a, حدثنا محمد بن فضيل بن غَزوان عن الوليد بن عبد الله بن جُمَيع عن ابى سلَمَة بن عبد الرحمن ابن عَوف قال كان مِن اصحاب النبى صلى الله عليه وسلم من اذا أُريد على شىء من امر دينه رايتَ حماليقَ عينيه فى راسه تَدورُ كانه مجنون

instances, even if the persons concerned had no wish to avail themselves of the dispensation or the cases were in detail not the same as that originally provided for in the tradition. Hence, what was meant to be a relief became, instead, a burden [1]).

The Reason for his Method The belief he held in the merit of good works [2]) was so strong that a rigid exegesis of the Ḳorân and of Tradition was the most natural thing to be expected of him. The same belief explains his persistent application of himself to a life of ascetic rigor and fasting [3]).

and for the Manner of his Life. His love of the ascetic life, in its turn, throws light upon the mystic character of his piety and his faith in dreams [4]). Solitude, hunger, and the absence of distracting comforts made the subjective life seem more real than the objective, and led Aḥmed to feel an aversion to a life such as other men lived; for in such a life the reality of the interior world which he had created for himself was shattered, and mysticism with its revelry of religious imagination dissipated [5]).

---

1) For illustration of his rigorous interpretation, see Goldziher, Ẓahiriten, pp. 87, 88 f., 103 l. 20 ff.; cf. p. 141 infra; Goldziher, Moh. Stud. II, 250.

2) cf. p. 164 and note 1 infra. Houtsma, De Strijd etc. 85, says that the close adherence to the letter of the Ḳorân on the part of the orthodox revived a strict conception of life such as was found especially among the Ḥanbalites. But we would call attention to the fact that there was at this time a deep current of popular sentiment favoring a stricter religious life, and this great tendency of the life of individuals and of society at large expressed itself in high views of the Ḳorân and a rigid interpretation of its precepts. The stricter conception of the Ḳorân then reacted and gave definite form to the life tendency of the nation and its members. It was the conception of life that affected the conception of the Book which was the rule of life, rather than otherwise. Such is my reading of the circumstances, but Houtsma's explanation will also find many advocates.

3) cf. Abu'l-Maḥ. I, 364, obituary notice of Yazîd ibn Abî Yazîd al-Azdî, containing a reference to his ascetic life and imitation of Aḥmed ibn Ḥanbal.

4) al-Maḳrîzî, p. 18, ونقل من كثير من السلف انهم رأوا الله تعالى في المنام كالامام ابى حنيفة والامام احمد بن حنبل رضى الله عنهما cf. pp. 92 f., 82.

5) Abû Nuᶜaim, 142 *b*, قال [Cod. inserts لى] بوران ابو محمد لابى

Reverence for Relics. This ascetic-mystic aspect of his character comprises a reverence for relics, which has found expression once or twice in the course of the preceding narrative [1]).

Foreordination of Events. To one holding such views as those of which we have been speaking, the belief in a predestined order of life is the only explanation of human events. Aḥmed appears to have held that there was no contingency, either in the actions which men do, or in the events through which they are called to pass [2]).

The Doctrine of Faith. The doctrine of Faith expounded by his friend Moḥammed ibn Aslam was, apparently, held by Aḥmed ibn Ḥanbal, likewise. That is, that Faith is in the spirit, is expressed by the lips, and is confirmed by the acts. His declaration that discipline and trial would serve to increase his faith favors such a view [3]).

Aḥmed's Attitude toward Patronage. His attitude toward patronage and favors on the part of rulers was that of an extremist, but there can be no doubt that his high con-

---

عندى خفٌّ ابعثُ به اليك فسكت فلما عاد اليه ابو محمد قال يابا محمد لا تَبعَثْ بالخف فقَد شغل قلبى علىّ

1) Abû Nuᶜaim, 144 a, ورايت ابى ياخذ شعرة من شعر النبى صلى الله عليه وسلم فيَضَعها على فيه يقبلها واحسب انى رايته [يضعها على عينيه ويغمسها فى المآء ثم يشربه يستشفى بها Marg. ورايته] قد اخذ قصعة النبى صلى الله عليه وسلم فغسلها فى حُبّ الماء ثم شرب فيها ورايته غير مرة يشرب ماء زمزم يستشفى به ويمسح به يديه ووجهه cf. p. 107.

2) note 2, p. 109; p. 151.

3) al-Maḳrîzî, p. 12, وكنت فى السجن اكل وذلك عندى زيادة فى ايمانى الخ The faith which was increased by his adversity appears to have been an inward exercise of the mind. cf. Moḥammed ibn Aslam's view p. 38 f.

ception of his vocation as a teacher led him to keep as clear of compromise as possible [1]). Surramanra would become his prison, he said, were he to stay there and teach while, at the same time, receiving the fixed salary of the Khalif [2]). Isḥâḳ ibn Râhawaih he said he would rebuke, if he ever saw him, for his truckling to the Emîr Abdallah ibn Ṭâhir [3]). The wilfulness of Aḥmed, doubtless, contributed to his opposition to a Court position; he was master of his own circle in his own way in Baghdâd, but at the Court such would have been impossible. And, then, his real hatred of easy and congenial conditions on the ground of religious principle presented a crowning obstacle [4]).

Aversion to Systematic Theology and its Result. The character of Aḥmed as a traditionist, and his aversion to generalization and deduction, prevented him from leaving behind any system of opinions. We may formulate for him in these days, but he would not have been willing to do so. Hence, the uninfluential character of the Ḥanbalite school. Their master's teaching was unsystematic, and much ground was lost ere his spirit and teaching could be put before the world in such a form as to accomplish any powerful effect. His personality in his lifetime and after his death was a great force in the Muslim world; and the personality seems yet to be as powerful in its influence as the opinions which he enunciated, though his following has never been great in comparison with that of the other three orthodox Imâms.

---

1) p. 112 infra, p. 141; cf. attitude of Mâlik ibn Anas toward Hârûn al-Rashîd, von Hammer, Lit. Gesch. III, 101, 102.

2) p. 142.

3) p. 145.

4) On this whole subject, cf. Goldziher, Moh. Stud. II, 39.

INDEX.

ᶜAbbâs, the client of al-Maʾmûn, 75.
ᶜAbbâsa bint al-Faḍl, 174.
Abd al-Aᶜlâ ibn Ḥammâd, 174.
Abdallah ibn ᶜAbbâs, 157, 159, 176.
Abdallah ibn Aḥmed ibn Ḥanbal, 20 ff., 26, 28, 146 ff., 150, 173 f.
Abdallah ibn Idrîs, 46.
Abdallah ibn Isḥâḳ, 140.
Abdallah ibn Masᶜûd, 102, 160.
Abdallah ibn Moḥammed, known as Bûrân, 88, 147, 148.
Abdallah ibn al-Mubârak, 11.
Abdallah ibn ᶜOmar, 158.
Abdallah ibn Ṭâhir, 18, 194.
Abd al-Malik ibn Abd al-Ḥamîd al-Maimûn, 26.
Abd al-Munᶜim ibn Idrîs ibn bint Wahb ibn Munabbih, 73.
Abd al-Raḥmân ibn ᶜAmr al-Auzâᶜî, 176.
Abd al-Raḥmân ibn Abî Hâtim al-Râzî, 173.
Abd al-Raḥmân ibn Isḥâḳ, 70, 74, 78, 101 ff.
Abd al-Razzâḳ, 12, 15 ff., 26.
ᶜAffân ibn Muslim, 86.
Ahluʾl-ʾAhwâ, 161 n. [1]), 163 n. [1]).
Ahluʾt-Tauhîd waʾl-ᶜAdl, 62 n. [1]).
Ibn al-Aḥmar, 73.
Aḥmed ibn ᶜAmmâr, 105.
Aḥmed ibn Abî Dowâd, 3, 4, 52, 55 f., 64, 93, 102 ff., 120, 121, 126 f., 142.

Aḥmed ibn Ḥanbal, his greatness and influence, 2 ff.; his biographers etc., 5, 173; birth, family and early years, 10; teachers of, 11 ff.; performance of the Hajj, 14; at Mecca, 14; at San^câ, 16; period of teaching, 18 f.; works, 19; Musnad, 19 ff.; his pupils, 26; method of teaching, 26; contemporaries, 27 ff.; friendship for mystics and ascetics, 41 ff.; his trial predicted, 49; regrets apostasy of his companions, 64 f.; cited before Isḥâḳ ibn Ibrâhîm, 70, 72; referred to in al-Ma'mun's letter, 77; refuses to recant, 80; ordered to Tarsus, 81; sent back to Baghdâd and his imprisonment there, 85; second citation, 89; discussion before Isḥâḳ, 90 f.; taken to al-Mu^ctaṣim, 91; trial, 93 ff.; discussions before al-Mu^ctaṣim, 101 ff.; ordered to be flogged, 107 ff.; set free, 111; relations with al-Wâthiḳ, 114 f.; invited to visit al-Mutawakkil, 139; conversation with Isḥâḳ ibn Ibrâhîm, 139; accused of ^cAlyite leanings, 140; second invitation of al-Mutawakkil, 140 f.; vow to renounce teaching, 142; royal gifts, 141, 143; fasting and sickness, 144 f.; consulted about Ibn Abî Dowâd, 142, 145; released by al-Mutawakkil, 145 f.; correspondence with his sons, 146 f.; his testament, 147 f.; returns to Baghdâd, 148 ff.; objects to his family receiving stipends, 150 f.; accused to the Khalif again, 152; al-Mutawakkil asks for his view as to the Ḳorân, 154; his letter in reply, 155 ff.; Yaḥya ibn Khaḳân visits him, 164; Moḥammed ibn Abdallah ibn Ṭâhir invites him, 164; fasting, 164; sickness and death, 165 ff.; his funeral, 172; his tomb, 172 f.; family, 173 f., testimonies of esteem, 175 f.; Aḥmed as a faḳîh, 177; habits of life, 178; characteristics, 179; religious character, 181; personal appearance, 182; *His Views*, 183 f.; on the Ḳorân, 184 ff.; on the Divine Unity, 187; on anthropomorphic attributes, 187 ff.; on interpretation of the Ḳorân, 189; on extra-Ḳorân sources of doctrine, 190 f.; on interpretation of Tradition, 191; the reason for his method and for the manner of his life, 192; reverence for relics, 193; foreordination of events, 193; the doctrine of Faith, 193; his attitude toward patronage,

193; aversion to systematic theology and its result, 194.
Aḥmed ibn Abi'l-Hawârî, 26.
Aḥmed ibn Ibrâhîm al-Daurakî, 64.
Aḥmed ibn Moḥammed ibn Hânî al-Ṭâ'î al-Athram, 26.
Aḥmed ibn Naṣr al-Khuzâ'î, 116 ff., 119, 127, 128.
Aḥmed ibn Rabâh, 90.
Aḥmed ibn Shujâ', 70, 78, 84.
Aḥmed ibn Yazîd ibn al-'Awwâm Abu'l-'Awwâm al-Bazzâz, 70, 77, 84.
'Alî (the Khalif), 54.
'Alî ibn 'Âsim, 92.
Abû 'Alî ibn al-Bannâ, the Fakîh, 173.
'Alî ibn Hishâm ibn al-Barîd, 12.
'Alî ibn al-Ja'd, 70, 84.
'Alî ibn al-Jahm, 140.
'Alî ibn al-Madînî, 12, 26, 31, 87, 174, 176, 177.
'Alî ibn Abî Mukâtil, 70, 71, 76, 84.
'Alî ibn Yaḥya, 79.
'Alkama, 176 n. [1]).
al-A'mash, 63.
'Ammâr ibn Yâsir, 84.
'Anbasa ibn Isḥâk, 84.
al-Aswad, 176 n. [1]).
Ibn A'yan, 180.
Ayûb ibn al-Najjâr, 46.
Ayûb al-Sakhtiyânî, 161.

al-Baghawî, 26, 174.
Bahr ibn Asad, 12 n. [3]).
al-Baihakî, 173.
Bakî ibn Makhlad al-Andalusî, 26.
Ibn Bakkâ al-Akbar Abû Hârûn, 70, 73, 84.
Ibn Bakkâ al-Asghar, 72, 74.
Abû Bekr, 54, 123.
Abû Bekr ibn Abî Shaiba, 174.
Bishr ibn Ghiyâth al-Marîsî, 48 and n. [3]).
Bishr ibn al-Ḥârith al-Hâfî, 45, 125.

Bishr ibn al-Mufaḍḍal, 12.
Bishr ibn al-Walîd al-Kindî, 70 f., 75 f., 80, 84.
al-Bokhârî, 26, 34.
Bughâ al-Kabîr, 90, 91.

Ibn Challikân, 176.

Abû Dâûd, 26.
Dâûd ibn ᶜAlî al-Ẓâhirî, 46.
Abû Dâûd al-Ḥafarî, 46.
al-Dhahabî, 176.
al-Dhayyâl ibn al-Haitham, 70, 71, 76, 84.
al-Dhuhlî, see Moḥammed ibn Yaḥya.
Divine attributes, The doctrine of, 39 f., 90, 187.
Divine Unity, 187.
Duḥaim al-Shâmî, 26.
Ibn Abî Dunya, 26.

al-Faḍl ibn al-Farrukhân, 70, 77 f., 84.
al-Faḍl ibn Ghânim, 70, 77, 84.
Faith, Doctrine of, 39, 193.
Abu'l Faraj ibn al-Jauzî, 48, 173.
Farwa ibn Naufal al-Ashjaᶜî, 160.
Fâṭima bint Aḥmed, 175.
Fiḳh, 13, 177.
Freedom of the will, 62.

Ghundar, 12.
Goldziher, I, 7.

Hairs of the Prophet as charms, 107 f.
al-Haitham ibn Jamîl, 29.
Hajjâj ibn al-Shâᶜir, 26.
al-Ḥakam ibn ᶜUyaina, 161.
Ḥammâd ibn Zaid, 11.
Ḥanbal ibn Isḥâḳ, 10, 26.

Ḥanbalite School, Origin of, 4 f., 194.
Abû Ḥanîfa, 30.
al-Ḥarbîya, 175.
al-Ḥârith ibn Asad al-Muḥâsibî, 41 ff.
Ibn al-Harsh, 70, 84.
Hârûn ibn Abdallah al-Zuhrî, 61.
Hârûn al-Rashîd, 47, 48, 50.
Abu'l Ḥasan ibn Abd al-Hâdî al-Sindî, 21.
al-Ḥasan ibn Aḥmed, 175.
al-Ḥasan ibn ʿAlî, 114.
al-Ḥasan al-Baṣrî, 160, 162.
al-Ḥasan ibn Ḥammâd al-Sajjâda, 70, 78, 80, 84.
al-Ḥasan ibn Moḥammed al-Khallâl, 173.
al-Ḥasan ibn Mûsâ al-Ashyab, 12.
Abû Ḥassân al-Ziyâdî, 70, 71, 77.
Abû Ḥâtim al-Râzî, 26.
Hayyâj ibn al-ʿAlâ al-Sulamî, 55.
Hishâm, 47.
Hisn, concubine of Aḥmed ibn Ḥanbal, 175.
Hudhaifa ibn al-Yamân, 162.
Abû Huraira, 159.
al-Ḥusain, Tomb of, 123.
al-Ḥusain ibn ʿAlî al-Karâbîsî, 32 f., 176.
Abu'l-Ḥusain ibn al-Munâdî, 173.
Hushaim ibn Bashîr, 11, 50.

Ibrâhîm al-Ḥarbî, 26.
Ibrâhîm ibn Ismâʿîl al-Muʿtazilî, known as Ibn ʿUlayya, 47.
Ibrâhîm ibn al-Mahdî, 12, 26, 76, 80.
Ibrâhîm al-Nakhaʿî, 162.
Ibrâhîm ibn Saʿd, 12.
Ikhlâs, Doctrine of, 76.
ʿImrân ibn Ḥuṣain, 102.
Isḥâḳ ibn Ḥanbal, 3, 10, 88, 112, 145, 150.
Isḥâḳ ibn Ibrâhîm al-Mausilî, 139 n. 1).
Isḥâḳ ibn Ibrâhîm ibn Musʿab, 56, 64, 70 ff., 83, 84, 85, 88, 89, 90, 139 and n. 1), 140, 178, 184.

Isḥâḳ ibn Abî Isrâ'îl, 70, 84.
Isḥâḳ ibn Râhawaih, 12, 14, 18, 46, 145, 176, 194.
Isḥâḳ ibn Yaḥya, 63.
Abû Ismâ'îl al-Anṣârî, 173.
Ismâ'îl ibn Dâûd, 64.
Ismâ'îl ibn Ibrâhîm ibn Bistam, 12 n. [3]).
Ismâ'îl ibn Abî Mas'ûd, 64.
Ismâ'îl ibn Ulayya, 11.
Îtâkh, the Turk, 141, 144.

Jâbir ibn Abdallah, 160.
al-Ja'd ibn Dirham, 47.
Jarîr ibn Abd al-Ḥamîd, 12.
Abû Ja'far al-Anbârî, 81.
Abû Ja'far ibn Dharîḥ al-'Ukbarî, 152.
Ja'far ibn 'Isâ al-Ḥasanî, 74, 79.
Ja'far ibn Moḥammed, 139.
Abû Ja'far Moḥammed ibn Jarîr al-Ṭabarî, 5, 9, 177.
Jahmîa, 37 ff.
Jahm ibn Ṣafwân, 37 n. [1]).
Jubair ibn Nufair, 160.
Abû Juhaim, 159.

Kaidar, Governor of Egypt, 61.
Kalâm, 32 and n. [2]), 41, 55.
Ibn al-Kalbî, the postmaster, 140.
Karrâmîya Murji'a, see Murji'a.
al-Khabâb, 160.
Khalaf ibn Hishâm al-Bazzâr, 12 n. [3]), 31.
Khâlid ibn Abdallah, 47.
Abû Ḳilâba, 161.
Ḳiyâs, 190.
Knowledge of God, 90, 101 f., 187.
Ḳorân, Orthodox doctrine of, 184 n. [5]).
von Kremer, A., 7.
Ḳubaisa ibn 'Oḳba, 12 n. [3]).
"Kun", its significance, 119 and n. [2]).

Kuṣṣâṣ, 24 n. [1]).
Kutaiba ibn Saᶜîd ibn Jamîl, 12 n. [3]), 70, 72.

Lafẓ al-Korân, 32 and n. [3]), 34 f., 46, 186.
al-Laith ibn Saᶜd, 176.

Abu'l-Maḥâsin, 5.
Ibn Mahdî, vid. Ibrâhîm ibn al-Mahdî.
al-Makrîzî, 8.
Mâlik ibn Anas, 11, 50, 117, 176, 188 n. [2]), 194 n. [1]).
Abû Maᶜmar al-Kaṭîᶜî, 70, 78, 84.
al-Ma'mûn, 3, 6 f., 19, 47, 48, 50 ff., 52 f., 54, 55, 82, 83, 84, 105, 122, 126, 130 n. [2]). His letters, 9, 56 ff., 63, 64, 65 ff., 74 ff., 83.
al-Manda, the Ḥâfiẓ, 173.
Marwân II, 47.
Ibn Masᶜûd, see Abdallah ibn Masᶜûd.
Miḥna, 1 n. [1]), 19, 47 ff.; in Egypt, 61, 113 f.; at Damascus, 61, 62; at Kûfa, 63; general survey, 124 ff.
Moḥammed ibn Abdallah al-Makdisî, 21.
Moḥammed ibn Abdallah ibn Ṭâhir, 164 and n. [1]), 167, 172.
Moḥammed ibn Abd al-Waḥîd, 21.
Moḥammed ibn Aḥmed, 175.
Moḥammed ibn Aḥmed ibn Abî Dowâd, 56.
Moḥammed ibn Aslam, 36 ff., 193.
Moḥammed ibn Ḥanbal, 10.
Moḥammed ibn al-Ḥasan, 29, 79.
Moḥammed ibn al-Ḥasan ibn ᶜAlî ibn ᶜÂsim, 70, 79, 84.
Moḥammed ibn Ḥâtim ibn Maimûn, 70, 78, 84.
Moḥammed ibn Ibrâhîm, 85.
Moḥammed ibn Isḥâk, 140.
Moḥammed ibn Isḥâk al-Ṣaghânî, 26.
Moḥammed ibn al-Jarrâḥ, 144.
Moḥammed ibn Makhlad, 174.
Moḥammed ibn Nûh al-Maḍrûb al-ᶜIjlî, 70, 78, 80, 81, 85, 119.
Moḥammed ibn Saᶜd, 64.

Moḥammed ibn Sîrîn, 161.
Moḥammed ibn Yaḥya al-Dhuhlî, 26, 46.
al-Muᶜaiṭî, 31.
Muᶜâwia ibn Ḳurra, 161.
al-Muhtadî, 122.
Murjiᶜa, 37 ff.
Mûsâ ibn Hârûn, 26.
Abû Mushir, 79.
Abû Muslim, 64.
Muslim, 26.
Musnad, 5, 19 ff.
Muᶜtamar ibn Suleimân, 12.
al-Muᶜtaṣim, 3, 6, 23 n. 2), 55, 62, 63, 85, 90, 93 ff., 114, 127.
al-Mutawakkil, 4, 6, 7, 19, 54, 63, 118, 122, 129, 130 ff., 163, 169.
Muᶜtazila, 2, 6, 48 and n. 2), 62 n. 1), 187 n. 3), 189 n. 1), 190 n. 1).
al-Muᶜtazz, 142, 143, 144.
al-Muṭṭalib ibn Abdallah, 77.
Muẓaffar, chamberlain of Abdallah ibn Isḥâḳ, 140.
Muẓaffar ibn Kaidar, 113.
al-Muẓaffar ibn Murrajjâ, 73.

al-Naḍr ibn Shumail, 70, 84.
Names of God, 90.
Ibn Nâsir, the Ḥâfiẓ, 173.
Abû Naṣr al-Tammâr, 70, 77, 84.
al-Nawawî, 176.
Abû Nuᶜaim, Aḥmed ibn Abdallah al-Ispahânî, 8.
Abû Nuᶜaim al-Faḍl ibn Dukain, 63, 87 and n. 1).
Nuᶜaim ibn Ḥammâd, 119.
Ibn Numair, 12.

ᶜObaidallah ibn Moḥammed ibn al-Ḥasan, 72.
ᶜObaidallah ibn Moḥammed Abuʾl-Ḳâsim, 26.
ᶜObaidallah ibn ᶜOmar al-Ḳawârîrî, 70, 79, 80, 84.
ᶜObaidallah ibn Yaḥya, 154, 183 f.

ᶜOmar ibn Abd al-Azîz, 123, 161 f.
ᶜOmar ibn Aḥmed al-Shammâ al-Ḥalabî, 21.
ᶜOmar ibn al-Khaṭṭâb, 54, 159 f.
ᶜOthmân ibn Saᶜîd al-Dârimî, 26.

al-Rabîᶜ ibn Suleimân, 119 f.
Rajâ al-Ḥiḍârî, 82.
Rationalism, vid. Muᶜtazila.
Raʾy, 190.

Saᶜdawaih al-Wâsiṭî, vid. Saᶜîd ibn Suleimân.
Saᶜîd ibn Aḥmed, 175.
Saᶜîd ibn Suleimân Abû ᶜOthman al-Wâsiṭî, 70, 78, 84.
Ṣâliḥ ibn Aḥmed ibn Ḥanbal, 26, 141, 146 ff., 150, 151, 164, 170 f., 173 f.
Ṣâliḥ al-Rashîdî, 104.
Samsama, 118.
al-Sarî al-Saḳatî, 45.
al-Shâfiᶜî, 2, 13, 27 ff., 49 f.
Abû Shuaib al-Hajjâm, 90.
Ibn Shujâᶜ, see Aḥmed ibn Shujâᶜ.
Shyites, 54 and n. 1).
Sîma al-Dimashḳî, 118.
al-Sindî, 75.
Sofyân al-Thaurî, 176.
Sofyân ibn ᶜUyaina, 11, 12, 13.
Steiner, H., 7.
al-Subkî, 8, 127, 172.

Tâbᶜiûn, 163.
Taḳîa, 65, 83, 88, 128, 129.
Tashbîh, 106.
Tauhîd, 62.
Ṭâûs ibn Ṭâûs, 161, 169 f.
Abû Thaur, 176.

Ibn ᶜUlayya al-Akbar, 12, 47, 70, 73.

Wâçil ibn ᶜAṭâ, 55 and n. 4).
Wakîᶜ ibn al-Jarrâh, 12 and n. 3), 13.
al-Walîd ibn Muslim, 12.
Abu'l-Walîd al-Ṭayâlisî, 26, 174.
al-Wâthiḳ, 4, 6, 55, 63, 114, 115 ff., 121, 127 ff.

Yaḥya ibn Abd al-Raḥmân al-ᶜOmarî, 70, 79, 84.
Yaḥya ibn Aktham, 52, 54 f., 56.
Yaḥya ibn Khâḳân, 143, 151, 164.
Yaḥya ibn Maᶜîn, 12, 16, 31, 64, 117, 128, 174, 176.
Yaḥya ibn Saᶜîd al-Kaṭṭân, 12, 176.
Yaḥya ibn Abî Zâ'ida, 12.
Yaᶜkûb Ḳausarra, 141.
Yaᶜkûb ibn Shaiba, 26.
Yazîd ibn Hârûn, 12 and n. 3), 26, 29 f., 52, 176, 180.
Abû Yûsuf, the Ḳâḍî, 12.
Yûsuf ibn Yaḥya al-Buwaiṭî, 114, 119.
Yûsuf ibn Abî Yûsuf, 79.

Zainab bint Aḥmed, 175.
Ibn al-Zayyât, the Vizier, 55.
Ziyâd al-Bakaᶜî, 12.
Zuḥair ibn Ḥarb Abû Khaithama, 64.
Zuḥair ibn Sâliḥ, 174.
Abû Zurᶜa al-Dimashkî, 26.
Abû Zurᶜa al-Râzî, 26, 175.

INDEX OF NAMES OCCURRING IN ARABIC FOOTNOTES.

(Names occurring only in Isnâds or as names of Râwi's are omitted).

بغا الكبير 92 f.
البغوى 174.
ابو بكر بن سماعة 15.
ابو بكر بن ابى شيبة 174.
ابو بكر الصديق 43, 123, 124.
البيهقى 173.
ابو جعفر الانبارى 81.
ابو جعفر بن ذريح العكبرى 153.
جعفر بن محمد النسوى 169.
جهم بن صفوان 34.
الجهمية 40 f.

الحارث بن اسد المحاسبى 33, 44 f.
حارث بن مالك 42.
حذيفة بن اليمان 34, 158.
الحسن بن احمد بن حنبل 174, 175.
الحسن بن احمد بن حنبل (الثانى) 174.
الحسن البصرى 156.
ابو الحسن التميمى 169.
الحسن بن حماد السجادة 70.
حِسن سُرِيّة احمد بن حنبل 174.
الحسن بن على الجعد 115.
الحسن بن محمد الخلال 173.
ابو الحسن بن المنادى 173.
الحسين بن احمد بن حنبل 174.
الحسين بن على (الشهيد) 124.
الحسين بن على بن يزيد الكرابيسى 33 f., 169, 177.

الحكم بن عيينة 157.
حماد بن زيد 12.
حميد 30.
حنبل بن اسحاق 171.
ابو حنيفة 30, 192.

خلف بن سالم 180.
الخبّاب 156.
ابو خيثمة 99.

ابو داود الحفرى 46.
ابو داود السجستانى 179.
دحيم الشامى 27.
ابو الدن 109.
الدينورى 166.

الذهبى 34, 170.

الربيع بن سليمان 49 f, 120.
رجاء الحضارى 82.

زهير بن صالح بن احمد 174.
زينب بنت احمد بن حنبل 174.

سعيد بن احمد بن حنبل 174.
سفيان بن عيينة 12, 15.
سلمة بن كهيل 13.
ابو سليمان الجوزجانى 30.

الشافعى 13, 14, 27ff, 33, 49, 102.

علقمة بن قيس 176.
ابو على بن البنّاء 173.
على بن الجعد 166.
على بن الجهم 132, 133, 136.
على بن عاصم 176.
على بن المدينى 31, 87 f, 174.
عمر بن الخطاب 43, 155, 156.
عمر بن عبد العزيز 123, 124, 157.

ابو غالب بن معاوية بن عمرو 151.
الغزالى 28.

فاطمة بنت احمد بن حنبل 174.
الفتح بن سهل 166.
ابو الفرج بن الجوزى 173.
فروة بن نوفل 156.
فضل الانماطى 191.
الفضل بن دكين 63, 87.

ابو القاسم النصرآباذى 44 f.
ابو قلابة 157.

الكرّامية 39, 41.
ابن الكلبى صاحب البريد 131.

ليث بن ابى سليم 166 f.

ابن ماسويه 135.
مالك بن انس 11, 116.
المامون 49, 51, 53 f, 65, 81, 82, 86, 109.

صالح بن احمد بن حنبل 131 ff, 148 f, 151 f, 164, 166 ff, 170 f, 173 f. 183, 190 f.

ابن طالوت 168.
عبد الله بن طاهر v. ابن طاهر
طاووس بن طاوس 157, 167.
ابو طيبة الحجام 17.

عباس بن مسكويه الهمذانى 110.
عباسة بنت الفضل 174.
عبد بن حميد 17, 18.
عبد الله بن احمد بن حنبل 20, 28, 137, 149, 166 ff, 171, 174.
عبد الله بن ادريس 46, 166.
عبد الله بن اسحاق 131.
عبد الله بن طاهر 18, 146.
عبد الله بن عباس 155.
عبد الله بن المبارك 11.
عبد الله بن محمد (المعروف ببوران) 83, 138, 192 f.
عبد الله بن مسعود 43, 103, 156.
عبد الرحمن بن اسحاق 97, 98, 99, 102.
عبد الرحمن بن ابى حاتم الرازى 173.
عبد الرزاق 17 f.
عبد العزيز بن ابان 20.
عبيد الله بن يحيى 148, 154.
عتاب 56.
عجيف 99.
عفان بن مسلم 86.

المتوكل 123, 124, 130 f, 148 f, 151 f, 154 f, 164, 167 f, 170.
محمد بن ابرهيم 85.
محمد بن احمد بن حنبل 174.
محمد بن اسحق بن ابرهيم 131.
محمد بن اسلم 40 ff.
محمد بن الجراح 135.
محمد بن الحسن 30.
محمد بن حنبل 10, 11.
محمد بن سيرين 157.
محمد بن عبد الله بن طاهر 148, 165, 167 ff.
محمد بن مخلد 174.
محمد بن معاوية 133.
محمد بن نصر صاحب الشرطة 153.
محمد بن نصر المروزى 33, 167 f, 170.
محمد بن نوح المضروب 81, 83.
محمد بن يحيى الذهلى 35.
المرجئة 40 ff.
المروزى vid. محمد بن نصر
المظفر حاجب عبد الله بن اسحاق 131.
معاوية بن قرة 157.
المعتز 134.
المعتزلة 49, 55.
المعتصم 92 ff, 101, 104, 108 ff, 112 f, 114, 115, 131.
معمر 18.
ابو معمر القطيعى 73.
ابن مندة 173.
موسى بن حزام 30.
ميمون بن الاصبع 109, 113.
ابن ناصر الحافظ 173.
نعيم بن حماد 119.
هارون الرشيد 49.
هشيم 12, 29.
هياج بن العلاء السلمى 55.
الهيثم بن جميل 29.
الواثق 115, 116, 119, 120.
واصل بن عطاء 55.
الوركانى 170.
وصيف 133.
وكيع بن الجراح 13 f.
ابو الوليد الطيالسى 174.
يحيى بن اكثم 53.
يحيى بن خاقان 134, 135 f, 151, 164.
يحيى بن سعيد القطان 30.
يحيى بن معين 10, 17, 65, 86 f, 99, 116, 174.
ابو يحيى الناقد 176.
يحيى بن هرثمة 133.
يحيى بن يحيى 18.
يزيد بن هارون 30, 53, 180.
يعقوب بن البختمان 135.
يعقوب المعروف بقوصرّة 132 f, 136.
يوسف بن يحيى البويطى 120.

CORRIGENDA.

Page 3, line 5, Read Abî for Abû.
„ 4, „ 3, „ „ „ „
„ 19, n. 1, Read cf. p. 114 and p. 142.
„ 23, n. 2, last line, Read cf. Arabic, p. 97, l. 2 ff.
„ 28, line 6, Read al-Shâfi^cî's for al-Shafi^cî's.
„ 38, note, l. 4 infra, Read Shahrastânî for Shahrastâni.
„ 46, line 2, Read Ayûb ibn al-Najjâr.
„ 47, „ 5, also Side-heading, Read al-Mu^ctazilî for al-Mu^ctalizî.
„ 53, last line, Read: made a jest.
„ 70, line 6, Dele comma after "Sa^cdawaih".
„ 73, „ 2, Read Muẓaffar for Muẓaffir.
„ 75, „ 12 infra, Dele comma after "him".
„ 83, „ 11 „ Read طِرسوس.
„ 96, „ 10 „ „ يَعُود for يِعُود.
„ 102, „ 4 „ „ وكانوا „ وكانو.
„ 109, „ 5 „ „ باسرع „ باسع.
„ 172, „ 17, Insert after "and": — confirmed their judgment.
„ 200, „ 10 infra, Read al-Khabbâb for al-Khabâb.

www.ingramcontent.com/pod-product-compliance
Lightning Source LLC
Chambersburg PA
CBHW020822230426
43666CB00007B/1067
* 9 7 8 3 7 4 3 3 8 2 7 7 0 *